Bill Beaumont

THE AUTOBIOGRAPHY

D1382550

Bill Beaumont

THE AUTOBIOGRAPHY

with Geoff Green

CollinsWillow
An Imprint of HarperCollinsPublishers

First published in Great Britain in 2003 by
CollinsWillow
an imprint of HarperCollins*Publishers*
London

This paperback edition first published in 2004

1 3 5 7 9 8 6 4 2

A CIP catalogue record for this book is
available from the British Library

The HarperCollins website address is:
www.harpercollins.co.uk

ISBN 0-00-715670-7

Set in Adobe Garamond by
Rowland Phototypesetting Ltd, Bury St Edmunds, Suffolk
Printed and bound by Clays Ltd, St Ives plc

Picture acknowledgements

All photographs courtesy of Bill Beaumont with the exception of:
BBC 11(t), **Blackpool Gazette** 2(tl); **Bob Thomas Sports Photography** 6(t);
Colorsport 4(m); **Edward A. Winpenny** 2(b); **Empics** 3(b), 8, 9(b), 10; **F.N.G.
Clarke** 6(b); **Gary Talbot** 13(b); **Getty Images** 1(b), 4(t), 6(m), 7(t & b), 9(t);
Ian Joy Photographic 11(b); **Lancashire Evening Post** 14(b); **Luke Unsworth**
13(t); **Mike Brett Photography** 1(t), 2(tr), 3(tl), 5(b); **PA Photos** 3(tr), 5(t),
12(b), 16(b); **Photography/Fellery House Studio** 7(m)

To my wife Hilary and our sons Daniel, Sam and Josh.

*Thank you for your support and encouragement and
for selflessly providing me with the opportunity to do a lot
of things I wouldn't, otherwise, have been able to do.*

CONTENTS

ACKNOWLEDGEMENTS

I would like to thank Geoff Green for helping me to write this account of my life and for all the years of friendship we have enjoyed as he covered, as a rugby writer, all aspects of my career as both player and administrator.

My thanks also to the lads I played alongside and shared dressing rooms with at all levels from my club, Fylde, to the British Lions. Rugby is arguably the finest team game in sport and you can't achieve what I did as a player without the help of others, both on and off the field.

And a special thank you to Hilary. Not only has she had to put up with my many absences as a player, businessman and rugby administrator but also had to spend hours poring through scrapbooks and photograph albums helping to research this autobiography.

FOREWORD

Clive Woodward

I was delighted to accept Bill's invitation to write the foreword for his autobiography.

Bill had a huge influence on my international career. He was captain when I made my debut for England against Ireland in January 1980, the same year he led England so brilliantly to the Grand Slam, England's first for 23 years.

On the day I replaced Tony Bond, who was very unfortunate to break his leg on what was an otherwise enjoyable afternoon. To win your first cap, as Tony and Bill would testify, is a great feeling and one of Bill's strengths as captain was to make the new caps feel welcome. I was fortunate to play in the remaining three games of the 1980 Grand Slam and they are memories that will always stay with me.

Bill captained England a further 11 times with me in the side and his influence on the team was huge. He was inspirational and a very good leader. To survive the slaughtering he received from his team-mates, including me, when he was ignored during his half-time team talk against Australia, while we were all distracted by a young lady called Erica Roe running across the sacred turf of Twickenham, showed his true mettle!

In total Bill played 34 times for England, 33 of them consecutively and on seven occasions for the British Lions on two tours to New Zealand and South Africa, the latter as captain. He stayed loyal to his club Fylde and retired prematurely at the age of 29 when surely further honours would have followed.

Once a player retires, it's often difficult to make the move from sport to business but Bill has made the transition effortlessly.

Bill's achievements on the field of play have been matched off it. An OBE in 1982, a successful career in broadcasting, notably *A Question of Sport*, and running a profitable textiles business, endorse his versatility and commerce skills. Bill has also remained dedicated to rugby. He is one of two RFU representatives on the International Rugby Board and earlier this year he was made Chairman of the British and Irish Lions Committee, underlining the worldwide respect for a man who has given so much to the game.

Enjoy the book, it contains the life of an extraordinary man and one whom I'm proud to call a friend.

Clive Woodward
England May 2003

PROLOGUE

A Glasgow pub may seem an unlikely setting for a defining
moment in English rugby history but The Drum and Monkey,
in the city centre, will always be associated with England negotiating our way back into the Six Nations Championship after
being unceremoniously kicked out of the competition four
years ago in a dispute that was as stupid as it was damaging. It
was a major bust-up over money – television money in this
case – that reflected badly on everyone concerned and went a
long way towards destroying trust between England and our
immediate rugby neighbours.

Over the years I fought many battles in England's cause,
having the scars to prove it, so I wasn't prepared to stand by
and watch us turfed out of a marvellously compelling tournament, even though there were some at Twickenham who had
been doing their best to extricate England from the Six
Nations in a deluded belief that our interests would be better
served by aligning ourselves with the big three from the southern hemisphere: Australia, New Zealand and South Africa.
Which is why I took the bull by the horns, jumped into my car

and drove north to thrash out a compromise deal over what the media, in their colourful way, called 'a pie and a pint'.

That last bit wasn't entirely true but I see no reason to spoil a good story and the media made the most of the combatants sealing a new accord over refreshments in The Drum and Monkey. The hard negotiating had actually been concluded in the Glasgow office of Allan Hosie who, as chairman of the Five Nations Committee, had announced our banishment to a startled rugby world 24 hours earlier. With the media pack in attendance, we simply retired to the pub – I was driving so had to settle for shandy – to wind down, the 'early doors' trade considerably boosted by our entourage!

Being banned from the championship wasn't exactly a new experience. It had happened three years earlier after England had broken with the tradition of collective bargaining and negotiated its own television deal with BSkyB without involving Scotland, Ireland and Wales. The difference then was that the ban had taken effect in the summer, leaving plenty of time for common sense to prevail before the competition could have been affected. In 1999 we were on a very different timescale as our banishment came as Clive Woodward was preparing his England side to face Scotland in the Five Nations Championship.

The fixture was scheduled to take place less than three weeks later. England had sold all their tickets for the game. Lucrative hospitality and sponsorship deals with the business world were in place and thousands of ordinary fans had bought tickets for the game. Yet, when the Rugby Football

Union Council held an emergency meeting to discuss the possibility of a ban, days before Allan Hosie's public pronouncement, members were talking about challenging the move in the courts. We were given legal advice that England would be able to resist a ban and the mood seemed to be that it wouldn't happen anyway, that the other nations were bluffing, and that we should leave it to the lawyers to sort out.

I stood up at the meeting to urge my colleagues to forget the legal route and use dialogue to extricate ourselves from a ban that would have had serious financial implications, not just for England but also for the other leading European nations because revenue from international matches is essential for the health of the game at large. I'm not suggesting that England shouldn't have been seeking a bigger slice of the financial cake from any television deal for coverage of international matches and I still argue our case on this issue on the Six Nations Committee, but we had gone about things in the wrong way. We are often, wrongly I believe, accused of arrogance but in this case I suspect there were those in the England camp who felt that we were bigger and better than the other home countries and therefore entitled to take advantage of the financial rewards on offer.

Some might suggest that doing the Drum and Monkey deal, instead of taking the other countries to court, cost England millions of pounds in television revenue. We will never know but I have always taken the view that problems can best be solved if people are prepared to sit down together and debate contentious issues sensibly. I told the Council that we owed more to the game than simply winning a legal argument – assuming we would have won – especially as bad feeling would have increased rather than diminished. We had to think about all those people, predominantly members of rugby clubs throughout the country, who had been going to Twickenham for the last 20 years or so to support the national team and who would have been perfectly justified in kicking us all out for the mess we had created.

My message to the other countries was not to give up on us. There were some at HQ, in particular personalities like Graeme Cattermole, RFU Chairman Brian Baister and Fran Cotton, who were doing their best to sort out the whole, sorry mess. Even so, it came as a shock when, a few days later, Allan Hosie told the world that England had been kicked out of the championship. I heard the news as I was driving home from work and decided to act very much on my own initiative, especially after Allan had been quoted as saying he thought he could still avoid disruption by sitting down with someone like myself and going over the various contentious issues. I rang Brian Baister and told him, 'I'm going to Glasgow tomorrow so get yourself up there and we'll sort it out together.'

I felt it important to have Brian with me because he was Chairman of the RFU and his views on the issue were very much in line with my own. I drove to Glasgow but Brian flew, Allan Hosie picking him up from the airport. We all met in Allan's office and, because I had told officials at Twickenham what we were doing, the telephone lines had already been working overtime. In the end we found enough common ground for Allan to reverse a decision that I felt should never have been made. I had known Allan a long time and disagreed with him on that occasion, believing his action to have been a bit over the top. I suppose the powers that be wanted to force the issue by banning us; they certainly succeeded if that had been the intention.

As a result of our deliberations we had to make concessions and didn't end up with as big a slice of the financial cake as I felt we were entitled to as the biggest rugby-playing nation in the competition. In that situation it wasn't equitable to have equality. That may sound double-Dutch but our share of television money has to be spread much farther because we have many more players and clubs to support than the other nations. Also, more television sets are switched on in England than anywhere else when the Six Nations swings into action and I will continue to fight for a better deal in future although I will do so sitting around a table rather than taking to the trenches.

So, a form of peace prevailed, although the whole thing could have been handled rather better by all concerned. Whilst the episode didn't reflect well on England, it didn't reflect too well on our neighbours either at a time when the leading nations in the northern hemisphere should have been pulling together to turn Europe into the dominant force in world rugby rather than continually hanging on to the coat tails of the only three nations to ever win a World Cup: Australia, New Zealand and South Africa.

From a personal perspective I'm delighted that my initiative

helped to keep England in the Six Nations without a court-
room battle that would have lined the pockets of the lawyers
if nobody else, although I did see a certain irony in finding
myself in the role of peacemaker for an organisation that had
once kicked me into touch too.

Being banned had become something of a habit because,
under the archaic amateur laws that prevailed until recently,
my reward for leading England to a first Grand Slam in the
Five Nations for 23 years, back in 1980, was to be outlawed
for having had the audacity to retain the proceeds of a book
written after injury had forced my premature retirement as a
player. I joined a long line of well-known players who were
denied the opportunity to put something back into the game
because they had cashed in on their fame, to lesser and greater
degrees, after hanging up their boots. Some, who had sacrificed so much during their playing careers, hardly benefited at
all financially but still paid a heavy price by being outlawed.
Many, like myself, felt very hurt at being treated in that way.
I'm sure I speak for most when I say that we never even
thought of being paid to play for our country. It was deemed
a great honour to be selected and I would have paid the RFU
for the privilege of donning the England shirt and taking the
field at Twickenham, walking all the way from my Lancashire
home if necessary.

Fortunately, the wind of change finally blew through rugby
union and players like my friend Fran Cotton and I, formerly
banished, were welcomed back into the fold. We have since
thrown ourselves into administration of the game with the

same enthusiasm and dedication we showed as players and were both involved in the creation of Club England, the arm of the RFU that has laid the foundations for what I am sure will be a great future for our country on the international stage.

Perhaps if we had been able to stay in the game after injury brought our playing careers to an end we might have helped to prevent England, the country that gave the game to the world, becoming so distrusted. It is bad enough that everybody wants to beat England; our scalp is more prized than that of any other country, with a passion. But it saddens me that the word of an Englishman is no longer held in the high regard it once was. That was brought home to me very forcefully when, as a member of the Six Nations Committee, I was a candidate to take over the chairmanship when Allan Hosie stood down. It was a role I felt eminently qualified to take on. I had captained my country for several years, led the British Lions in South Africa in 1980 and had fought to preserve the viability of the Six Nations – a tournament that would lose much of its appeal without England's involvement. Competing against me for the position was Jacques Laurans from France. He is a nice man and I have no beef with Jacques (if the French will pardon the expression) but I felt I had better credentials to take on the job. So the show of hands around the table felt like a stab in the back as Scotland and Ireland, in particular, combined to ensure that I didn't win the vote. I did have the support of the Welsh representatives but I had no illusions about how England was regarded after a display of tactical voting with the sole intention of keeping English hands off the reins.

There is no doubt that the deep wound, opened by the bitter row over television money, had continued to fester, as was made plain to me after the meeting when I talked to the two Irish representatives, Syd Millar and Noel Murphy. When the British Lions toured South Africa in 1980, with me as captain, Syd went as manager and Noel as coach. Although we didn't win the series the three of us had worked very well together as a management team and I regarded them both as good friends. I still do. But they had been mandated by the Irish RFU to support Jacques and, when I asked why they had voted against me, the explanation was simple. 'We trust you Bill but we don't trust England.' So, despite our friendship, I was guilty by association of a crime they clearly felt very strongly about. I was an Englishman.

So, in a few short years, I had been turned away by England after leading my country to overdue success and rejected by friends within the international community for no other reason than my nationality. Both were bitter blows, but I didn't shun England when they invited me back into the fold a few years ago and I won't turn my back on our Celtic neighbours either because I believe very strongly in the Six Nations Championship and have established close friendships over the years with players and officials from the three other home countries.

There was a certain irony in the vote for chairmanship of the Six Nations Committee being taken in Dublin. I have had three major disappointments in the Irish capital: it was there that I suffered defeat when I was first capped by England, there that I failed to secure chairmanship of the Six Nations, and there that the vote was taken this year to grant the 2007 World Cup to France rather than England.

I was disappointed that the exciting English concept of a 16-team tournament, backed by a Nations Cup for a further 20 countries, wasn't adopted. The formula would have generated a lot more money, with the extra revenue enabling the Nations Cup to take place alongside the main event and enabling developing rugby countries to immerse themselves in the atmosphere of a World Cup. The English format allowed for a Super Eight play-off that would have given another chance to countries that lost a game in a hard pool.

It was not to be and, whilst it will take time to heal the wounds, we will gain nothing from remaining at loggerheads. We should all be working together to develop and improve rugby in the northern hemisphere, both in domestic and international competition, and England has a great deal to offer in that respect, having set the standard in recent seasons. And, by being completely open with our neighbours, we will hopefully regain their respect.

CHAPTER ONE

Childhood, school and family life

If the meeting with Allan Hosie at The Drum and Monkey was fairly critical for the wellbeing of English rugby, the meeting between my parents and doctors at Preston Royal Infirmary shortly after my birth on 9 March 1952 was even more critical for the wellbeing of William Blackledge Beaumont. I had arrived somewhat prematurely by Caesarean section and, within days, had gone down with pneumonia. My chances of surviving beyond a few more days were deemed to be so minimal that I was actually christened in hospital as it was felt that I would never make it to a church. Not much of a vote of confidence for someone who, despite arriving a month earlier than expected, had still weighed in at a pretty healthy-sounding nine pounds.

The will to 'hang on in there' must have been pretty strong, even at that early age, because I confounded medical opinion by coming through the crisis, aided by a new drug so revolutionary that doctors had to obtain permission from the Ministry of Health in order to administer it to me. That wasn't the end of my medical saga, unfortunately. Hospital staff expressed concern that I couldn't keep anything down and was throwing up with messy regularity. If *they* were puzzled by this phenomenon, my mother certainly wasn't. Having seen it all before, she was able to make an instant diagnosis: I was suffering from a hereditary condition – that had also afflicted her brother – known as Pyloric Stenosis, which occurs when a skin forms between the gullet and the stomach, preventing anything from being digested. A fairly simple operation rectified that little problem – my uncle had been less fortunate, spending his first 12 months being fed minute amounts of food on a tiny salt spoon.

My wife Hilary and I have three sons and, thankfully, none of them inherited the condition. Quite the contrary, they've never had a problem digesting anything and have been eating us out of house and home ever since!

So, after a longer than average sojourn in the hospital's baby unit, I finally made it to the family home in Adlington to join my parents, Ron and Joyce, and sister Alison. She was two years my senior and brother Joe arrived four years after me.

Adlington was a working Lancashire village where everyone seemed to be employed at either the local weaving mills or at Leonard Fairclough's, a large construction company responsible, at that time, for building bridges on the new motorways that were mushrooming all over the place. It was a small community and we were a tight-knit family with our own lives tending to revolve around the family textile business – a cotton and weaving mill founded in nearby Chorley by my great grandfather, Joseph Blackledge, in 1888.

My mother's family, the Blackledges, had always made their way in the commercial world but the Beaumonts were academics. A succession of teachers, who had the unenviable task of trying to impart knowledge to a largely unresponsive pupil, would suggest that I leaned more towards my mother's side of the family, despite the fact that my paternal grandparents were themselves both teachers. My grandfather, Harry Beaumont, had started teaching at Blackpool Grammar School – the Alma Mater of my old adversary and friend Roger Uttley – after the First World War and started a rugby team called the Bantams. He had been badly wounded fighting in Mesopotamia, now Iraq, and was awarded the Military Cross. My father carried on the academic tradition by winning a place at Cambridge University after serving in the Royal Navy during the Second World War. He had been put in charge of a motor torpedo boat so maybe it was from him that I acquired my own interest in boats. It all started when the family owned a house on Lake Windermere, and I've been messing about in them ever since. When they sold the property some time later we rented cottages in the area for summer holidays, and Hilary and I still keep a caravan on the waterfront in the Lake District because the boys took up my interest in water-skiing, although I spend most of my time in the boat these days. I even ventured back into the world of learning that I spent so much of my youth trying desperately to escape from, in order to study navigation. Lakes are pretty straightforward but I fancy myself as something of a seafarer these days and I reckon it helps if you know what you're doing!

My grandparents fully expected my father to follow them into teaching once he had graduated from Cambridge but he had other ideas. He chose to go down the commercial route and took a job as a sales representative with a company called Bradford Dyers' Association, which was a great move from my point of view because he ended up endeavouring to sell his wares at the Blackledge mill in Chorley. He walked in one day hoping to secure a little business but secured a wife instead. My mother had joined the armed forces after leaving school and had experienced an 'interesting' war, working as part of the back-up team for our 'foreign agents', who would regularly be sent into occupied France and other theatres of the war. Once peace had been restored she had joined the family business and, as luck would have it, was there the day my father popped in.

By that time my father had started playing rugby at Fylde, having also played at Cambridge as an undergraduate. I don't think he had any great pretensions in the game but, like the majority of players, he was a great enthusiast for the sport and made it as far as the second team. The club played a lot of games in the Manchester area in those days and he used to call in to see my mother on his way back to Blackpool. She wasn't over keen on rugby at that time and, after they married, he never played again. In any case he was busy because, when he asked my grandfather for my mother's hand in marriage, he was asked, in turn, when he could start work in the family business. He really threw himself into the job and did a great deal of work on developing the sales side of the business whilst my grandfather and uncle concentrated on manufacturing. The job involved a good deal of travelling and I can recall times when he would go off to Australia on business trips that lasted as long as two months.

Apart from those trips we were always together as a family and, until the age of eight, childhood was an uncomplicated affair that revolved around playing football and cricket in the garden or on the rec with the local lads. We didn't have a care in the world in those days and the only person who would get upset at times was my father, when our games of football and cricket made a mess of his pride and joy, his garden. He was a budding Alan Titchmarsh, and would spend hours pruning the roses, weeding and continually mowing the lawn – an activity I deemed a complete waste of time although, whilst not inheriting his green fingers, I have been known to tell off my own boys for doing a pretty good job of wrecking our garden.

It is a case of going full circle because the lads have always turned our garden into a rugby, soccer or cricket pitch, according to the season or inclination at the time, and you often can't move for cricket bats, rugby and soccer balls and golf clubs. Our boys are of the fairly boisterous variety, now rapidly growing into men, and, as they are all into one sport or another, we are now the proud owners of two washing machines and two tumble driers because just one of each simply wouldn't be enough to cope with the mountains of muddy, sweaty playing kit they manage to accumulate in just 24 hours.

The Blackledges were always heavily into cricket and the game dominates the summer months at the Beaumont homestead, whilst rugby league is a favoured activity in the winter when uncle Jack Partington, who used to play in either half-back position for Broughton Park, Fylde and Lancashire, happily joins in. He hasn't any children of his own to wear him out so he turns up with boundless energy and goes through a sort of second childhood, which the boys take full advantage of. That takes the pressure off me, allowing me, unless I get roped in, to sneak off and read my newspaper.

The boys, Daniel (20), Sam (17) and Josh (11), have always been crazy about sport. I've never been a pushy father, preferring to let them pursue the sports that interest them and to find their own level. But I have always been there with support and advice when needed. Interest in, and an aptitude for, sport must be in the genes and they certainly take after me when it comes to size. At birth, Danny weighed in at 8lb 13oz, Sam at 9lb 7oz and Josh tipped the scales at 10lb 5oz. Like any father, I was just delighted that they were born healthy and that Hilary was fine. We were living in Longton, near Preston, when Daniel was born and I had a bad habit of driving around with nothing other than fresh air in my petrol tank. Hilary was convinced I would run out of fuel if I had to take her to hospital in a hurry, but fortunately we made it to Preston Royal Infirmary when Hilary went into labour, without running dry. It wasn't the easiest of deliveries and, like many fathers before me, I sat around for hours anxiously awaiting his arrival and feeling like the proverbial spare part.

When Sam was born he looked just as he does now; his features haven't changed at all. Both he and Danny had little hair at birth but Josh had a mass of black hair when he arrived on the scene, his brothers christening him 'Bear' – a pet name they still use. Despite being born the size of a three-month-old baby, however, he has still, unlike his older brothers, to graduate to the pack on a rugby field. All three boys took to the game immediately, Daniel developing as a front-row forward and Sam as a second row while Josh, who looks like being the tallest of the three eventually, is currently playing junior rugby at fly-half – a position his father once graced! They also play a lot of cricket, soccer, tennis and golf. It is a case of indulging in whatever is in vogue at the time. During Wimbledon fortnight, for instance, it is tennis, whereas when the World Darts Championships appears on television, I notice that the dartboard suddenly reappears.

It hasn't been easy for the boys, because having a high-profile sportsman for a father can work against you and I feel that Daniel, in particular, has had a raw deal. He's a bright lad but very sensitive and he has had to cope with the expectation that comes from the Beaumont name. He played at Fylde from an early age, turned out at tight-head prop for Lancashire Clubs' Under-15s, and is now hooking at Manchester University where he is studying for a business degree, but he was largely ignored by school selectors and when he dropped the ball or did something wrong, even at the age of seven playing mini-rugby, he would have to put up with stupid comments such as, 'You of all people should know better than that.'

Sam is the quiet one and, at the moment, the tallest of the three boys. He played for the Lancashire Under-18s A-team a year early and has a good knowledge of the game. That may come from the fact that the boys have accompanied me to World Cups, been taken on British Lions tours and used to join me in the commentary box when I was working for television. They have watched a lot of top-class rugby and had the advantage of being in the company of people who have played the game at the highest levels, so they have a better than average understanding of what is happening on the field.

I have always found having to stay on the sidelines and not get involved in the boys' sporting activities at school frustrating, but I could see it being difficult for a schoolteacher being scrutinised by a former British Lions captain. So I stand back and try to help the school in other ways, such as fundraising so that the school team can undertake tours overseas.

At present young Josh seems to be least affected by the famous father syndrome. When his brothers were born, there was quite a bit of media interest and their pictures appeared in newspapers and magazines, to be followed later by happy family features. By contrast there was no fuss whatsoever when Josh arrived and he may well escape the goldfish bowl. In any case he is one of those annoying little characters who confidently take everything in their stride – in his case probably because of having to compete with older and bigger brothers –

and he is naturally good at every sport he attempts. He captains rugby and cricket teams, and competes in the school swimming team as well, even though he hasn't bothered joining the swimming club. He also regularly embarrasses both Hilary and me on the golf course! I remembering partnering him in a fathers-and-sons tournament at the Royal Lytham course in which we had to play alternate shots. Josh decided very early on in the round that *I* was the weakest link! At another time I had been due to play in a tournament during the festive season and we were sitting around at home with nothing particular to do so I said to Josh, 'Come on, let's go and hit a few balls down at the golf range.' When we got there we bumped into Paul Eales, a PGA European tournament professional, who told me he had just been reading a new coaching manual but added that there was no point in lending it to me because I was beyond help. When I suggested that Josh might benefit he said, 'I can't do anything with him because he already has a swing to die for.' Josh's temperament is such that I suspect he will ride out any family references and cope with the inevitable question, 'Do you play rugby and are you as good as your dad?'

The great thing is that, whilst they are all very different in character, each of the boys has inherited our love of sport. And, as parents facing the difficulties of modern society, Hilary and I take great comfort from the fact that they enjoy the ethos of rugby and cricket and socialise within that environment, just as we always did. It is an environment in which I have always felt comfortable because it attracts people from all walks of life and is very family-orientated. Family life is very important for

Hilary and I and, whether playing football and cricket on an Algarve beach, skiing in France or water-skiing in the Lake District or at our home in Spain, the important thing is all being together. Our impromptu games of cricket and football on foreign beaches have often attracted other holidaymakers who ask to join in. They were always most welcome but we had to take care where we elected to play after inadvertently finding ourselves playing cricket on a nudist beach on one occasion. We were blithely unaware until a bather suddenly appeared between batsman and bowler. Sam's eyes were like organ stops!

The boys have accompanied me on Lions tours and to World Cups. They also go to Twickenham with Hilary and I and join in the traditional get-together in the car park with Fran Cotton, Steve Smith, Roger Uttley and their families. (I remember how, during the last Lions tour to Australia, Josh had his face painted – they'd never seen anything like that before in the committee box!) Importantly, they aren't blasé about this, always making a point of thanking us for taking them.

I didn't have the same opportunities for travel that my boys have enjoyed throughout their lives but I had a very happy childhood nonetheless – the carefree routine only being broken when I started attending the Council School in Adlington and adopted a stance that was to stay with me throughout my scholastic career. I took very little notice of the bookwork and thought only about getting into the playground with a ball. Lessons were merely an unwelcome distraction but I was about to be doused in ice-cold water – metaphorically speaking. When I was eight I was packed into the car and driven to Kirkby Lonsdale, on the edge of the Lake District, to be introduced to Cressbrook Preparatory School, which was to become my home for the next few years. To say the experience was a shock to the system would be putting it mildly. It took me a long time to settle in and I was very homesick. Years later I can recall asking my mother how she could have sent me away from home like that but it wasn't easy for her either. She said it had been the worst week of her life because Alison, who was ten at the time, went off to boarding school in Harrogate on the Thursday, I went to Cressbrook on the Friday and my father flew to Australia on business the following day. From having a house full of people she was suddenly left with just four-year-old Joe to look after.

I don't think our three boys would have appreciated a boarding-school regime, and anyway Hilary and I always enjoyed them being at home with us so that we could sit down together to chat and find out what they had been up to. Of course, things were different when I was young and, by sending my siblings and me to boarding school, my parents were only doing what was the norm for people in their social circle. As I say, I wasn't happy at first but you get used to it and there was the saving grace of sport being available to me almost on tap. Another good thing from my point of view was the headmaster, David Donald – a great guy.

Interestingly, the head boy at the school was someone I would come to know very well through rugby in later life:

former England centre John Spencer. He subsequently had no recollection of me because he was in his final year at Cressbrook before going on to Sedbergh, but those of us in the first year knew who he was because of the position he held in the school's pecking order. Since then, of course, we have become good friends and have worked together for many years in rugby administration.

Arriving at Cressbrook was certainly traumatic. We slept in dormitories and it was lights out at 6.30 p.m., followed by the cruel wake-up exercise of a swim in the freezing pool at 7.15 the following morning. Little wonder, then, that I hated the countdown to returning there after our very occasional holidays. I was so determined not to go back one term that I hid in a tree!

Unlike the local schools my pals attended back in Adlington, we had few holidays and our parents were only allowed to make three visits each term, although they were permitted to turn up to watch us play for the school at soccer, rugby or cricket. Being a boarding school, the routine was very different from most schools. A typical day, for example, might comprise lessons in the morning, sport in the afternoon and then more lessons at four before supper and bed. The sporting routine in my first year was soccer in the winter and cricket during the summer months. Fortunately, I enjoyed both games.

Cricket was probably my greatest love and I still like nothing better than sitting down to watch a game, whether it is a Test Match at Old Trafford or just a knockabout on the village green. The game was in the blood; my maternal grandfather was such an enthusiast that he was one of the founders of the Northern League. My uncle, Joe Blackledge, was not just a good cricketer but also Lancashire's last amateur captain, taking on that role for the last time in 1962, by which time he was probably past his prime and his timing was not as good as it had been. I remember Dad picking me up from school and taking me to watch him play at Old Trafford but Uncle Joe ducked into a ball from Butch White of Hampshire and was knocked out. To add insult to injury the ball fell on to his wicket, so he was out in more ways than one!

Uncle Joe played at our local club, Chorley, and that's where you would find me during the school holidays. I was a wicketkeeper and opening batsman, and played quite a lot of my league cricket in the same team as both the father and the uncle of former England fly-half Paul Grayson, who also had a spell playing cricket at Chorley. Another cricketing pal was Paul Mariner, who went on to play soccer for the Chorley Town team before moving on to Plymouth Argyle, Ipswich Town, Arsenal and England. As the youngest players in the team, we tended to knock around together. Paul ended up coaching in America and we have rather lost contact, but I still bump into his parents when I am out and about in Chorley.

I have never tired of watching cricket and, fortunately, our boys developed the same avid interest in the game although Hilary thinks it is akin to watching paint dry. I had to explain that cricket is a wonderfully social game, just as rugby was when I was a young player. It is also a very unforgiving game, cruel almost. More than any other team game, the spotlight is on the individual, and luck can play an important part in success or failure. Some guy might be dropped five times and go on to score a century whereas the next guy could be out first ball to a brilliant catch.

When I first started playing rugby at Fylde I continued opening the batting at Chorley in the summer months, usually in the second team, but all that stopped when I got into the pattern of touring every year, either with England or the British Lions. I did make my 'cricketing comeback' a number of years ago, however, when we went to live in Wrea Green, a pretty village not far from Blackpool. It is the archetypal English village, complete with church, pub and houses surrounding the village green and duckpond. The captain of the village cricket team was my neighbour, Richard Wilson, and he persuaded me to turn out for them even though I protested that I hadn't swung a bat in earnest for years. When I dug out my old bat it seemed about half the size of everyone else's and the same could be said for the kit, which was so tight it almost gave me a squeaky voice, although I did just about manage to squeeze into the flannels! (There was, however, one memorable occasion when I split my trousers and had to nip home for running repairs, holding up play for about 15 minutes. Then it started to rain so the lads claimed they would have won the game if I hadn't forced the fabric!) It may have been beginner's luck but I took a catch in the gully off the third delivery of my 'trial' game and took another later when fielding at deep midwicket. We lost the game but I made 51 not out and they thought they had discovered another Ian

Botham! The Grapes pub served as the clubhouse and, in the euphoria of getting a few runs – and a bravado fuelled by a few pints – I signed up to play for the team on a regular basis. Unfortunately, I never played quite so well again but at least I could walk to the ground from home . . . and the clubhouse was always a considerable attraction!

My playing days, apart from in the garden and on the beach, are definitely over now but I enjoy watching our youngest, Josh, playing for the Under-11s side. Golf is more my game these days although I don't profess to be very good. I got into the game because that's how rugby players traditionally pass the time when they're away on tour and aren't involved in training. Even now, it's a good excuse to get away with my pals for a few days, although when it comes to competitions I leave Josh to represent the family. As I said earlier, he is something of a natural with a golf club in his hands and won the Royal Lytham Under-17s Championship when he was only ten.

Daniel and Sam are also good golfers, so I never have any shortage of partners, though that proved costly when I played in a competition with Daniel last year. He wanted a car and I had been planning to buy him a very basic model. Young men have their own ideas, however, and he was keen to have one of the new breed of Mini. As I was pretty confident that my pocket wouldn't be at risk, I wagered him that he could have the Mini if he beat me in a club competition. My pre-round confidence evaporated on the sixth hole when it took me 12 shots to get out of a bunker. Unsurprisingly, Daniel ended up with the Mini. To my pals at the golf club that sand trap is now known as Mini Bunker!

My interest in soccer developed through being taken by a neighbour to watch Blackburn Rovers, and my first major sporting outing was to Wembley to watch England beat Scotland in the days when the two nations met on an annual basis. It is a pity that the old cross-border rivalry isn't given an airing on the field of play these days, as it is in rugby union, but I suppose the opportunity for rival fans to cause mayhem is a good enough reason to have called a halt.

Even though my father had played for Fylde, my main interest in rugby as a boy, living in Lancashire, was limited to rugby league. Wigan was just a few minutes away so I was more interested in the feats of Billy Boston than in what was going on at Twickenham, although we did watch the internationals on television and I also have a vague recollection of being taken to watch Fylde. While in my final year at Cressbrook, in 1964 I was also taken to Edinburgh to watch England play Scotland at Murrayfield, though I little thought at the time that I would one day lead England to a Grand Slam at the same venue. For all of us it was just a great weekend away from the confines of the school. Sport provided me with many opportunities to escape the academic life. I was a typical lad in many respects, and lazy when it came to schoolwork. Deep down, I expected to end up working in the family business, so there was no academic incentive, despite the efforts of my grandparents when Alison and I went to stay in their bungalow in Blackpool for the summer holidays. They had turned the front room into a small classroom, complete with three desks, and they gave private lessons. I remember being there one summer when Sir Stanley Matthews' son, who developed into a good tennis player, was having lessons.

For some reason the family also had the habit of staying at Blackpool's Norbreck Hydro for three days every year; a massive treat, because it had an indoor swimming pool. My father would travel with his garden spade in the boot of the car and we would take it on to the beach and spend all day building dams. Those breaks were always over far too quickly, and then it would be back to Kirkby Lonsdale and the school routine.

Initially, soccer was the winter sport at Cressbrook, and I played in goal. I suppose it linked very well with my wicket-keeper role when playing cricket. I don't think we won many matches but I was just happy to be involved, preferring the sports field to the classroom. We weren't allowed to neglect our studies but I had little thought of cap and gown at that stage in my development. So it was perhaps a little ironic that I ended up, much later in life, with two honorary degrees – one from Manchester University and the other from the University of Central Lancashire. I couldn't help wondering as I received those what my father would have thought could he have seen me standing, resplendent in gown and mortarboard, before 500 students and their parents, while someone delivered a eulogy outlining why Bill Beaumont was being honoured with a degree!

After initially concentrating on soccer we switched to rugby at Cressbrook and, although I started out at prop, I quickly made a dramatic move to fly-half. They didn't have anyone else and I fancied my chances because I had quite a good boot on me. I wasn't that big in those days, only starting to grow rapidly from my mid-teens, but I can't claim to have been the quickest fly-half in the business. I did have my moment of glory, however, shortly before leaving Cressbrook, when I dropped a goal against a school side that hadn't conceded a point for two years. I was quite proud of that!

Most of my contemporaries when they left Cressbrook went to Sedbergh, Will Carling's old school, but my father had other ideas. The plan had been for me to go to Repton, but that was a soccer school so father opted instead for Ellesmere College in Shropshire, where the headmaster was Ian Beer, who had been at Cambridge University with him. Ian, of course, had a distinguished rugby career and represented Cambridge on the RFU committee for many years, being honoured with the Presidency in the 1993–94 season. From Ellesmere he went eventually to Harrow, where Roger Uttley was the rugby master. I spoke at a dinner in Ledbury for Ian many years later, and when he introduced me he dwelt more on my lack of academic achievement than on my sporting triumphs. In response, I observed that this didn't say a lot for the teachers. Touché.

By the time I moved to Ellesmere College I was used to life as a boarder but it still came as something of a shock because I switched from being a big fish in a little pool of 90 pupils to a small fish in a sea of nearly 400 boys. Most of them were older and bigger than I was. Ian Beer's later comments on the study front were fully justified because I found academic life a real drag and simply couldn't be bothered with learning unless it was a subject in which I had a particular interest – which usually meant one involving a ball! I enjoyed my rugby at Ellesmere although I had no thought initially of pursuing it seriously. If I indulged in boyhood dreams, they involved opening the batting for Lancashire at Old Trafford. Indeed, I took so little interest in rugby that the only name that meant anything to me was Richard Sharp, the England fly-half. Yet I knew all I needed to know about our leading cricketers and also vividly remember watching England win the soccer World Cup in 1966. Apart from Fylde I wasn't aware of other rugby union teams but was always keen to discover how Blackburn Rovers and Blackpool had fared in the Football League.

The sporting facilities at Ellesmere were excellent and that helped me through my school years. If you are into sport then, wherever you are – at school, college or just generally in the community – you will always have mates, and in my time at the college we were a pretty mixed bag. Because we were very close to the border there, quite a few of my rugby mates came from Wales and one of those was Mark Keyworth, who played his club rugby with Swansea and got into the same England team as I did in 1976. We suffered a whitewash in what was then the Five Nations Championship and that was the end of Mark, unfortunately. Those were the bad old days of English rugby when players came and went, often without trace, with frightening regularity. A lot of my fellow pupils also came from abroad – the sons of servicemen, diplomats and businessmen who were based overseas – and I recall one boy staying with my family in Adlington for a month in the school holidays because he wasn't able to join up with his parents. I suppose I did a lot of growing up at Ellesmere as well as involving myself in the usual pranks that healthy, energetic teenage boys get up to. We used to sneak out of school, I remember, to visit the local pub. Fortunately, it had three entrances, so we had our look-out and our escape route all worked out in case a master walked in and caught us supping ale. There was also a girls school not far away, which now and again joined ours for the occasional concert, but we tended to regard girls as though they had arrived from another planet. The problem with boarding schools in my time was that they were almost monastic in some respects. The interaction of a mixed-sex school is, I think, far healthier.

I continued to concentrate rather more on my cricket than anything else but also played for the school team at rugby, usually at fly-half or full-back. There were no invitations to take part in county or international trials but I somehow don't think I would have made the grade in the back division, so I've no grumbles on that score. But, since I have started to take note of what goes on, I can't say that I have ever been greatly impressed by schoolboy selections. Some youngsters are pushed all the time by their masters, and if the latter also happen to be selectors you know who will get into the teams. I was interested to read in *The Daily Telegraph* how Ben

Cohen, who has developed into a tremendous wing, played in England schoolboy trials but never got a look-in because he didn't go to the right school.

Some schools, invariably those in the independent sector, have a tradition of producing rugby talent and, over the years, some senior schools have offered scholarships to promising youngsters based on their sporting, rather than academic, ability. With regional and national selectors being drawn from leading schools, there was always a feeling that their own pupils had an unfair advantage in the pecking order. Today, fortunately, boys from schools that are not as well established in a rugby sense can still progress through the club structure now that we also have regional and national age-group sides drawn from clubs as well as schools.

Selectors also seem to ignore the fact that some players are late developers, this being an aspect that worries me about the current academies, valuable though they are. Not everyone plays top-class schoolboy rugby and, despite what we achieved later, neither Fran Cotton nor I ever played for Lancashire Schools. Fran did make it to a trial in his final year at school but that's as far as it went, although, knowing Fran as I do, I'm pretty sure this provided him with a goal to aim at. I have also found that some players peak early. They achieve a great deal at schoolboy level but can't cope with not being top dog when they progress to the senior game, so they simply drift away. The door has always got to be open for players who don't make it into the academies.

At club level things have changed. When I played the game

the county side was the avenue in the North towards national recognition, whereas in the Midlands clubs like Coventry, Moseley, Leicester and Northampton provided the route to international status. Now, however, international players are likely to be drawn from any of the 12 professional clubs in the Zurich Premiership, and, whereas clubs like Bath and Leicester dominated almost unchallenged for long periods, enabling them to attract the best young talent, there is now a far better spread of talent throughout the entire Premiership. Any player performing well in that competition is going to attract the attention of the national coaches and, with England selection being down to head coach Clive Woodward, there is none of the horse-trading that I suspect went on between selectors from different parts of the country in the old days.

Since I was a youngster, much more has been done through the clubs in terms of developing players, largely through the introduction of mini- and junior rugby. That was essential because of the way team sport was discouraged at many schools simply because someone had the daft idea that life shouldn't be about winners and losers. They didn't want youngsters to feel either the elation of victory or the pain of defeat but, whatever they say, life is competitive and I feel sorry for those kids who will grow up with no real knowledge of the concept of team sports. I have a real passion for such sports because I believe they mould you for life generally. You learn how to work together, how to show humility in success and how to cope with setbacks. Regardless of what some of the politically correct brigade might desire, we are not all equal and never will be. And, wherever you go in life, there will always be someone in charge.

I left Ellesmere when I was 17, with no inkling of what the future held for me. At that time I assumed I would work in the family business, play cricket for Chorley and perhaps play rugby at my father's old club, Fylde. Occasionally I have to pinch myself when I think back to how I was suddenly pitched on to a rollercoaster ride that brought its share of joy and heartache but one that, despite the dips and the empty feeling in the stomach these brought, I wouldn't have changed anything.

CHAPTER TWO

Remember you're a donkey

My rugby future was being mapped out for me while I was still at Ellesmere College. Father sent a letter to Arthur Bell, the long-serving Fylde secretary, offering my services and pointing out that, although I had been playing full-back towards the end of my school career, I was a bit on the slow side and would probably end up in the pack. So it was with a considerable degree of trepidation that I set off for my first training session at the ground in St Annes, making sure that I arrived in plenty of time. I needn't have worried because I was to find that not everyone displayed my enthusiasm for training.

I quickly got used to the pattern of training twice a week and discovered that work and family commitments affected attendance levels. Only half of the team would bother to turn up on a Monday, when one of the lads would lead us in some fitness work and, when we reassembled on Thursday evenings, we would meet in the back bar at the club and mess about flinging a ball around until someone suggested that it might be a good idea if we actually went outside and got started; a decision that would be put off for as long as possible if it happened to be wet and cold, which it invariably was. Even then most of the discussion, if we were scheduled to play away from home, usually concerned whether or not we were staying at our host club and making a night of it. Coaches were unheard of in those days and it was invariably the captain who called the shots on the training pitch. Afterwards, the routine was to down a couple of pints, in some cases rather more than that, and then to eat as many portions of fish and chips as we could lay our hands on. Today's coaches and nutritionists would have had a fit if they could have seen us but it was a very different game then. Had I played in the professional era, I somehow couldn't see myself surviving on pasta and salad! When I was captain of England, my Friday-night routine would be to settle down at home with Hilary to a prawn cocktail followed by a steak and a bottle of wine, which I am sure would be frowned today.

Training might have been somewhat haphazard in those days but the one thing there was in abundance was club loyalty. Today, away from the professional end of the game where players are tied to contracts, loyalty doesn't seem to last from one week to the next. Well down the league system there are players who will move clubs simply because they are offered a few quid for doing so. I'm glad that I stayed faithful to Fylde throughout my playing career. We may not have been one of the biggest clubs in the business but we had a decent fixture list and rugby clubs then tended to have a strong family atmosphere. Many of my best friends are lads I played with in my early days at Fylde.

Arriving for that first training session was rather like the first day at school. I was a new boy among men and the only player I knew was the captain, Mike Hindle, who also played at prop for Lancashire (I knew him because he was also in the textile trade). My father had introduced me to Mike and he had facilitated my club membership, but it was to be some time before we rubbed shoulders on the same pitch. I was picked to make my debut at full-back for Fylde's sixth team against a Manchester junior side called Burnage and that was my one and only appearance in the club's back division. The following week I was in the back row forwards and, never having had any rugby ambition other than to play the game, happily settled into the routine. I may well have stayed at that level for ever because there was a tendency for the lower sides to hang on to anybody who was as prepared as I was to run around like a mad young thing for 80 minutes. However, a selector called Roy Gartside turned up to watch the sixth team, and even though my team-mates somehow contrived not to give me the ball, Roy must have spotted some talent since I was eventually picked to play for the third team at Percy Park in the North East, probably because some of the regular team members didn't fancy the trip. So off I went – having told my mother to expect me home about 10 p.m. – all bright-eyed and bushy-tailed, clutching a one-pound note, which constituted one-third of the weekly allowance I received from my father.

It was the first time I had ever travelled any real distance with a senior side and I was an innocent abroad. The game went well and, although I found senior rugby harder physically, it was played at a pretty pedestrian pace after what I'd been used to at school. Only afterwards did I realise that I had a lot to learn about club rugby. We went into the clubhouse for a pint of beer and a bite to eat and I asked one of my new team-mates what time the coach would be leaving for home. It came as a surprise when he told me we were on a 'stopper' and wouldn't be leaving until midnight. I was 17, wasn't used to drinking – not more than a couple of pints anyway – and we ended up in a pub called The Jungle near the docks in North Shields, where I found myself surrounded by the local clientele, who all seemed to have had their faces stitched at some stage in their careers. A few years later I was battling it out with All Blacks, Wallabies and Springboks, but at that stage in my development I was a young lad straight out of public school and I was crapping myself. I was absolutely petrified and determined not to make eye contact with any of them in case they took exception to my scrutiny and decided to 'fill me in'. My pound didn't last very long either but I was subsidised by the older players and gradually started to get into the swing of things. I was even chirpy enough to ring home from a transport café at Scotch Corner to tell the folks that I would be home later than planned. It was after 2 a.m. when my mother answered the call, handed the telephone to my father and told him, in no uncertain terms, that I wouldn't be playing rugby again. I stumbled into the family abode at about the same time as the milk arrived on the doorstep, having discovered the delights of rugby touring. The 'choir' sang most of the way home on the coach, and as the vehicle didn't have an on-board toilet we had to hang out of the door to relieve ourselves until one bright spark decided it would be a good idea to lift the floorboards and pee down the hole. The only problem with that was that our offerings merely hit the drive shaft and sprayed all over the place.

At the same time that I joined Fylde, I started a textile technology and business studies course at Salford Technical College and, not surprisingly, gravitated towards the college rugby team. I played in the back row alongside a former England Schoolboy, Richard Jazwinski, who was playing club rugby at Broughton Park. He was a very good player and went on to represent Lancashire, and, during that time, I played against Nigel Yates, who was a centre at Sale and went on to become a senior referee.

I graduated to the second team at Fylde and also made the move into the second row, but at the start of the following season it was felt that I was too small for the position in which I was later to make my name, so I was demoted back to the third team to learn how to prop. It was in that position that I made my first-team debut against Waterloo in November 1970, when the team were short, but I afterwards returned to the position I was to occupy for the remainder of my career and, a year later, had established myself in the first team.

The only time I was ever dropped by my club was at Christmas during that season, when Roger Uttley, who was studying at university in Newcastle and playing for Gosforth (now the Falcons), returned home for the holidays and was picked ahead of me for the Boxing Day game against our oldest rivals, Preston Grasshoppers. I wasn't very happy to see this total stranger, to me anyway, suddenly walk in and take my spot, and I had a quiet chuckle to myself when 'Hoppers' won.

Looking back it is quite incredible how my playing career has interwoven with Roger's over the years, our rivalry extending over a considerable time. When I started playing in the second row for Lancashire he was playing for Northumberland and was already an established international. I owe my England debut to Roger because I was called into the side when he had to pull out through injury. He also captained England ahead of me – I then took over the captaincy from him, only to lose it back again later. We were intense rivals, and I think we both felt more comfortable when I was fully established as captain and he came back into the national side in 1980 as a flanker. I had made my mark and the selectors weren't going to bring Roger back as captain again. I think we always respected each other and we have been good mates ever since. Hilary and I thoroughly enjoy his company – and that of his wife Christine.

My elevation to the second row at Fylde had again only come about because they happened to be short in that position one day, but once in the engine room of the pack I never looked back. Having worked my way through to the first team, I made my senior debut at second row against New Brighton; a side that, like Fylde, was more of a force in those days.

Certainly, the side I played in would beat the current Fylde team without too much difficulty. Brian Ashton was at scrum-half and he was a class player with a good understanding of the game, as has been proved since with his coaching success at Bath and with England. He currently has the vital task of looking after the country's Academy players who are being groomed for the national side. He toured Australia with me in 1975 when he was really on top of his game and he would surely have been capped had he been able to stay Down Under, but he had to return home to be with his wife after she had miscarried the baby they were expecting. It is a tragedy that he never won his cap because he then went to live and play for a time in Italy and so was largely lost to us. When he finally returned it was to move into coaching, where he has played a considerable role in helping to change the way English backs play. He was not just a top player but is a bloody good bloke too and he is ideally suited for the development role he has taken on.

Another Fylde player who came close to representing his country during my playing days was wing Tony Richards. He and Brian were my regular travelling companions and Tony was Lancashire's wing for many years, playing in England trials but without getting the call he wanted. Despite the passing years, I still see quite a bit of Tony because he is an enthusiastic worker for The Wooden Spoon Society, the rugby charity.

By the time I had established myself in Fylde's first team I was starting to take the game very seriously and I did find it frustrating that not everyone in the side had the same approach to training and preparation. The difference in attitude became more apparent when I started playing for Lancashire. Suddenly I was in the company of players of international calibre and it didn't take long to work out why. They were a dedicated and very single-minded bunch. Coming second best was not on their agenda and you never had to worry that anyone might be slacking on the field.

Still, Fylde had a reasonable fixture list, which provided me with the opportunity to play against powerful clubs, none stronger than Coventry in those days. They could almost field a side of internationals and when I picked up a match programme and saw the quality of the opposition I started at last to acquire real ambition. I remember playing against Moseley at The Reddings one day and their side included England half-backs Jan Webster and John Finlan, John White and Nigel Horton. On that occasion I had an excellent game against Nigel and decided that I rather liked the game of rugby union. He clearly had a long memory because, a year later, he smacked me at the first line-out and gave me a hard time generally. I was suddenly made aware that this rugby business wasn't as easy as I had been starting to think it was.

Lancashire would run a series of trial games, and I played in these in the hope of breaking up the experienced second row combination of Mike Leadbetter and Richard Trickey. Both played in the North West Counties team that became the first English provincial side to beat the All Blacks – at Workington in 1972, during which I stood on the terraces to cheer them on. Mike did win an England cap but only in a 35–13 defeat against France at Stade Colombes in Paris. Under the scoring system then, that was quite a hefty thumping but England were hardly front-runners in the Five Nations during that particular era. There was a lot of chopping and changing and Mike wasn't the only one-cap wonder by any means.

Richard was travelling reserve that day in Paris – they didn't have replacements at that time and you were only there in case someone was taken ill before the game – and that's as close as he got to a cap. That was a pity because he certainly deserved one – the old Sale warhorse taught me a great deal. He was limited in ability and not the purest of line-out jumpers but you couldn't fault him for commitment. He was the fittest bloke I had ever encountered and was a massive influence on my career. At that time he was working as a sales representative and he would get up at 5 a.m. every day in order to get all his calls done by 2 p.m. so that he could devote the rest of the day to his punishing training routine. He could literally run all day and was ultra-competitive. The lads at Sale tell how, after he had retired and taken up coaching, he would race against them, claiming he had beaten them all, despite his age. On investigation, you discovered that he only won the last of a series of 50 sprints, by which time the players were hardly capable of standing, let around galloping 100 metres!

In 1972, just three days after the aforementioned victory over the All Blacks by the North West, I made my county debut alongside Richard because Mike Leadbetter had taken a knock in that game. Richard made more than 100 appearances for Lancashire and he soon handed out advice that ensured

I didn't get ideas above my station. In his gruff, forthright way, he told me, 'Don't try anything fancy. No sidestepping or selling dummies or trying to drop a goal – just stick your head up the prop's backside, shove like a lunatic and contest every blasted line-out no matter where the ball is meant to be thrown. We've plenty of prima donnas in the backs to provide the tricks as long as we provide the ball. Just remember you are a donkey, and behave like one.' As a young man who was already awe-stricken at finding himself in company with players like Fran Cotton and Tony Neary, not to mention 'Tricks', I nodded my head vigorously in accord. I certainly wasn't prepared to try debating my role with him. The game was against Cumberland and Westmorland, now rebranded Cumbria, and I soon realised just how fit Richard was when I saw the speed with which he arrived at the breakdown ahead of me. I fared all right at the line-out but the pace of the game was a new experience and one and that made me determined to put in even more work on my fitness. Fortunately, I enjoyed training and even turned a corner of the factory into a gymnasium so that I could work out during my lunch break.

I wasn't picked again during that campaign but I was selected for the following season's opener at Durham and found myself sharing a room with Richard. It seemed that I still had a lot to learn from this iron-willed man with an equally iron constitution. It was freezing cold but off went the central heating and the windows were flung wide open. Stuffy hotel rooms were not to his liking so I shivered and didn't argue – I was still in awe of the man. Then there were the mealtimes. I enjoy a good trough as much as the next man, but I have never seen anyone eat quite like Richard. He gorged his way through a mammoth meal in the Royal County Hotel, dragged me off to a back-street pub for a few pints and then, while watching the midnight movie, demolished an enormous plate of sandwiches in the room while I tried to sleep. The following morning he was full of beans, metaphorically speaking, and dragged me, bleary-eyed, down to the restaurant for the sort of breakfast that would have rugby's modern-day nutritionists slashing their wrists in anguish. He walked it off by frogmarching me up the hill to the cathedral, apparently some sort of ritual for him and one that I continued in the following years. The walk seemed to have the desired effect because not only did it help him to walk off breakfast, it also gave him an appetite for lunch!

In the Lancashire camp they tell the story of how Richard and Fran Cotton attempted a monster meal the evening before once again taking on Durham. As coach John Burgess wasn't due to arrive until the day of the game because of business commitments in Russia, there wasn't the same control over what the players ate. Normally it was a set meal but the players this time were allowed to tackle the à la carte menu instead and both Richard and Fran had ordered so much food that their meals could only be accommodated on two large platters – each – and the unbelieving waiters actually carried the platters around the room so that other diners could see what was about to be attempted. I wasn't there but I'm told Fran retired hurt while Richard sent clean platters back to the kitchen. If Burgess had known about it then their overworked guts would have been had for garters.

John Burgess was not a man to fool with. When I first made the Lancashire squad I was petrified of him. He was a bit of a control freak but I had the greatest admiration and respect for him. In many ways he was ahead of his time because his organisational skills were second to none and he really thought about his rugby at a time when sides tended to go through well-tried motions. Before every Lancashire game he would provide each player with a dossier on the opposition and he had newspaper cuttings of all their previous matches. Goodness knows how he found the time to do it all and run a major engineering company at the same time.

He knew exactly what everyone had to do in every corner of the field and nobody in the Lancashire camp argued with him, not even the top players. A great motivator, he also had tremendous pride in his county and country, although his experience of coaching England wasn't a happy one. I suppose that when he reached that level he probably needed more than motivation, organisation and set-piece plays. Sadly, there were those in the England camp who regarded him as someone from a different planet.

I'm certain that he was far more comfortable with players such as Cotton and Neary, who thought the world of him, as indeed I did. He more or less transformed northern rugby after it had slipped into something of a backwater. We weren't a force in the land by any means but Burgess changed that, in no small part due to his honesty, which invariably shone through. As a player the last thing you want to hear is that you haven't played well but he would certainly let you know if he thought you had had a bad game, and it didn't matter if you were a many-times-capped international either. He was a massive influence on all our playing careers and I don't think many of us would have achieved what we did without him. I for one owe him a great debt of gratitude.

I played for the county throughout the 1973–74 championship campaign but injured my Achilles' tendon and had to withdraw for the final against Gloucestershire – a game we lost and that sparked a sequence of three successive title wins for the West Country side. Battles with Gloucestershire were always pretty memorable because both counties took the championship very seriously and, in some respects, it is sad that this particular element has gone out of rugby. When I played it was imperative that you figured in a successful county side because that was the best route to an international cap, considering the strength, or rather weakness, of club rugby in the north.

Injury kept me sidelined for three months but there was something to look forward to. Lancashire were due to tour Zimbabwe (Rhodesia as it was then) and South Africa in the summer and I was fairly confident of being included in the squad. I had succeeded in forcing out Mike Leadbetter and there was no serious challenger so far as I could see, so I assumed that I would be renewing my second row partnership with Richard Trickey. I had yet to meet a player who later proved capable of challenging the very best – Maurice

Colclough. He was a complete stranger then but was destined to become my partner in an England Grand-Slam-winning team and on a British Lions tour. Maurice, a big, redheaded student from Liverpool University, was poised to have a memorable tour but for all the wrong reasons. That he enjoyed a drink was never in dispute and he would have made his Lancashire debut earlier but for the fact that he had to withdraw because of a judicial appearance he had to make in Dublin. In his youthful exuberance he had apparently stripped off in order to swim across the River Liffey and I can only assume that this didn't go down too well with the local gardaí. Maurice was picked to play in Lancashire's second tour game in Bulawayo but after a heavy night of carousing he was not really in the best state to sally forth into battle. He tried to fortify himself with a glucose drink, but whilst that provided the propulsion for a wonderful break out of defence it obviously wasn't too easy to digest because he threw up spectacularly the minute he hit the deck after being tackled. That didn't endear him to a management that took its rugby very seriously. He had a lot to learn about our Lancashire rugby culture.

CHAPTER THREE

Your country needs you

Touring clearly suited me because I always seem to return from my travels a better player. That probably had something to do with playing in good company, and very often against more demanding opposition. The trip to Zimbabwe and South Africa, from a purely personal point of view, had gone very well and I was ready, on my return, to make a determined effort to break through into the England side, knowing full well that this would probably mean renewing my rivalry with Roger Uttley.

Tonga paid a visit to the UK during the autumn of 1974 and played against the North at Birkenhead Park just four days before they were due to take on England Under-23s at Twickenham. I was involved in both games, teaming up with Gosforth's Terry Roberts in a North side that also included my Fylde pals Brian Ashton (who had joined Orrell), Tony Richards and fly-half Ian McDonnell, and I was subsequently included on the replacements' bench by England.

As I had already taken Monday and Tuesday off work to play for the North, I telephoned Twickenham to ask if it would be in order if I turned up on the Friday rather than Thursday, on the grounds that I didn't want to push my luck – family business or not. They said that this was all right but assumed I would be in London in time for the Friday-afternoon training session, so I suspect I wasn't the most popular guy in town when I actually arrived during the evening, having done a full day's graft at the factory. My punishment was to be dragged from my warm and comfortable bed very early the following morning to practice line-out work with skipper John Raphael, who was also the hooker. I was such an innocent abroad that I didn't even possess a tracksuit, so I went through the line-out ploys in the car park clad in a pair of jeans and a sweater, relying on one of the other lads to lend me a tracksuit to wear that afternoon so that I wouldn't look completely out of place sitting on the bench.

Twickenham was an entirely new experience for me and I couldn't get over the size of the dressing room. I was used to the cramped boxes that seemed to be the norm at a lot of clubs so it took some time to adjust to the luxury of space and the sight of rows of individual baths rather than the traditional communal bath. The top players, I decided, as I settled down on the bench to watch the match, were very cosseted. I wasn't too concerned when Trevor Cheeseman, who was playing at number eight, had to leave the field suffering from concussion early in the second half. Coventry flanker Mal Malik, who later took over Rugby Lions, was the back row replacement so I fully expected him to be sent on to fill the gap. You can imagine my surprise, and delight, when they switched Neil Mantell from the second row and sent me into the fray. In the excitement of it all I forgot the line-out calls that I had been hastily trying to take on board in the car park that morning but I still managed to perform well in that department, helped by scrum-half Steve Smith, who let me know when the ball was coming my way. I was also reasonably busy in the loose in the time remaining, so felt pretty pleased with myself when the final whistle sounded. And I had my first England jersey, albeit not the one I really coveted.

The important thing was that I was 'in'. I had been involved in an England team and it was down to me to prove to the selectors that I was worthy of consideration for the senior side. Things are very different today because there is no selection committee, and I am sure that in days gone by deals were done at times rather than the best 15 always being selected. Now responsibility rests with one man, Clive Woodward. In the 1970s, however, England still relied heavily on a series of trials and I found myself picked alongside Roger Uttley in a North side that took on the Midlands at Headingley's old ground at Kirkstall. Roger was just back from the British Lions tour to South Africa and that was the first time we had appeared together. It looked as though I would be up against Nigel Horton, who jumped at four, because Roger was a recognised front-jumper. But Fran Cotton, who skippered the side, asked Roger to take on Horton and allow me to jump at the front.

Roger was already an established international and hardly needed to prove his credentials but it was still a magnanimous gesture when he agreed to the switch without a moment's hesitation.

I was quite surprised after the game when the Midlands hooker, Peter Wheeler, walked past and said, 'Hello Bill.' I didn't think he would have a clue who I was so I was chuffed that established players seemed to be aware of me. There was another surprise in store when I told Fran Cotton that I hoped he would have a good Christmas and he responded that he would wish me seasonal greetings the following weekend when we travelled to Twickenham for the final trial. I would, he assured me – and you don't argue with Fran – definitely be involved in that game. And he was right.

Roger Uttley and I found ourselves on opposite sides rather than as partners. He was picked to play for England and had been due to partner Chris Ralston, while I packed down alongside Nigel Horton for the Rest, but Nigel was elevated when Ralston pulled out and my new partner was Bob Wilkinson from Bedford. As you only meet up just before the game you are never really sure what the team is going to be and there was no time to work out line-out drills. To give you some indication of what it was like, our skipper – Bristol's Dave Rollitt, who was a bit of a character to say the least – approached me in the dressing room and enquired, 'And who the hell are you, may I ask?' Hardly a vote of confidence when even your skipper hasn't a clue who you are, but he did add that, since I had been selected for an England trial, I couldn't be 'completely useless'. I grew to enjoy Dave's caustic brand of humour and soon discovered what a good bloke he was.

I certainly felt a little inadequate and our preparation was such that I had worked out the opposition's line-out signals long before I had sorted out our own. Hardly surprising then that we went down 38–22 but I wasn't too disheartened because I had made one or two useful contributions in the game, and I did have the familiar faces of Tony Richards and Steve Smith in the side. Trial games were always difficult games to play in because sides often comprised players who knew little about each other and it wasn't easy developing an understanding on the field. That's why I was able to work out the opposition's line-out signals before our own. Indeed, the games were often such a poor indicator of ability that it wasn't unusual for experienced internationals to find a convenient injury to avoid having to play in them. Some of the established players took the not unreasonable view that it was better to rely on past reputation rather than subject themselves to trial games – many of which were messy and disjointed affairs.

It was normal practice to stay down at Twickenham after the final trial for a squad training session and, after Christmas, I was one of 30 players called back for another session. I was really made up just to be there and was determined to shine and prove a bit of a nuisance to the senior players. Conversely, when I was England captain, I just wanted the rest to stop being a nuisance!

In trials and squad sessions it's possible to look out for your mates. I remember how Fran Cotton and Mike Burton in scrummaging practice seemed to work a little routine. Fran had been at tight-head with Stack Stevens at loose-head and they swapped over so that Fran was up against Burto. They made it look as though Fran was murdering him, with the result that he was kept at loose-head, which ensured that Burto got in at tight-head. In the end it was all in vain because, before they were due to play for England, Burto was sent off in a county championship game by Alan Welsby, the Lancashire referee – that being the occasion when he bowed to the crowd as he walked off. The result was that Stack returned at loose-head with the versatile Fran moving back across the front row.

England were due to open their Five Nations Championship campaign against Ireland in Dublin on January 18 and I was starting to take more than a usual interest in the deliberations of the selectors. On the day that I knew the team would be announced, I was on business in London with my uncle Joe, and I bought the first copy of the *Evening Standard* I spotted as we walked to our hotel. I somewhat feverishly scanned the sports pages and could hardly contain myself when I saw that I had been named as one of the six replacements. Needless to say, work was put on hold while Uncle Joe and I went for a couple of beers to celebrate. As I had expected, Roger Uttley had been named as the front-jumper, with Chris Ralston as his partner rather than Nigel Horton, who had been alongside him in the final trial.

Back in the 1970s the team was traditionally announced almost two weeks before the game and, in the case of a first cap, it was usual for the lucky player to stand down from his club side that weekend. I suppose that was done partly to ensure the player didn't miss his big moment by getting injured seven days before his international debut but, as I had only been named on the bench and because I just loved to play at whatever level, I turned out for Fylde against Nuneaton. So you get some idea of the enormous jump in standard players often had to make those days, whereas now the standard is so high in the Zurich Premiership that the step up to international level isn't quite so daunting.

Two years earlier England had gone to play in Dublin in spite of warnings from the IRA that there would be dire consequences if they did so. Their reception that day had been rapturous because both the Scots and the Welsh players had refused to travel to Dublin after receiving death threats, purportedly from the IRA. After the Nuneaton game I saw John Elders, an England selector who had formerly coached Northumberland, talking to Arthur Bell, the Fylde secretary. Arthur was holding a letter he had received from the IRA warning the supporters and I not to make the trip. The IRA needn't have bothered because not even a charge of the Light Brigade would have prevented me from travelling to Lansdowne Road. Admittedly I was only due to sit on the bench and might not even get on to the field, but I wasn't prepared to take the chance of missing out. The rest of the England squad responded in the same way and, once again, we were given the warmest of welcomes by the Irish, as I have always found to be the case – except when dealing with rugby politics. Whether you are playing, or just travelling as a spectator, Dublin is a wonderful place to be on a rugby international weekend.

I was entering new territory and didn't know anything of the protocol of playing international rugby. So I telephoned Tony Neary, who was working as a solicitor in Manchester, to find out what the procedure was and, as a result, joined him on the train from Manchester to London on the Thursday morning, having walked from my home to Adlington station, humping my bag, to catch the local train – a far cry from today when players very often fly to training sessions. On the way down I pumped Tony for information on the etiquette of playing for England and he was very helpful, being an old hand at that sort of thing.

There was a surprise awaiting me when we arrived at the Stoop for the training session. Robin Cowling, the Leicester prop, dropped a hint that I could be in the side, which was subsequently confirmed by Alec Lewis, the chairman of selectors. Apparently Roger Uttley had knackered his back eating an apple pie on the train – which just goes to show how sensitive his back was! – so I was to take his place in the training session. I may have resented Roger taking my place in the Fylde side when I initially got into the first team but, one way or another, he seemed hell-bent on helping my career thereafter through his own misfortunes. Alec said they hoped Roger would recover in time to play but thought I should partner Chris Ralston during the session to see how things went.

Alec is a lovely guy but I think he should have turned to an established guy like Nigel Horton or a more experienced player like Nick Martin. After all, I was just 22, had hardly ever played outside the north of England and had just one England trial to my credit. Having said that, I would have been massively disappointed if they had brought someone else into the squad and I suspect that John Burgess, who was coaching the side then, had pushed for my inclusion. I had established myself in the Lancashire team and had done really well on the county's tour of Zimbabwe and South Africa, so that may have led the selectors to believe that I was ready. Roger wasn't at the team's hotel so he was obviously receiving treatment elsewhere and I faced an anxious wait to see if he was going to recover in time. The answer to that question came at the crack of dawn on Friday morning when Alec awakened me to announce I was definitely playing. Offering his congratulations, he shook the hand of a very bog-eyed William Blackledge Beaumont who was still trying to come to terms with what day it was. It was like a dream come true but – perhaps because I was so naïve – I don't think I grasped the full significance of the occasion as I should have done. I did relay the news to my parents but, because it was such a last-minute thing, they weren't able to get across to Dublin in time to watch the game live.

We flew to Dublin and stayed at the Shelbourne Hotel along with the Irish side. It is highly unusual for the rival teams to stay under the same roof but at that time it was common practice in Ireland for security reasons. Each side stayed on different floors of the hotel and I remember finding myself in the lift at the same time as Irish hooker Pat Whelan, who was also making his international debut. He asked me if I had any spare tickets for the game. There was me thinking we had to be kept apart like caged animals until the first whistle!

For security reasons we weren't encouraged to leave the hotel and go walkabout, so we spent Friday afternoon and evening playing cards. When I ended up winning what was then quite a lot of money, Steve Smith said, 'You lucky bastard. You're not only getting your first cap but you've won £50 as well.' Not surprisingly, I was pretty worked up about the next day's match, but I found myself sharing a room with Chris Ralston and he was so laid back that he was almost horizontal. He would lie on his bed quietly smoking a cigar, and the last thing I saw as I went to sleep, as well as the first thing I saw when I awoke the following morning, was the red glow of its tip. The bedroom was a fog of cigar smoke.

Chris wasn't keen on John Burgess, both he and Andy Ripley were of the opinion he had arrived from an entirely different planet. They particularly didn't enjoy being hugged and kissed by him, but players like Fran, Tony Neary and myself were used to his ways and knew just how passionate he was about everything. He drove Rippers mad, but Chris would just stand and look on in disdain as he had the forwards going through different forward moves with players flying off in different directions. Chris didn't get picked to tour Australia at the end of that season and some time later, when he was playing at Richmond, he said, 'If you see that bastard Burgess, tell him I'm still playing top-class rugby.'

It was Fran Cotton's first game as skipper, Tony Neary was

at open-side and Steve Smith was on the bench, so there were one or two familiar faces around. Peter Dixon and Andy Ripley completed the back row, with John Pullin and Stack Stevens joining Fran up front. Jan Webster and Alan Old were the half-backs, Peter Preece and Peter Warfield were in the centre and David Duckham and Peter Squires were on the wings, with Peter Rossborough at full-back. We had a police escort to Lansdowne Road, where I found the dressing rooms were horrible, dark and dank, and I was so nervous I spent about half-an-hour in the loo. I didn't know anything about Ireland but I knew quite a bit about the player I would be up against – Willie-John McBride. He was winning his sixtieth Irish cap that day and was a hero after leading the British Lions on an unbeaten tour of South Africa the previous summer. He and I have met many times since and we have regularly spoken at dinners together. There is a tremendous aura about the man and I could understand why he was such a great captain and respected player. I don't think he was the world's best second row but he was a very impressive guy and I could imagine the impact he would make when he walked into the dressing room. It was his final season, and probably a journey too far for him. In the dressing room Fran, who had great respect for the Irishman, told me not to worry because he considered McBride to be past his best. I wish I had felt as convinced at the time.

Players have little superstitions and I liked to take the field last – something I was unable to do for much of my career except when I was playing for my club – so Dave Duckham, who in fact liked to do the same, kindly told me I could bring up the rear as it was my first international. I wasn't quite prepared for the wall of noise that hit us as we ran out, and the actual match passed by in a complete whirl. I remember the first Irish line-out. Willie-John glared at me and I was petrified because I didn't want to make a mistake. Whelan threw the ball to him at the front and the great man clambered all over me to win it. Fran delivered a quick pep talk and, at the next Irish throw, I managed to beat him to it and palm the ball back to Jan Webster who found touch farther down-field. I felt a lot better after that, I grappled with Willie-John after Ireland had taken a short penalty, and we ended up with a scrum when he was unable to release the ball. At least, after that, I felt I had got involved but I'm the first to admit that my contribution wasn't great. Our hooker, John Pullin, didn't throw the ball to me even once at the line-out, a tactic that I suspect had been planned beforehand in a bid to keep the pressure off me as much as possible.

We lost the game 12–9 with Billy McCombe proving the match-winner for Ireland, but we had murdered them up front, where Ralston gave Moss Keane a very hard time in the second row and Andy Ripley got the better of Willie Duggan, who I later came to know as quite an entertaining tourist. I know I'm not the first player to say that his international debut went by in a flash but that's exactly how it seemed, the sheer pace of the game taking me by surprise. That may explain why I wasn't able to make the impact in the loose that I had always endeavoured to do since moving into senior rugby.

Largely through the efforts of the pack, we actually led 9–6 with time running out, but our full-back, Peter Rossborough, slipped as he went to take a pass from scrum-half Jan Webster and McCombe swept up the loose ball to score and add the conversion. I remember slumping on to the bench in the dressing room afterwards and bursting into tears in sheer frustration as I tried to sort out in my mind what I might have done wrong or could have done better.

From the team's point of view I believe England would have been better served if, instead of me, the selectors had opted for Nigel Horton or any one of several other decent second rows who had been around rather longer than I had and, as a result, were more experienced. I suppose common sense prevailed in that I wasn't picked for any of the remaining games that season, but even though my debut hadn't been the outstanding success I had hoped for I was happy to have joined what I saw as a very exclusive club and determined to work even harder at my fitness and to learn from the experience.

John Burgess consoled me in the dressing room afterwards and I soon perked up because I was about to embark on the real business of a rugby weekend in Dublin. The fact that I can't remember anything of what happened after the dinner, a very sociable affair as you might expect knowing what good hosts the Irish are, is neither here nor there. There were, I was assured, not just players but also thousands of fans experiencing what you might call 'lost-weekend syndrome'. My abiding memory of that dinner is noting the affection with which Willie-John was so obviously held when he stood up to make his traditional speech. He had long been my idol and, having played against him and experienced the remarkable presence of the man, I was more determined than ever to make it as a rugby player.

Roger Uttley had recovered from his back injury so was able to resume instead of me when England played France at Twickenham. I had expected nothing less but at least I was named on the bench so I assumed I couldn't have done too much wrong in Dublin. For a moment towards the end of that game it looked as though Roger, having provided me with my first cap, would provide my passport to a second, as he was led from the field with blood gushing from a gash on his ear that later required 18 stitches. I was dispatched to the players' tunnel to prepare myself for combat but found the team doctor, Leo Walkden, busily taping Roger's head before sending him back into the fray.

England lost that game, too, 27–20, and that led to changes that didn't help my cause as the selectors frantically tried to avert a whitewash. Andy Ripley was left out and Roger Uttley moved into the back row. Although that left a vacancy in the second row they brought back Nigel Horton to partner Chris Ralston and, with a second row now in the back row, England needed a back row player rather than a second row like myself on the bench.

In those days England had an appalling record against Wales in Cardiff and 1975 was no exception. We were beaten 20–4 and that led to the axe swinging once more with Horton, Peter Wheeler and John Watkins the victims. Fran Cotton was ill, so

Mike Burton was brought in to replace him and, in typical Burton fashion, he asked if he was also taking over the captaincy. There's nothing like cheek, but it was Tony Neary who took on that responsibility for the first time.

Scotland were on for a rare Triple Crown when they travelled to Twickenham for the final game of a disappointing English season and they should have won the match. Dougie Morgan missed two simple penalties late in the game and England hung on to win 7–6 – hardly the best preparation for a summer tour to Australia. By that stage I had increased my training schedule, having acquired a rather better understanding of what was required to play consistently well at the top level, and I went back to enjoying my club rugby at Fylde. There was also greater recognition, because I was picked to play for the Barbarians on their traditional Easter tour to South Wales, travelling down in my maroon Austin Maxi along with Tony Richards, Dave Robinson – a tough Cumbrian farmer who played for Gosforth and later became an England coach – and my old partner Richard Trickey.

We partnered each other again in the opening game against Penarth. I wasn't included against Cardiff but was back in the side for what proved to be a very hard game against Swansea. That's when I came up against Geoff Wheel for the first time. Swansea had a decent side at that time and we had to play well to win but I was convinced that my own game was improving all the time, having started playing against the best second rows in Britain. I was also keen to be seen playing well because I was desperate to earn a call-up for the tour to Australia. My reasoning was that England had experienced a poor season and that a tour was the ideal vehicle for bringing on one or two young players.

When the touring party was announced it was just one of many botch jobs by the selectors and it is not difficult to see the wisdom of having one man responsible for picking the side, as Clive Woodward, England's head coach, does now. He has other experienced coaches he can talk to, but at the end of the day it is his decision and, in the case of failure, his neck that is on the block. I always felt that selection by committee was flawed and that too many good players were denied an opportunity because of wheeler-dealing, one selector supporting a player from a different region in return for securing support for a protégé of his own. That is hardly the way to mould a successful side. Nowhere has bad practice been more apparent than in schoolboy rugby, where the old-school-tie network still works today.

While I had been confident that the selectors would give one or two young players an opportunity, including me, I hadn't expected them to go overboard. Far too many experienced players were jettisoned and it wasn't difficult to work out why I was in the touring party when I saw that the experienced Chris Ralston and Nigel Horton were being left at home. Of the four half-backs in the party only one had actually won a cap, Bedford fly-half Neil Bennett having made his debut against Scotland in the final game of that season's Five Nations Championship. Alan Wordsworth, the other fly-half, and scrum-halves Brian Ashton and Peter Kingston, didn't possess a cap between them. I found it absolutely staggering that they had completely ignored what I regarded as the best half-back pairing in the country, Steve Smith and Alan Old.

Peter Rossborough and Tony Jorden had both played at full-back that season but were ignored, while the untried Peter Butler and Alistair Hignell were called up. Of the four second rows Roger Uttley was clearly very experienced but I had just one cap and the other two, Bob Wilkinson and Neil Mantell, were uncapped. Perhaps the selectors had decided on a very experimental approach because Australia had performed poorly on their last visit to the UK but, as I was to discover, Australians are tough nuts to crack in their own backyard.

I felt sorry for our coach, John Burgess, because he soon found himself condemned to making what he could of a thoroughly bad job and the tour was to end his dream of turning England into a major force in world rugby. Before transforming the fortunes of Lancashire and the North West, Burgess had spent hours picking the brains of former All Blacks coach Fred Allen and studying the way the best side in the world went about its preparation. He had so much to offer England but was denied the opportunity by ludicrous selections and undisguised hostility in certain quarters. Players like Fran Cotton, Tony Neary and I knew what John was about. We knew what made him tick and what he was trying to achieve but I suppose he was considered by some to be nothing more than an uncouth and loud-mouthed northerner. Yet, he never threw in the towel and, although his coaching ability was never allowed to blossom at international level, he did become a leading administrator in the game before being honoured with the Presidency of the RFU.

The opening game against Western Australia was a bit of a cakewalk but we lost the second game, against Sydney, 14–10. I almost lost more than the game because, for no apparent reason, I was clobbered by Steve Finnane, Sydney's international prop, as we ran across the pitch following the action. It was a mindless and unprovoked attack that left me out cold. There is no place in the game, at any level, for such behaviour but Finnane had a reputation for that sort of thing. During the same game he flattened Mike Burton and Steve Callum, a mystery player who suddenly appeared in the touring party from Upper Clapton but was barely heard of again. Two years later Finnane broke the jaw of Graham Price during a Welsh tour of Australia, so the guy built up quite a history of violent behaviour.

When I eventually came round from Finnane's pile-driver, I was persuaded by Tony Neary to leave the field and was joined on the treatment table – thankfully not literally, considering the size of the pair of us – by Fran Cotton. He had trapped a nerve in his back and was unable to take any further part in the tour. As we were to lose Tony Neary with damaged ribs in the first Test you could say that some of our heaviest artillery had been put out of commission.

Not all the Aussies were out of Finnane's mould, there being some guys you would happily have a drink with. One of those was a guy who became chief executive of Foster's Lager. I met him during the 2001 British Lions tour to Australia and he told me he had made his debut for Sydney that day and had subsequently watched my career with interest. I was more than happy to enjoy a few beers with him, but I have never had any desire to socialise with people like Finnane who go around whacking people off the ball when they don't know it's coming and are in no position to defend themselves.

My chances of a Test place seemed to have diminished because I wasn't involved in the 29–24 win over New South Wales, figuring instead in a surprise 14–13 defeat at the hands of a New South Wales Country XV. A place on the bench was the best I could hope for and that's what I ended up with for the first Test in Sydney, and what an unpleasant game that turned out to be. The Aussies were capable of playing some breathtaking rugby so I couldn't understand why they picked abrasive characters like Finnane who seemed more intent on intimidating than playing rugby against us.

Tony Neary injured his ribs midway in the first half and I was sent on to the battlefield. From a personal perspective it went quite well because I ended up front-jumping against a guy called Reg Smith and won my fair share of ball at the line-out. Though I say it myself, I had my best game of the tour in the loose and, after helping England to victory over Queensland in midweek with Bob Wilkinson as my partner we were picked as a pair for the second Test. So I won my third cap on merit instead of as a replacement, although I wish it could have been a more auspicious occasion. If we thought the first Test was bad then I am afraid we had seen nothing.

The Aussies launched themselves at us with all the ferocity

of caged animals that hadn't been fed for a long time, and I had trouble believing what was going on. Barry Nelmes, the Cardiff prop, won the ball at the kick-off but was tackled and, while he was on the floor, a pack of Aussie forwards raced in and started kicking him. Nowadays two or three players would have walked for that. The first line-out was just as bad. Mike Burton, never short of a quick riposte, said something to one of the Aussie forwards who was then heard saying 'Burton's got the biff on' to his team-mates who immediately piled into us. About four of them waded into me and I ended up needing stitches. My boys watched the incident on a Brian Moore video nasty that we somehow acquired recently and they thought it was absolutely hilarious that Dad had been unable to fight his way out of the situation. It was quite a long hike down the corridor to the dressing rooms at Ballymore and, as I was having the stitches inserted, I could hear studs clomping towards us. The next minute Burton walked in and slumped on to a bench, and when I asked what was wrong with him he told me he'd been sent off.

Nowadays a replacement prop would have been sent on as cover, with a flanker having to drop out to make way for him. Things were different then and sides had to cope as best they could. I should have stayed off but I thought bollocks to that, I'm going back on. I didn't want to be replaced in the first international I had actually been selected to start in. As a result I raced back to the pitch and joined John Pullin and Barry Nelmes in the front row. I was well fired up, but I had played at prop previously, albeit at nothing even approaching that level, and coped all right, losing only one put-in against the head all afternoon. One scrum did collapse and I reckon my opposite number, Ron Graham, who is now an Australian rugby administrator and a good guy, could have killed me had he been so inclined. That he didn't seemed rather odd, considering all that had gone on before!

I discovered later that Burton had delivered a late, late tackle on Doug Osborne, the Aussie wing and after the earlier fracas there was only one way he was going . . . and that was off. Mike took it badly, feeling he had let everyone down. I felt particularly for John Burgess because, through no fault of his own, everything was going wrong. Perhaps with a more experienced side things wouldn't have got quite so out of hand but the Aussies did have something of a reputation at that time and they had one or two players who just appeared to go looking for trouble. Sledging, as favoured by their cricketers, is one thing but unprovoked violence is a different matter and it is a wonder that nobody received a serious injury.

Steve Finnane had already shown his colours but their flanker Ray Price and hooker Peter Horton could also put it about to some tune. What I couldn't understand was that Horton was actually English and a teacher to boot. He was into Pom-bashing big-style and I only hope his language was rather better in the classroom. Price was a very talented player and turned up in England to play rugby league at Wigan. I met him at Central Park one day and with tongue in cheek said, 'I remember you Bill. You cut easily.'

It had been a disastrous tour and, even though I had

collected my third England cap, I still hadn't played on a winning side. Although I had made my debut the previous season England had only managed to win one Five Nations game – by a solitary point – and worse was to come. John Burgess resigned as national coach and, in the following season, England suffered a whitewash. A time of gloom and doom for English rugby but it wasn't all bad news for me because I met my wife Hilary.

Just before the start of the following season I was invited by a friend of mine to a girl's twenty-first birthday party but I declined, saying that it didn't seem right to attend when I didn't even know who she was. The following day I did attend a pre-season barbecue in St Annes that had been organised by one of the lads at Fylde, and ended up chatting to the attractive young lady whose party I had decided I couldn't possibly have attended the previous evening. Had I known it had been Hilary's birthday party I'm pretty sure I would have been first on the doorstep. We got along fine but it wasn't long before I was ensconced in a corner chatting about rugby with the lads and I didn't notice her again. Not that I was seeing too well by the end of the evening because one of the lads had been messing around with a golf club and a ball hit me in the eye. That forced me to withdraw from the club's two opening games against Coventry and Cheltenham, so I was not exactly a happy bunny. The first game I was able to play was a home fixture against Gloucester, a side packed with quality players and captained by Mike Burton. John Watkins, John Fidler, Peter Kingston, Peter Butler and John Bayliss were also in the line-up but I was determined to do well because I had trained hard during what had been left of the summer and wanted to get my season off to a good start. Fylde would usually settle for any sort of victory against a side of Gloucester's quality but we really got the bit between our teeth and beat them 31–3. I remember that we scored a try in the last minute of the game and then caught the restart and ran it back at them to score again. It was that sort of day and was about to get better.

In the bar afterwards I bumped into Hilary who had gone to the game with her sister and brother-in-law. She didn't know anything about rugby but her brother-in-law was quite keen and when I ran on to the field at the start of the game she was able to say that at least she knew the big guy with the number four on his back. Apparently he was quite impressed that she'd been chatting to an international rugby player but she couldn't understand what all the fuss was about. Anyway, she told me later that she hadn't been too impressed by my performance that afternoon because I hadn't been running around doing spectacular things with the ball. It took me some time to teach her that forwards have a very different but equally important role and that beating Gloucester 31–3 was not something you did every day.

My initial impression of Hilary was enhanced at our second meeting and I asked her out on a date. Unfortunately, I had forgotten the Lancashire trials so I had to hastily reschedule and, as it was, our first date coincided with Lancashire playing Cumberland and Westmorland in a warm-up game, for-tunately at Fylde's ground – a game in which the father of Sale

Sharks wing Mark Cueto was playing for the opposition. I wore my England blazer to impress and took her for a drink at the Grapes pub in nearby Wrea Green, not realising that we would one day be married and living just around the corner.

That was the start of a fine, if at times complicated, romance bearing in mind that rugby was tending to dominate my life and Hilary was a student in Manchester, preparing to become a French teacher. She shared a house with two other students and that's where we did most of our courting. Although it was often a case of snatching a few hours together between work, training and Hilary's studies we got engaged the following February. Fortunately, Hilary grew to love the game, which was just as well considering that, with three rugby-daft sons, it does rather dominate our lives. Instead of watching me play she now watches the boys and the only difference is that these days she has three times as many sets of dirty kit to wash and iron!

Throughout the ups and downs of my career, both in rugby and in business, Hilary has been my greatest supporter, confidante and friend – in short, the love of my life – and without her I would never have achieved half the things I have achieved. We are both basically shy people who enjoy nothing more than spending a quiet time with our family and, in a way, we had to force ourselves to do things that were being demanded of me because of the high profile I had acquired. I'm fortunate that she was always there to encourage me. If she hadn't been, there is a lot that would have been left undone. During the early years of our marriage she had to endure long separations that would have put a strain on many marriages but she coped with those well and has proved a wonderful mother to our children. She has held the ship steady during my absences and even now is involved in the business, becoming a director a few years ago. Since moving into household and upholstery fabrics, the feminine touch has been much appreciated and there is no problem when it comes to decision making because that is something we have always done together.

For my sins, I became a Lloyds Underwriter in the 1980s and, like a lot of people from the world of sport, I lost a lot of money in that venture, but with Hilary's help I worked my way through it. We were fortunate having the family business to fall back on.

Our engagement coincided with England having an even more disastrous time in the Five Nations Championship and I'm just grateful that Hilary and I were better at selecting our partners than the England selectors were at picking a side that might actually win something. With John Burgess gone from the scene, England elevated their Under-23 coach Peter Colston into the hot seat and it really was a baptism of fire. Peter's one saving grace was that we did manage to beat Australia, even if we lost everything else.

At least I was picked to play for England in what was effectively a trial game against the North and Midlands at Leicester. (It would be interesting to discover just how many different permutations of trials the selectors devised during what you might regard as some of the bleakest seasons in England's history.) The game at Leicester was hardly a confidence-booster because we were beaten by a combined divisional side led by Peter Wheeler. The selectors' axes were not merely sharpened after that but used with bloody effect, and seven members of that side were dispatched. Thankfully, I wasn't one of those beheaded, and I also survived a narrow victory over the South at Gloucester when three more changes were made for the final trial at Twickenham just before Christmas.

I held my place as we won 39–21 and the selectors picked us *en bloc* to take on Australia. Sadly for Roger Uttley he had been forced to pull out of the trial through injury, his place taken by Andy Ripley. The team included three new caps: Barrie Corless, the Coventry centre; Mark Keyworth, my old team-mate at Ellesmere College who was playing for Swansea; and a scrum-half who appeared to come from nowhere and who almost as quickly went back there. Mike Lampkowski, who was of Polish extraction, played for Headingley and had been a member of the North and Midlands side that beat England in the trial game. He was a very powerful player and extremely committed. He could batter his way through all but the best defences but he lacked that one ingredient that is so necessary to a scrum-half: he couldn't pass a ball quickly and accurately and, at international level, you aren't afforded the luxury of time.

As debut games go, Lampkowski's wasn't too bad. It can sometimes happen that a new boy gets an adrenalin rush and plays better than he will ever play again. Certainly, the lad played out of his skin, despite his limited repertoire, scoring a try, and many were left thinking we had unearthed a real find. For obvious reasons, we were very keen to beat Australia but it turned out to be a very different Aussie side, especially in terms of attitude. The only Test they in fact managed to win was against Ireland in Dublin. We recorded what, at the time, was the biggest ever victory over our Commonwealth cousins from Down Under. Even with Steve Finnane, Peter Horton and Stuart MacDougall in their front row the game passed without incident, although the 23–6 scoreline may have given us a false impression of just where we stood in the pecking order. In those days the Aussies were nowhere near the force they have been in the last decade.

Having earned the first three of my four caps against Australia, it was great, from a personal point of view, to be given the chance to play against the other countries in the Five Nations Championship. Yet it was a campaign to forget as we suffered a whitewash that had more to do with the selectors than the guys out on the park. We were well beaten by Wales, but then Lampkowski and Martin Cooper were up against Gareth Edwards and Phil Bennett so the first chinks were seen in the scrum-half's armour. The difference in class was patently obvious and Lampowski's form had reached crisis level by the time we had succumbed to Scotland 22–12 at Murrayfield. Alan Old had been drafted in to partner him but passes were flying all over the place and he made a number of suicidal breaks, which resulted in him spending much of the game under a pile of Scottish bodies. Panic set in but the selectors kept faith with Mike and, instead, dropped our key line-out jumper at the back of the line, Andy Ripley, and replaced him with Leicester's Garry Adey, who was much smaller and never reappeared in England colours once the campaign finished. Dave Duckham was injured so my Lancashire colleague Mike Slemen won his first cap in the 13–12 defeat by Ireland at Twickenham and, that time, Lampkowski paid the ultimate price after another poor game in which his inadequacies were once again exposed. I must confess to feeling sorry for him. It wasn't his fault and he was being asked to do a job that, quite clearly, he was incapable of doing. Nobody helped him to either improve his service or iron out some of the wrinkles in his game.

While Mike stayed in the side we simply couldn't set up our backs, and I couldn't believe that the selectors could ignore the claims of Steve Smith. I know he was a mate but when you play alongside a player you discover what sort of contribution he is capable of making and there was no doubt in my mind at that time that Smithy and Alan Old made up the best half-back pairing in the country. They were ignored for too long and it is interesting that both played key roles in the tremendous success of the North side that so comprehensively beat the All Blacks at Otley in 1979. There is an irony about Smithy being forced out by Lampkowski. He had been told by the selectors at the trial stage to concentrate his efforts on getting the ball out to the backs quickly, which is exactly what he did. Then, when he was left out of the side, he was told that he hadn't been taking defences on in quite the manner that Lampkowski had. If that wasn't double-Dutch then I don't know what is. Smithy was penalised for obeying instructions and not playing his natural game. In any case, he had the ability to play it whichever way they wanted and was experienced enough, once on the field, to determine the tactics rather than adhere slavishly to whatever battle plan had been concocted in the dressing room.

Even when the selectors finally turned to Smithy that season, having dropped Lampkowski, they still contrived to get it horribly wrong. Initially they paired Steve with Moseley's Martin Cooper for the game against France in Paris but Martin was getting over an injury and, before we flew out on the Thursday, he was subjected to the most rigorous fitness test I have ever seen. If he had started out fit there is no way he would have been at the end, and, surprise, surprise, he was ruled out of the game.

At that stage it was patently obvious to everyone involved that Alan Old, who had already been named on the replacements' bench, was the player who should be called in at the eleventh hour. All except for the selectors who plucked another name out of the hat and Chris Williams, the Gloucester fly-half, was rushed out to the French capital to earn his one and only cap, while poor Alan sat and watched us go from bad to worse.

When I think of how organised things are today in the England camp it is difficult even trying to comprehend just how chaotic it used to be. You really did have to be involved to understand how bad it was and I had sympathy for Chris because an international debut is tough enough anyway without it being made even more difficult by going in unprepared, and having to join a losing side that was very low on morale.

France hammered us 30–9 and seven members of that side – Garry Adey, Bob Wilkinson, John Pullin, Peter Butler, Ken Plummer, David Cooke and Chris Williams – were never seen again. I had only been on one winning side in eight international starts but survived to fight again. It was little wonder we were so poor because the standard of selection was awful and too many of the players, myself included, simply weren't playing at a competitive enough level on a regular basis. By that stage I had found club rugby pretty well pressure-free and it was only in the county season that the standard was high enough to be meaningful. Even then there was a big disparity in terms of the ability of the county sides and, with a side as strong as Lancashire had become, there were a limited number capable of asking serious questions of us. Gloucestershire would always do that and, in the northern region, Northumberland enjoyed a dominant spell with a side based largely on the successful Gosforth club. It has been very different since the game went professional and the best players have been confined to a smaller club elite, much though some in the game hate the thought of any form of elitism at club level. With top players scattered around a great many clubs, it was a mammoth, costly and time-consuming task for selectors to traverse the length and breadth of the country checking on form.

The present England management not only has its senior squad available for training on a regular basis but is also able to monitor progress by taking in just six games every weekend. Very often those games are spread over three days and, even if Clive Woodward and his coaches can't always get to games they have the facility of watching match videos. Nothing is left to chance and most countries now envy our domestic competition.

The 1976–7 season dawned with me in good condition and spirits. I was due to get married, Lancashire were sweeping all before them, Fylde even had a good run in the John Player Cup, rugby's equivalent to the FA Cup, and the British Lions were due to go on tour to New Zealand the following summer. My hope was that I might possibly be in with a chance of a Lions tour providing that I stayed in the England side and performed well. I thought my chances had been enhanced when a combined North and Midlands side crushed Argentina 24–9 at Leicester, just seven days before the Argies lost by a mere point to Wales in Cardiff. A lot of good it did me. England had a new selection committee, headed by the genial Sandy Sanders and including Mike Weston, Derek Morgan and Budge Rogers, and I was dropped down to the Rest side for the final trial. Not only was I fed up over my demotion, I also had to abstain from seeing in the New Year in traditional liquid fashion because the administrators, in their infinite wisdom, decided to play the trial game on New Year's Day. The only saving grace was that I was in some fairly good company, with Steve Smith and John Horton at half-back and Dusty Hare at full-back. All three were with me when we performed the Grand Slam three years later. We dominated the line-out, largely through the efforts of Andy Ripley who had been given a roving commission at the line-out with me and the other second row, Barry Ayres, acting as decoys. At the interval the sides were level so Barry and I were promoted to the England team in place of Bob Wilkinson and Roger Powell and the seniors ran out comfortable 20–3 victors. That ensured that I was in the starting line-up when the Five Nations began but, even though selection improved that season, there was still a glaring omission – Tony Neary.

I had played alongside Tony for Lancashire, the North and England ever since I had broken through into the senior ranks and knew he was an enormously talented player. Peter Dixon was another badly treated by a succession of English selection panels although, under Sandy, they got it right that season by including him. As they also picked Roger Uttley as captain, England could have had a back row of Uttley, Dixon and Neary. They had to wait until Otley two years later to discover just what they had been missing: three great-thinking footballers and first-rate ball-handlers, who played Graham Mourie's All Blacks off the park to record a memorable victory that, I suspect, still rankles with the New Zealanders.

We beat the Scots 26–6 at Twickenham and were almost getting giddy with excitement when we beat Ireland at a muddy Lansdowne Road. For the second successive game the English pack took control, although it was fly-half Martin Cooper who got over for the only score of the game following a good break by current broadcaster Alistair Hignell – another talented footballer whose fearless tackling provided much-needed solidity in defence. As a cricketer of county standard he also had good hands.

Nobody needed reminding that we were just two games away from a Grand Slam but our next outing was to be against the same French side that had demolished us twelve months earlier. We faced the same fearsome pack but, in 1977, we gave as good as we got and should have won the game, which ended 4–3 in favour of the French. Even then they were assisted by Alistair missing five out of six kicks at goal and further helped by a very dubious try scored by their centre François Sangalli after everyone other than the referee had been convinced that full-back Jean-Michel Aguirre had knocked on. The French boys admitted afterwards that they felt we had deserved to win.

Michel Palmie played in the French second row that day, as he had a year earlier, and we got to know each other quite well. At one stage we served on the European Cup committee together, and I soon learned that when he was present at the meetings held in Dublin it was not a good idea to stay overnight unless, of course, I wanted to get completely wrecked. He played for Béziers, and when Hilary and I went on a camping holiday in that region in the summer of 1978, I decided to give him a call. He came round to the site to take us back to his place and caught me doing the washing-up. I never lived that down and he demanded to know, 'Why is a man doing the washing-up. What is a wife for!' I won't relate Hilary's comments here, but he became a good friend and we rarely pass through that part of the world without popping in to share a glass or two – or maybe a few more – with Michel.

That defeat ended our Grand Slam hopes but I had other things on my mind because Hilary and I were married three days later, four days before I turned out to help Lancashire beat Middlesex in the county final. To say that Hilary was a very understanding young woman would be to understate the case but, by then, she had grown accustomed to the inconveniences of having an international rugby player as a partner. Fortunately, she had grown to enjoy both the game and the company, and had become part of the social scene at Fylde, doing her stint on the ladies committee and helping with some of the unglamorous work behind the scenes such as ensuring that numerous starving players didn't go hungry after games.

Our honeymoon had to be put on ice until the end of the season. Or at least that was the plan. In the meantime we travelled to Cardiff to take on Wales for the Triple Crown and my one great regret is that I never played in a winning England side at the National Stadium. Even before the new Millennium Stadium replaced it, the old stadium had lost some of its aura, but when I was playing it was an intimidating venue. As you waited like Gladiators in the dressing room you would hear the biggest choir in the world giving full voice, and that was worth a few points start to the Welsh. The current England side isn't at all intimidated by travelling to Cardiff, but Wales have been a very pale shadow of what they once were.

Wales won the game 14–9. We played badly and I didn't perform well against Geoff Wheel, which annoyed me because I knew the British Lions party to tour New Zealand was due to be announced a couple of weeks later. Knowing that they would take four second rows, I had held on to the hope all season that I might just scrape in but Geoff Wheel got the call rather than me and was due to have Gordon Brown, Nigel Horton and Allan Martin as his travelling companions. Geoff withdrew from the party later. I heard the news on the car radio, and my heart almost missed a beat as I waited for the name of his replacement to be announced. When it turned out to be Moss Keane I couldn't believe it. I had played against Moss on a couple of occasions and thought myself to be the better player.

The Lions were travelling without a specialist front-of-line jumper but that wasn't the only piece of poor planning; I also felt the management team was wrong. The late George Burrell went as manager and though he was a nice bloke he was rather dominated by coach John Dawes, who virtually ran the whole show through Phil Bennett. John had captained the successful Lions in New Zealand in 1971 but he wasn't the world's best coach and I suspect he had pushed for Phil, who had captained Wales, to be given the job in New Zealand. Phil is a nice guy but rather shy and he lacked the personality of Willie-John McBride who had led the all-conquering Lions in South Africa three years earlier. Indeed, Phil was the first to admit that he shouldn't have taken the job and, by the end of the tour, he had lost form and was homesick, something that seemed to afflict the Welsh lads more than the other nationalities.

Once I had heard about the inclusion of Moss Keane I was so brassed off that I booked a honeymoon in Majorca during the time when the Lions were away, and when the factory closed down for the annual Whitsun holiday, Hilary and I took ourselves off on a camping holiday to the Lake District with our long-standing friends Steve and Sue Braithwaite. In fairly typical Lake District fashion the weather was terrible. It poured down so, in the end, we packed up and returned home. We arrived back on a Monday evening and I suggested to Steve that we take the wet tents to the factory where they could dry out while the workforce were away on holiday. When I went into the office I took a telephone call from Malcolm Phillips, a Fylde member and Lions selector, telling me that Nigel Horton had broken his thumb playing against Otago and would be in plaster for six weeks. I was about to become a Lion.

CHAPTER FOUR

Lion cub

Although I realised I was the Lions sixth-choice second row I wasn't going to quibble, and I started hastily clearing the decks at work. The adrenalin at that stage was flowing and my first task was to ring Fylde secretary Peter Makin. I had been appointed captain for the following season but told Peter that, as I wouldn't be starting the new season because of the tour, I wanted scrum-half Micky Weir to take on the role. Micky took on the responsibility and did a fantastic job – such a good job, in fact, that I never achieved my ambition of becoming club skipper. As I became even more heavily involved with England I decided to put the club job on the back burner until I stepped down from the international arena, but injury put paid to any such plan.

Micky and Peter came round to wish me all the best and speed me on my way, and Hilary travelled down with me, but it was a somewhat pensive William Beaumont who arrived in

London to collect his gear and jet off to the other side of the world. Instead of feeling over the moon, I felt heartbroken. I remember wondering why on earth I had agreed to travel. I had just got married, my honeymoon had been postponed yet again and I experienced the same empty feeling that had marked my return to boarding school as a youngster.

I had to meet John Lawrence, secretary of the Four Home Unions Committee, at a Club in London in order to be measured up for my Lions blazer and flannels, so we set off a little late to drive to Heathrow to catch the flight to Auckland which, just to stop me getting bored, was dropping in at Los Angeles, Hawaii and Fiji *en route*. If I had mixed feelings about having to leave Hilary to join the Lions, I felt all the more like turning around and going back home when a crash in the underpass on the approach to Heathrow effectively brought traffic to a standstill. There was nothing else for it. I had to grab my kit-bag and my new Lions outfit and leg it through the tunnel to the check-in desk at the terminal, arriving only just in time for the flight. It was a very hot day and I was saturated in perspiration, so I felt sorry for the poor devil who had to spend all those hours sitting next to me on the aircraft.

It seemed like forever before the plane touched down in Auckland. I had been told to wait in the arrivals hall where I would be met by a New Zealand rugby official who would en-sure I was placed on the correct onward flight to Christchurch on the south island, the Lions' next port of call after travelling from Invercargill, where they had beaten Southland. By that stage, with the first Test approaching, they had chalked up eight straight victories. I was handed a bundle of Auckland newspapers to hand over to a guy called 'Doc' Murdoch. He was a great guy: a Kiwi who was travelling with the Lions as a sort of physiotherapist-cum-baggage man. Quite apart from working on our bodies he also had responsibility for moving mountains of kit around the country. He had worked with the Lions in 1971 and was chuffed that they asked especially for his services again. As a mark of respect for someone who was popular with the entire party, we ended up paying for him to travel to Fiji with us at the end of the tour.

When I arrived in Christchurch, feeling shattered from having spent more than 30 hours squashed into an aircraft seat in the economy section, I was met by crisp, frosty weather and Russ Thomas, the New Zealand official who later managed the All Blacks side that the North beat so memorably at Otley two years later. Russ took me to meet my fellow Lions, and I remember Willie Duggan, the Irishman, saying to me, 'If you have any bloody sense you will get on the next plane back home.'

As I was to discover, that particular tour was marred by atrocious weather and it was usually a case of mud, glorious mud. The photograph of a bedraggled Fran Cotton became the company logo when he set up Cotton Traders with Steve Smith and people still walk around with the picture on the front of their tee-shirts. It didn't take me too long to work out that it was a far from happy tour. Some Lions tours have been noticeable for a wonderful spirit, whereas others have all but fallen apart; this one definitely fell into the latter category (to some extent, the 2001 trip to Australia wasn't exactly a bundle of laughs either). In the end it all comes down to good, firm management, and that's something they had in abundance in South Africa in 1997 when Fran went as manager and had Ian McGeechan and Jim Telfer as a well-balanced coaching team right out of the 'good-cop, bad-cop' mould.

It is a strange experience walking in to meet a large group of people who are to be your travelling companions for the next few weeks and I was pleased to see the reassuring faces of players like Fran, Tony Neary, Peter Wheeler and Peter Squires. Derek Quinnell, who I had never met before, also made me very welcome, offering me some of his kit when he learned that mine had been lost in transit.

The Lions were due to play their ninth game against New Zealand Universities on the Tuesday before the first Test in Wellington and I had to sit and watch the side suffer its first defeat. Gordon Brown injured his shoulder and had to be replaced by Allan Martin – an injury that also kept Broonie out of the Test. Moss Keane suffered concussion but was considered to have recovered sufficiently to be fit enough to start in the Test team alongside Allan. That wouldn't have happened today because he would have been sidelined for three weeks as a very understandable and necessary precaution. I can only assume the management wasn't prepared to pitch me straight into a Test match.

Defeat didn't rest easily with John Dawes, and the training session the following morning was the hardest I had ever taken part in. There was no way anybody would have been fully recovered in time for the Test match. Dawes came in for a lot of criticism for that session and Fran, as hard and conscientious a trainer as you could wish to meet, accused him of literally burning out the Test team. It was no wonder the selected players looked lethargic when they went down 16–12 in the Test at Athletic Park. The session was only my second since arriving, and although I had tried to keep in shape during the summer I wasn't as finely tuned as players who had been touring for several weeks. Yet I was determined to demonstrate that I was worthy of my place in the squad and, although blokes were dropping like ninepins, I willed myself to keep going.

When the Test side was announced I was staggered to discover that Fran had been left out, but then I couldn't understand why they had take Ireland's Phil Orr as a loosehead rather than Ian McLauchlan in the first place. Trevor Evans got the vote at open-side ahead of Tony Neary, another selection I couldn't understand because Nero proved to be the missing link from the pack when he was eventually included for the final Test, by which time it was too late.

The weather was as miserable as ever on Test day and the authorities even had to call in a helicopter to use its rotor blades to spread the pools of standing water across the rest of the pitch. They then played a warm-up game, so the pitch was in an even worse state when the main event got under way. The line-out was a shambles from the Lions point of view and I was learning quickly that some referees in the southern hemisphere seemed quite happy to settle for a free-for-all. The

Lions missed Gordon Brown's presence and I felt it would have been a different story if he and the injured Nigel Horton had been paired together to take on Andy Haden and Frank Oliver.

The killer moment came when the Lions were attacking and had engineered an overlap. All Black wing Grant Batty anticipated a delayed pass from Trevor Evans to Phil Bennett and galloped in from long range just before half-time. Phil had been struggling anyway after Willie Duggan had landed on his shoulder quite early in the game – an injury that meant he was unable to lead the Lions in the next match against a South-Mid-Canterbury and North Otago Select XV. That job went to Terry Cobner who had also taken over responsibility for coaching the forwards. I was pleased about that because I had already spotted serious deficiencies in the two games I had witnessed. There was a lack of set-piece basics and no apparent organisation at kick-offs and drop-outs. I was selected to make my Lions debut in the game alongside Allan Martin and felt more confident with Cobner taking charge. I was also boosted to see that he would be joined in the back row by Nero and Derek Quinnell. My luck was in because with Peter Wheeler as hooker I knew the ball would be thrown in well at the line-out.

Fran, who had roomed with me that week, told me I would always remember Timaru because a Lions debut is such a special occasion. He couldn't have been more right. The build-up with Cobner was good and we rattled off a 45–6 victory. I was up against a 6-foot-and-8-inches-tall second row but he didn't pose me any real problems and I felt I had had a good game. I believed that I was at least on board the bus, so to speak, and I looked forward to the next encounter. I didn't play in the next game against Canterbury – a game the Lions won narrowly – but was paired with Moss Keane against West Coast Buller in Westport. We rattled up another 45 points without reply and I even managed my first try in a Lions shirt!

They say that every cloud has a silver lining but the opposite can be the case, as for me when I found myself sharing a room with Moss Keane and Willie Duggan. What an experience that was. Lovable they may be but conventional they most certainly are not and the room was a complete tip from start to finish. There had always been a degree of order in my life and I found it difficult coping with the mountains of bags, kit and dirty washing, not to mention the used plates and glasses and overflowing ashtrays. What a disorganised pair! As for training, Willie absolutely loathed it, yet on the field he was always capable of pulling it out when it mattered. The two of them were wonderful tourists and good mates.

We beat Wellington 13–6 in my absence but I was picked to play against Marlborough-Nelson Bays at Blenheim four days before the crucial second Test. For the first time I was paired with Gordon Brown and he came up to me and said he'd heard a whisper that if we played well together we would be picked in the Test side. I told him there was no way they would pick me because I felt I hadn't played enough to make an impression. Broonie wouldn't have it though, and said we ought to try to work really well as a pair. It went okay but I was absolutely knackered after an hour and he told me to pull my finger out. My response was to tell him to go for it if he wanted to be in the Test team but that I didn't think I was up to it. He bullied me into even greater effort however and we were both picked in the side the following day. Fran and Peter Wheeler replaced Phil Orr and Bobby Windsor in the front row, with Quinnell taking over from Trevor Evans in the back row, but there was still no place for Nero. They also dropped Peter Squires – in my view mistakenly – and replaced him with Gareth Evans, from Newport.

It was hard to comprehend that I was about to start in a British Lions Test match when just a month earlier I had been camping in the Lake District with Hilary and contemplating a belated honeymoon in Majorca. Needless to say the telephone lines were burning that day.

Cobner must take a lot of credit for the build-up to the game in Christchurch. Normally on a tour the squad splits fairly quickly into a Test side and a midweek side, often referred to as the Dirt Trackers, but that hadn't happened in 1977. Indeed, it was only at that stage, the week of the second Test, that the senior side started to come together. That had made life difficult for Terry in terms of working out a forward strategy based on the differing abilities of what was considered to be the senior pack, and there had been no overall pattern to the play of the Lions.

With Terry's leadership we opted to play the mauling type of game so beloved by Pontypool in the 1970s – a style that made the Welsh club, already famed for its front row of

Charlie Faulkner, Bobby Windsor and Graham Price, into one of the most feared in the northern hemisphere. It may have been considered boring by those who enjoy a flowing game, and in the final analysis it may have been overdone on that tour, but we at least started playing to our strengths, and the style was to give us the win we so desperately needed.

Our preparations having gone well, Terry took the forwards into the shower room to get us fired up, so, with the adrenalin flowing, we got off to an explosive start. Throughout the tour, the New Zealand forwards had been jumping across and barging at the line-out, being allowed to get away with it by the match officials. We decided to match like with like and succeeded in knocking the stuffing out of the All Blacks. With the attention we received I had difficulty making two-handed catches, but I was able to palm the ball down at the line-out to our sweeper, Derek Quinnell, and, while Broonie outplayed Andy Haden in the middle, Willie Duggan was winning more than his share at the back.

As one might have expected the All Blacks didn't take too kindly to being dominated up front, because we out-scrummaged them as well, and things kicked off a bit. Phil Bennett was felled by a late tackle from Kevin Eveleigh, the New Zealand flanker who was up to skulduggery throughout a game that was played on the now almost obligatory mud-heap. It was a terrible game of rugby. Everyone was fighting and kicking and you just got carried along with it. That has never been a side of the game I have had much time for, but if you don't fight then you feel as though you are letting down your mates. A lot of brawls start because of peer pressure within a team and that day I ended up doing things I had never done before and have never done since on a rugby field.

Our fired-up opening had given us a 13–3 lead by the end of the first quarter. Phil Bennett kicked three penalties and it was his kick-and-chase that set up a try. He regained possession to combine with Broonie, Derek Quinnell and Ian McGeechan to send JJ Williams away. The Welsh wing used a supporting Andy Irvine as a decoy as he scampered over the line. Bryan Williams kicked a couple of penalties for the All Blacks but missed one late in the game as they came back at us. The closing stages were pretty frantic but we held on for a win that the partisan crowd didn't like and that the All Blacks weren't exactly overjoyed about either. We, of course, were delighted to have squared the series.

I had been pleased with my performance but perhaps shouldn't have been too surprised at being in the side because one of my team-mates had suggested it might be on the cards. At a formal dinner after the first Test – an unusual occurrence on a Lions tour – Moss Keane had introduced me to Frank Oliver, whom he had played against that afternoon. Moss predicted that I would be playing as Frank's opposite number in the second Test. At the time, I had yet to play a game, having only just arrived in New Zealand, but Moss clearly rated me higher than sixth in the second-row pecking order.

The tour suffered from weak management, as was evident after that successful Test. A dance had been organised in our honour at a local rugby club but the players decided they wanted to stay at the hotel and celebrate in their own way. We had previously accepted the invitation and I thought it very discourteous of us not to turn up. That was an occasion when the management should have put its foot down and insisted that we attend a function that people had put a lot of effort into organising. When I was captain of the Lions and England I always made sure that we honoured our obligations. Perhaps the decision had been prompted by the animosity of the All Blacks in the game and shown afterwards by some of their supporters. Not only did the latter give full voice to their feelings but some of the comments were also of the nasty variety and one chap even threw beer at JJ Williams. All the more reason why we should have turned up at the function. As it was, three of their players came to our hotel to join us for a drink, which only made us look worse.

In some respects a siege mentality was creeping into the squad. Despite being in the land of the long white cloud, surrounded by beautiful scenery, there was very little by way of entertainment and we spent an awful lot of time hanging around our various hotels, the standard of which was generally poor. Playing golf offered some release but that wasn't always possible. I remember on one occasion Gordon Brown and I having to call off a round with the Governor General before the first Test because the rain was coming down like stair rods. Living in the UK you might think we would have been used to cold, wet weather but that's not what you want or expect when you go away from home. On a long tour it is important to have quality leisure time and it helps enormously if the sun shines so that you can relax by the pool or on the beach, play golf or tennis, or simply go for a walk. The tour I led to South Africa in 1980 was, despite all our injury problems and the fact that we lost the Test series, a much happier affair; I used the New Zealand experience to ensure that this was so.

The seeds of professionalism were probably sown on tours like that 1977 visit to New Zealand where the players were placed in poor hotels, devoid of facilities, despite the fact that the event was generating a lot of money for the host nation. Though I would never have thought of getting paid for playing the game I enjoyed, I can fully understand why players started to demand some recompense for the growing pressures of performing at the highest level, with the attendant sacrifices that had to be made.

We won our next four games in the build-up to the third Test, the biggest winning margin being the 34–15 defeat of Auckland, which some wrote up as our best performance of the tour. Once again I partnered Gordon Brown and we then had a full week's break before the Test match at Carisbrook Park in Dunedin. Unfortunately it wasn't a long enough break for Brynmor Williams, who had injured a hamstring and was a doubtful starter, while the other scrum-half, Dougie Morgan, was suffering from a groin strain. Brynmor eventually made the starting line-up but we suffered an immediate setback when Ian Kirkpatrick scored a try in the opening minute after centre Bruce Robertson had kicked ahead. I'm afraid I rather had a hand in the try, literally, because I had palmed the ball back at the first line-out, having got to it ahead of Frank

Oliver. I had been aiming for Peter Wheeler but my direction was poor and it was gobbled up by Brian Ford, the All Blacks wing. He set up a ruck from which, to our complete surprise, they decided to run. The result was the try, and that proved a hammer blow from which we never recovered even though the pack dominated the All Blacks. Brynmor did produce a blind-side break that led to a try for Willie Duggan but he limped out of the action early in the second half to be replaced by Morgan. We kept battering away up front but it was all going wrong behind and both Phil Bennett, who by that stage had so obviously lost his confidence, and Andy Irvine missed penalty chances they would normally have gobbled up.

The All Blacks had done their homework and, perhaps sensing that we more than had the measure of their pack, they kept the action away from the forwards as much as possible. They also introduced a new flanker in the shape of Graham Mourie, of whom much was to be heard in the following years. He had tremendous pace, read the game well and in many respects reminded me of Tony Neary, who we had again failed to get on to the field. Having played many, many games with Nero I was as puzzled by the Lions rejection of him as I was when he was similarly pushed to one side by the England selectors.

We won a lot of ball for our backs but they appeared to lack the confidence to play the adventurous game favoured by the opposition, kicking too much away or indulging in lateral running. In some respects it was almost a role reversal in that era for an All Blacks pack to be outplayed by the Lions but a

Lions back division to be given the run around by the All Blacks. The result in that game, of course, meant that we could no longer win the series.

By the time we reached the final Test at Eden Park, Auckland, both Terry Cobner and Derek Quinnell had been ruled out through injury. Jeff Squire took over from Derek and Tony Neary won his first and only Lions cap as well as taking over the role of pack leader. The changes made no difference to our forward effort and once again we had the All Blacks scrum under tremendous pressure. Indeed, we dominated the forward exchanges even more completely than we had in the previous test and with Doug Morgan and Phil Bennett kicking far better than at Carisbrook we deservedly led 9–3 at the interval.

In the second half, Morgan kicked a penalty and then scored a try courtesy of Lancashire. Nero won the ball at the tail of a line-out, Fran Cotton and I combined on the peel to set up a maul in midfield and Doug was left with the simple task of picking up the ball and scampering over their line. It was a move we had executed many times for Lancashire and one we had also introduced to England. We should have pulled away to level the series but the host nation trimmed our lead to three points and then Doug missed a fairly simple penalty that would have sewn things up. The game moved into injury time and it still looked as though we would achieve our objective until Phil Bennett failed to find touch and Bill Osborne gathered the ball and kicked towards the corner. Steve Fenwick caught the ball but failed to make a mark and was tackled by Osborne. Somehow Peter Wheeler got his hands on the ball but he was hit by Mourie and the ball went loose to Lawrie Knight, who dived over the line. We had lost 10–9 and all the hard work of the pack had been in vain. I was choking with disappointment and could see Phil Bennett in tears. For the tour captain defeat is even harder to bear, if that's possible.

I had only arrived in New Zealand at about the half-way stage of the tour but, as intimated earlier, it hadn't taken me long to work out that the tour was beset with problems that came about largely through weak management. George Burrell, the manager, was a delightful man but he let John Dawes dominate and make too many mistakes. I'm not going to pillory John for that because we are only human and all make mistakes from time to time but I think both he and George became very sensitive to media criticism, with the result that we ended up a very insular bunch. Looking back I wonder what our image must have been like. There was one occasion when the management had planned a closed training session, but when we arrived a crowd of mainly youngsters had turned up to watch. John was all for driving off there and then but Fran Cotton stood up, said he couldn't believe what we were doing, and led us all off the bus to train in front of them. We should have been encouraging those kids, and – with that in mind – I vowed to make the tour to South Africa in 1980, for which I was offered the captaincy, a far more open and interactive affair, involving the local community as much as possible.

I hadn't really known John Dawes before the tour. I had shaken his hand once after a game and regarded him as something of an icon for the way he had led Wales and the 1971 Lions. He had clearly been a good captain and player but that didn't necessarily make him a great coach, and the longer I played top-class rugby the more I came to realise that it wasn't necessarily a natural progression. Some of the best coaches had never played international rugby and that included John's opposite number, All Blacks coach Jack Gleeson, who was an excellent coach but was uncapped, having come through their provincial system.

I don't know what happened before I joined the tour but maybe there had been a feeling that, having won the series there in 1971 and then swept undefeated through South Africa three years later, the Lions expected to win again. But the thing I respect about the New Zealanders is that they welcome you with open arms yet then make no bones about the fact that they want to beat you. That starts the minute you step off the aircraft and, as a sportsman, I respect that attitude and wish it was more evident in our own sporting make-up.

It may not have been a particularly happy tour but the good things to come out of it were the friendships I forged with a number of players and, in particular, Gordon Brown, who never played international rugby again after that tour. We would play golf together, and after we had both retired from the game we would get together with our families. Very often we found ourselves speaking on the same bill at sportsmen's dinners, at which I always insisted on batting first because

Gordon was a better and more natural orator than I was. He was a warm man with a wonderful sense of humour and a fund of amusing stories and anecdotes. We even went on supporters' tours together and he came to speak at the Fylde dinner when I announced my retirement from the game. He had made his Scotland debut in 1969 against South Africa but hadn't played in the Five Nations Championship prior to the 1977 Lions tour. In many respects he was a big-match player who didn't always play like a British Lion. I can vouch for his talent, having played against him on a number of occasions (Fylde versus his club, West of Scotland, being a regular fixture). News that he was suffering from cancer came as a terrible shock and I can't tell you how I felt when I heard that it was terminal. Yet he was a fighter to the very end and even appeared at a dinner in his honour shortly before he died, where he was given a wonderful reception.

The last time I saw Gordon was when I travelled to Glasgow to speak at a dinner to raise money for a hospice. John Beattie, the former Scottish number eight, who had toured South Africa with my Lions side in 1980, was at the dinner and I asked him how Gordon was. He said he was very ill, at a hospital just up the road. I asked the organisers of the dinner if they would mind if I missed the meal, promising that I would return in time for my speech. They were very good about it and a girl from the hospice took me to the hospital and on to the ward. It was something I felt I had to do because I was sure I wouldn't get another opportunity. I asked staff on the ward if I could see him but they said he was very poorly and not allowed visitors. So I asked if they would let him know that Bill Beaumont was there, only to hear a voice from a side-room telling me to go in. It was Margot, his wife, who was there with their grandson. Gordon was lying on the bed with tubes everywhere and I didn't know what to say, so we had a bit of a hug and then started to chat about the good times we had enjoyed together and the scrapes we had got ourselves into. Reluctantly, I had to drag myself away, indicating that I was speaking at a dinner. I knew he was dying, he knew it too, and we were aware as I left that we would never see each other again. Margot followed me out and thanked me, saying that she would see me again soon. So it proved. Shortly after the news broke that the great Broon of Troon had died – an announcement that saddened the entire rugby world – I received a call from his brother Peter, himself a former Scottish international, asking if I would act as a pall-bearer. I replied that I would be honoured to do so. The other pall-bearers were Peter, Gordon's son and nephew, Fran Cotton and Roger Uttley. It was a terribly sad occasion but Gordon wouldn't have wanted us to grieve for too long and through the tears I was able to picture that wonderful man and natural comic as I had known him, as the heart and soul of any party – a truly great character.

After my return from the 1977 tour I had planned to take a complete break from the game until October, shortly before the county championship season started, but I was selected to play in a British Lions side against the Barbarians at Twickenham in a game arranged to celebrate the Queen's Silver Jubilee. The game raised a magnificent £100,000 for charity – a figure we were understandably delighted with – but, not for the first time, the issue of the treatment of players' wives raised its head. It had long been a bone of contention among players that their partners were never invited to the dinner after international matches, but we had assumed the organisers would stretch a point for a charity game. It rankled with the players that their wives and girlfriends had to entertain themselves until very late on the Saturday evening after an international, only then joining up with us for the traditional disco. We reasoned that they should be allowed to enjoy the whole weekend experience with us, our resentment intensified, especially when we were playing away, when we saw members of the committee enjoying gin and tonics with their wives in the team hotel. Things have changed now, thankfully, but back then, in the build-up to that Jubilee match, there was something of a rebellion, the Welsh players, who were heavily represented, refusing to take part unless their partners were included. In the end the authorities relented to a degree. Partners could accompany us but the venue was hastily changed from the London Hilton, where England traditionally stayed after international matches, to the Star and Garter at Richmond. It had quite clearly been a reluctant gesture on their part but we put their pettiness behind us and concentrated on taking part in what was a somewhat unique occasion and one that turned out to be quite memorable. It was there that I had my first meeting with royalty. Prince Charles – introduced to the teams before the game – asked if I wore my headband to keep my ears warm or to stop people pulling them! The same thing happened two years later when I was introduced to Prince Philip before a Calcutta Cup game.

We won the game and I resumed my planned break from rugby. It didn't last very long, though, because I had a call from Malcolm Phillips asking if I would play for England in a game against the touring American Eagles at Twickenham. He said the selectors were picking a largely experimental side with an eye on the future, and that I was to be one of the handful of experienced players who would be expected to hold everything together on the field. After the Lions tour I was feeling a far more mature player but still considered myself as something of a new boy in international terms. So it came as a shock when he rang later to confirm the arrangements and dropped the bombshell that I was to captain the side. I hadn't captained any side since my schooldays, not even Fylde or Lancashire, but I assumed it was just a one-off situation without any special significance and pushed it to the back of my mind. There was another shock in store, however, when I attended a business meeting in Harlow and found half-a-dozen rugby writers waiting to interview me. At that stage I couldn't even imagine the pressure that a national captain is under and it was all rather novel at the time. Later, however, when I was well established as England captain, I had to rearrange my life completely in order to cope with demands on my time. Unlike today, when the players are full-time professionals, I had a full-time job to do, and at home Hilary and I found we had to take the telephone off the hook in order to be able to eat a meal in peace. Not that I'm complaining, because I regarded being asked to captain my country as the greatest honour that could have been bestowed upon me. I like to think that I acquitted myself well and always endeavoured to find time for people.

The game against the USA was a pretty low-key affair, so delivering a team talk to a group of largely younger players didn't prove too onerous and we won comfortably enough. I found that I even enjoyed the role of captain and was quite pleased when I was then invited to lead the North in the Divisional Championship. In those days the North had by far the strongest divisional side and we hammered a hapless London before beating Midlands 22–7 in the final. Recording three wins from my first three games as a skipper was very pleasing but I assumed that when the national selectors got around to picking an England captain they would turn to experienced campaigners like Fran Cotton or Peter Wheeler. I was wrong. I was named as England captain for the game against the Rest in the final trial at Twickenham and that's where my winning sequence ended when the sides drew 15–15.

Although I felt there were better-qualified players to take on the captaincy, I was named again for the opening Five Nations game against France in Paris in 1978 and was thrilled that the selectors had shown confidence in me. Later, when I was firmly established, I would be consulted on issues such as selection and tactics but not when I was a novice captain. It was more a case of providing a quick pep talk before the game and saying a few words at the post-match dinner. By the time I had led England to a Grand Slam, however, I was very involved and worked very closely with the coach, Mike Davis, and a small group of senior players who were able to contribute massively both on and off the field.

Our preparations for the French game were disrupted by the weather, with heavy snow delaying our departure from England. Nigel Horton was playing in France at that time and was awaiting our arrival, but we had to practise on this side of the English Channel as we waited for clearance to fly. We had already lost Fran Cotton with a knee injury sustained in a practice match against Buckinghamshire and it didn't do a lot for morale when our physiotherapist Don Gatherer, who was playing hooker for Bucks, took two heels against the head from Peter Wheeler. Mike Burton was drafted in for Fran. Never short of an opinion, Burto declared that there was no way our pack would cope with the French unit so we would be best served by spinning the ball wide as often and quickly as possible. That led me into my first major team talk as skipper and I told the players we needed to take on the French in the area where they probably felt they had an advantage – up front. I told them that I was prepared to scrummage myself into the ground if necessary and to challenge Michel Palmie at every line-out, generally making life as difficult as possible for him. Allowing the French forwards to take the upper hand would, I said, be tantamount to disaster and we would end up completely humiliated. Asserting myself like that was something of a new experience for me as I had always been content to take a back seat and concentrate on doing my job as a second row to the best of my ability. Mike Burton very quickly voiced his support and we agreed to take on the French pack from the first whistle. Once that had been decided I left it to our coach, Peter Colston, and chairman of selectors Sandy Sanders, to do all the talking and saved myself for those few moments when we would all be together as a team before leaving the dressing room.

England hadn't won in Paris for 14 years. While we didn't stop the losing sequence, ending up on the wrong end of a 15–6 scoreline, we did at least acquit ourselves pretty well, having given our hosts something to think about by leading 6–3 at the interval. We had our problems, though, because centre Andy Maxwell, from New Brighton, injured his knee so badly that he never played again, Peter Dixon suffered a collar-bone injury and prop Robin Cowling dislocated a shoulder. When Robin was injured we had used up our quota of replacements so he bravely battled on even though that meant he never played again that season.

Alan Old had played at fly-half and contributed two drop goals but was surprisingly dropped for the next game against Wales at Twickenham. Johnny Horton was drafted in while Bob Mordell took over from Peter Dixon in the back row and Barry Nelmes was at prop for Cowling as Fran Cotton still hadn't recovered from his own knee problem. The weather at Twickenham was of the New Zealand variety and it was no day for running rugby. In the end it was decided on penalty kicks and Wales pipped us 9–6 because Phil Bennett managed to land three out of four attempts while Alistair Hignell could only manage two from six opportunities. One had looked pretty straightforward and would have levelled the scores but it wasn't to be, although we did have the satisfaction of pushing the two strongest sides in the championship all the way.

Cotton and Dixon were back for the visit to Murrayfield to take on Scotland a month later and we won 15–0 after destroying the Scottish pack. That may have been because of our scrummaging practise at Peebles two days earlier against a local club pack. We pushed them all over the place for a few minutes and then they gradually got stronger so that we were only managing to get a slight nudge on them. At one point Fran demanded more weight from the second row, which surprised me because I had always prided myself on my ability in the engine room. When the session finally ended we discovered the reason for the dramatic improvement in the Peebles scrummaging. When we had started out they had a normal eight-man pack. We had failed to notice that they had kept adding more players so that we were actually taking on a sixteen-man unit!

I had to make my first on-field executive decision in the game at Murrayfield. Scrum-half Malcolm Young had been kicking the goals but he was best from short range and I didn't think he had a prayer when we were awarded a penalty near the touchline and more than 50 metres from the Scottish posts. Dave Caplan, a dentist from Leeds, had been brought in at full-back in place of Alistair Hignell, and while he was a very exciting runner he was not a recognised goal-kicker. Nor was centre Paul Dodge, but I knew he had a big boot on him so I tossed the ball to Paul and asked him to give it a whack, knowing we had nothing to lose. Sandy Sanders admitted afterwards that he thought I had lost my marbles but had to compliment me on an excellent decision when Paul smacked the ball straight between the sticks.

Sometimes you have to act on your instincts and, knowing that Paul had the power if not the consistent direction of a kicker such as today's Jonny Wilkinson, I just felt that in a one-off situation he might come good. Partly thanks to Paul, I was at last able to deliver the victory speech that I had been planning for some time instead of a hastily rejigged speech congratulating the opposition on taking the spoils. We then went on to beat Ireland at Twickenham and I was more optimistic about the following season. I felt increasingly comfortable in the captaincy role and looked forward to a serious challenge in the Five Nations.

Before that we had to take on the touring All Blacks the following season and I was annoyed because there was virtually no preparation for a tilt at the best side in the world. All the other northern hemisphere countries had squad sessions before taking them on but we met as usual on the Thursday before the game. We had clearly not learned the lesson of our earlier 13–13 draw with Argentina when once again we had been hopelessly ill prepared. No disrespect to Argentina but if we couldn't beat them in our own backyard the signs were hardly promising for our chances of toppling the All Blacks.

Fran Cotton was out of the equation due to an Achilles' tendon injury and the selectors revealed their own Achilles' heel by picking a recognised loose-head, Barry Nelmes, to play at tight-head. They compounded the felony by then playing John Scott, a recognised number eight, alongside myself in the second row, and selected Roger Uttley at number eight – another poor decision. Not only was Roger only just back from a lengthy spell out of the game through injury but, unlike John, he could play with equal ability at lock. Roger, an experienced campaigner, also saw the folly of the selections and, like myself, wasn't surprised when we were well beaten.

I was annoyed about the amateurish build-up to the game and couldn't understand why our leaders insisted on dragging us from Bisham Abbey, where we were staying, into London to visit a theatre on the Friday evening. Clambering into bed at midnight after a coach-ride back from the city was hardly my idea of the ideal preparation for a tough international. Graham Mourie's All Blacks won 16–6, but the winning margin could have been far greater because we were well beaten up front. I sensed at the post-match dinner that I might become the sacrificial lamb, it being common practice in those days to blame the captain for any inadequacies that were actually down to those picking the team. The cold-shoulder treatment was much in evidence and I awaited what I felt would be an unfair decision. Fortunately I was able to divert my attention to playing for the North against the All Blacks and, not for the first or last time, it was my native region that caused the tourists more problems than the national side. They managed to beat us only 9–6, but then the northern selectors knew what they were doing.

By that time Malcolm Phillips had become a respected

friend and I didn't hold him personally to blame for England's selectorial blunders. He telephoned to let me know the teams for the traditional trial game. I was still a member of the England side but captaincy had been handed back to Roger Uttley. I was so annoyed that I calmed myself down by going for a 10-mile run, venting my spleen on the pavements near my home.

Roger led the side when we played Scotland in the Five Nations opener at Twickenham but, despite crushing their forwards, we still only managed a draw. Shortly before the end of the match Roger injured his leg and I resumed the captaincy, little knowing that the job would be mine until my enforced retirement through injury three years later. The selectors again named Roger for the visit to Ireland but he had to withdraw from the team on the morning of the game when he went down with flu. Although I was delighted to take command again it would have been unnatural not to feel some sympathy for Roger, luck seldom having been on his side throughout his injury-ravaged career. Conversely, I had an amazing run as an international, never once being dropped.

Because of all that had happened to me, my self-esteem was somewhat low and I made a decision that I lived to regret but that helped to shape me for the future. A strong wind was blowing down the Lansdowne Road pitch, so I had a chat with the senior players about whether or not we should take first use of it if I managed to win the toss. My own gut feeling was that we should play into the wind in the first half, and the players agreed with me. There is often little benefit to be gained from the elements in the early stages of a game because the players are too busy bedding in and testing out their opposite numbers. The selectors intervened and told me to play with the wind if I won the toss. I called correctly and decided to follow their instructions. We lost the game 15–6, the players were unhappy and I vowed never again to be a selectors' lackey.

The lesson I learned is that I needed to be my own man. If the selectors didn't like the decisions I made, then they had the sanction to turf me out. At least I would be doing things on my own terms and I valued the advice of senior players who were tuned in to the modern game rather more than that of people who had played many years earlier and often didn't understand what was going on. Fortunately, that situation doesn't apply today because they have a squad system and one man is in charge. England's head coach Clive Woodward is his own man and he makes the decisions, rightly or wrongly, and takes it on the chin when things go awry.

There is a different relationship between managers, coaches and players these days. The exchange of ideas is encouraged and there is no way that Clive wouldn't talk to Martin Johnson about tactics and the strengths and weaknesses of opponents. Des Seabrook, the former Orrell forward who proved himself to be an excellent coach of both Lancashire and the North, would plan strategy with experienced players like Fran Cotton, Mike Slemen and I, and I was delighted when Mike Davis took over as England coach and quickly realised the importance of working with his players. There is nothing players hate more, at any level, than being treated like a bunch of school-kids whose opinions are of no consequence.

Before we took on France in the next game at Twickenham, I insisted that we hold a squad session the Sunday before. Lancashire had always had a club culture and extra training sessions were regularly built into preparation at the insistence of the players. If things weren't going right we were prepared to devote even more of our hard-earned free time to working on our deficiencies. I wanted England to do the same and we had a very tough training session. It was well worth it, because France, the reigning champions who had already beaten Wales and were fully expected to take our scalps too, ended up on the losing side. We pipped them 7–6, with the help of Nigel Horton and John Scott taking them to the cleaners at the line-out. I felt I had re-established myself as skipper, and despite losing against Wales in the final championship match in Cardiff I was confident I would stay at the helm.

Budge Rogers took over as chairman of selectors, and Mike Davis, who had been coaching England Schoolboys, was appointed as the new coach. Their first task was a tour to the Far East and I returned far more optimistic about England's future because the pair prepared far more thoroughly than their predecessors. As a result, it turned out to be one of the most enjoyable tours I have ever undertaken. Very much an experimental tour, it showed that several players were not up to international standard. Far better to find that out in Japan rather than in the middle of a Five Nations match. If some were clearly not going to make the grade, however, it became just as clear that many relatively new faces had the necessary ability. That number included my Lancashire colleague, wing John Carleton, fly-half Huw Davies, centre Paul Dodge and a big redheaded second row who was to become very well known to me in the near future, Maurice Colclough.

We won our matches, discovering at the same time how important it is to think about the game. Because of their size most people wouldn't give the Japanese a prayer but they were the most inventive rugby players we had ever encountered. When you line up against a second row who stands just 5 foot 8 inches tall you rather expect to have an easy ride at the line-out but you realise you have miscalculated when their hooker throws in to the feet of the prop standing at the front. He jumped in the air to allow the ball to pass beneath his feet and while I was preparing to leap like a salmon, my opposite number simply bent down, picked up the ball and set up a ruck. On other occasions their forwards would start jumping up and down like Jacks-in-a-Box and the hooker would throw the ball to someone about to leap into the air rather than someone on his way down. Like the grand old Duke of York's men, we didn't know whether we were meant to be up, down or neither up nor down!

The tour wound up with wins against Fiji and Tonga and there is no doubt in my mind that we laid some of the foundations for our Grand Slam success the following season. Mike started out in a rather schoolmasterly way but had the sense to change his tack as the tour progressed and I had a good feeling about things when we returned home. The plan was to take a holiday but the North selectors had other ideas. They were organising a welcome party for the next touring All Blacks, and my presence was required on another tour that also had a major influence on England's success.

CHAPTER FIVE

A slam at last

I will always look back on the year 1980 with enormous pride. I led England to their first Grand Slam for 23 years and also captained the British Lions tour to South Africa. Within a 12-month period I also took part in the most memorable victory any side has ever achieved at the expense of the All Blacks, which had occurred just before Christmas the previous year.

England's success and my invitation to lead the Lions were largely because of a decision made by some of the North's leading figures to plot the defeat of the All Blacks, who were due to tour during the latter part of 1979. The North West had become the first English provincial side to beat the tourists, back in 1972 at Workington, and there was a burning desire to repeat the process, only this time the All Blacks would be taking on the North as a whole. As well as dominating the largely unloved Divisional Championship – because we were always more committed to it than the rest of the country – the North had a massive tradition of performing well against touring sides.

Talent in the north had always been spread around a great many senior clubs rather than being concentrated into just two or three big clubs, as happened in other regions. That's why the county championship was so important and the most realistic achievable target for many players was the North team. That was the best route into the international side, and because that system was in place players didn't feel the need to switch clubs. That's why I was happy to spend my entire career at Fylde, even though the club was not packed with international players like some of those in the Midlands and the South West. For the same reason Tony Neary, once England's most capped player, stayed with Broughton Park when he could have walked into any side in the country. There was a real passion about playing for the North and I suppose we had a bit of a chip on our shoulders. We certainly never needed motivating, especially when we played against London!

So the North side was a proving ground. In 1978, when Graham Mourie's All Blacks won all four internationals against the home nations, the North gave them a tough time at Birkenhead Park and pushed them closer than England had managed a week earlier.

The first I knew that the scheduled game against the All Blacks at Otley in November 1979 was to be targeted was when the North West announced that it would be touring South Africa. The idea was to lay the foundations for the game at Otley and it was decided, even though it was a North West tour, to invite one or two guest players from the other side of the Pennines. That number included experienced back row Peter Dixon and up-and-coming prop Colin White, who were both playing at Gosforth. Des Seabrook had done a tremendous job with Lancashire and he was to coach the side.

I was approached to lead the touring side but I had just returned from England's tour to the Far East and said that, as an amateur, there was a limit to how much time I could take off for rugby. Quite apart from anything else, there would have been no time left for me to enjoy a holiday with Hilary. She had uncomplainingly given up our honeymoon for rugby and never complained when I had to spend summer months on tour with England or the Lions. She understood that playing rugby was a major part of my life but there had to be a limit, and this was to be it. It is an indication of just how seriously the powers that be were taking this tour that they came up with a compromise. Hilary was to travel with us, and they arranged for Lancashire and Scotland hooker Colin Fisher to take his wife June to provide Hilary with some company when the boys were . . . well, just being boys!

It certainly gave Hilary an insight into what rugby touring is all about and she probably came back far more broad-minded. 'Court' sessions are a regular feature of any rugby tour and it was inevitable that she should end up in the dock and be fined for something silly, like having too many outfits or spending too much time in the shops. They should worry; it was my credit card that was getting hammered!

We played our opening game in Stellenbosch and then tackled Western Province, Natal, Orange Free State, South Eastern Transvaal and Northern Transvaal. It was a very demanding tour but that's what Des wanted. The players bonded well together and there were plenty of lighter moments, but since this book is for family reading I won't go into those! One amusing moment was seeing Peter Dixon sent to the sin-bin. He walked straight to the ice-cream van in the ground, bought an ice-lolly and sat down behind the posts to enjoy it while we laboured away in the sunshine. I somehow can't see that happening at Twickenham.

Once the season started Lancashire swept all before them to win the northern title in the county championship and to secure a place in the semi-finals. We were running hot and it was obvious to everybody that Lancashire would form the nucleus of the side to face the All Blacks. In the end ten Lancastrians were chosen and Sale had five players in the side, a reflection of the club's strength at that time.

Kevin O'Brien, of Broughton Park, was at full-back and that game, plus his performances for Lancashire, helped to propel him into the Ireland side that season. Lancashire's back line of John Carleton, Tony Wright, Tony Bond and Mike Slemen had played so well in the county championship that it was picked *en bloc*, although I felt sorry for Peter Squires who had played in a poor Yorkshire side. Alan Old was at fly-half and Steve Smith at scrum-half – even though that selection went down like a lead balloon with the England selectors because they wanted the North to pick Nigel Melville.

Gosforth's Colin White, who had demonstrated his ability in South Africa, was at loose-head, with Fran Cotton on the other side of the scrum, while Andy Simpson, who spent longer than anyone else sitting on the bench for England without ever getting on to win his cap, was at hooker. I was joined in the second row by Jim Syddall and the back row was one that England should have picked for many years – Roger Uttley, Peter Dixon and Tony Neary. New Zealand's line-up was Richard Wilson, Bernie Fraser, Gary Cunningham, Mark Taylor, Stu Wilson, Eddie Dunn, Mark Donaldson, Brad Johnstone, Andy Dalton, John Spiers, Andy Haden, John Fleming, Ken Stewart, Murray Mexted and Graham Mourie. Allan Hosie, who seemed to play quite a major part in my life one way or another, was the referee.

We had prepared really well for the game and the media guys couldn't believe it when they turned up to watch our final training session and it only lasted a few minutes. There was no point in going on *ad infinitum* because we knew that everything was right. It was at that session that Geoff Cooke, who had been coaching Yorkshire and was a North selector, approached Steve Smith and questioned whether practising a particular move was advisable. Smithy just turned to him and said, 'Piss off Geoff. We are playing New Zealand in 24 hours and don't you think we know what we are doing.'

I remember being supremely confident we would win the game because we had an exceptional team and our planning had been first class. We also had four England captains in the pack and a wealth of experience. Furthermore, we spotted an immediate weakness when New Zealand picked two open-sides in Mourie and Stewart (sure enough, they didn't get the best out of either in the game). We knew that both players liked to hang off the rucks and mauls ready to launch an attack or get up quickly on the opposition in aggressive defence rather than get involved in the wrestling matches. So we planned to drive it close and commit people before moving the ball wide.

When Des Seabrook came into my room at the hotel for the final team talk, Mike Weston indicated that a lot of the side were not in the frame for England's game against the All Blacks the following week. He said the selectors had already made up their minds, so he suggested that we went out there to show them, which is exactly what we did. The North had picked a team to win that game. Peter Dixon wouldn't normally have been involved because we knew it was going to be his swansong, but what a way to go for a player who was so shabbily treated by a succession of England selection committees.

Graham Mourie won the toss and elected to play with a fairly strong tailwind, which suited me because, as indicated earlier, I always preferred to start into the elements, reckoning that the first 20 minutes of a big game is often spent sizing one another up. Not that much sizing up went on in that game. The All Blacks must have been surprised to see us take the field wearing what looked uncannily like a British Lions strip. Our planners had thought of everything!

We roasted the New Zealand pack and the boys were pretty

awesome in defence too. That afternoon nobody took a backward step and we took the game to our opponents at every opportunity. We made the first tackle count, put them under pressure at every scrum and, in terms of physical confrontation, had experienced internationals who could look after themselves. By the end of the game we had certainly proved ourselves to be stronger mentally and physically than the guys we were up against.

We took the lead through an Alan Old penalty, for which the wind was so strong that Tony Neary had to steady the ball for him. Because of the strength of the wind it would have been pointless Alan trying to kick for position so Smithy took over responsibility for drilling the ball on the deck. With half an hour gone he managed to pop the ball into the left-hand corner, the All Blacks made a mess of clearing the danger and Mike Slemen was on to the loose ball in a flash and popped it up to Smithy who finished what he had started by scoring in the corner.

In fairness to the All Blacks they came back at us in the second half but we dug deep and had the advantage by then of the wind at our backs. Tony Bond, having a great game in the centre, powered his way over for a brace of tries and we were home and dry despite a try by Stu Wilson for the tourists. Our efforts culminated in pushing the New Zealand pack off their own ball close to their line and Oldie picked up to dance his way over. Alan handed the ball to Kevin O'Brien to take the conversion, which, unfortunately, he missed. When I asked Alan why he had given the kick to Kevin he said it was to give the lad a go because he thought it would be good experience for him. It was that sort of team.

The crowd went mad at the final whistle and it was a fantastic feeling in the dressing room afterwards. We had not just won the game; we had also stuffed the All Blacks 21–9. Their skipper Graham Mourie was very gracious in defeat. A delightful guy, he said we had deserved the win, adding that they didn't like playing against sides wearing red shirts: a reference to being beaten by Munster, who also play in red, and, of course, the Lions.

I was back facing Graham and his All Blacks a week later, in an England shirt, and a lot can happen in such a short space of time. Like getting the selection wrong. After our triumph at Otley the selectors should have been bold enough to pick more of that North side than they did. The most glaring mistake was at fly-half, where they totally ignored the claims of Alan Old. Some thought he was past his best so they picked Les Cusworth for his first cap. Nothing wrong with Les, of course, but he was a running fly-half and they wanted him to switch from his natural game and kick – something he was ill-equipped to do whereas Oldie could have kicked us into positions all afternoon.

The other mistake was playing Mike Rafter in the back row instead of Roger Uttley, a decision that left poor old Roger absolutely gobsmacked. Don't get me wrong. Rafter was a great player and, on the ground, was better than Tony Neary, which is why he was known as Rafter the Grafter. He was also a top bloke but his inclusion left the back row with the wrong balance. John Scott was at number eight, Peter Dixon having announced his retirement, so there was never any hope of the North back row being included *en masse* anyway, well though it had performed at Otley.

We ended up losing 10–9 and, after the confidence boost of a week earlier, I was very frustrated as I left the field. When I was asked at the post-match press conference how I thought the game had gone I said I had been disappointed by the performance but, and I'm not sure why I did it, I stuck my neck on the block by declaring that we would win the Five Nations Championship. People were quick to point out that we had won the Wooden Spoon the previous season and just lost to New Zealand at Twickenham, but I simply had the feeling that we had enough good players to win the title.

Although I felt the selectors had got it wrong, I was encouraged by the way the new chairman Budge Rogers and coach Mike Davis were prepared to listen to the senior players, and I believe that attitude played a major role in our ensuing success that season. During the Far East tour I had got to know Budge and Mike quite well and they involved me in team selection for the first time. Budge also told me that I was to be captain for the season and that had boosted my confidence enormously. Until then you never knew from one game to the next if you would be on the field, never mind in charge. If the captain isn't sure of his selection then it must have a demoralising effect on the rest of the team. The New Zealand match was Mike's first at home and I know he learned a great deal from it, developing into a respected coach. He had stepped up from coaching

England Schoolboys, but had the playing pedigree and grew into the job fairly quickly. Mike was in charge and had the final word, but he was prepared to listen and that was like a breath of fresh air.

England opted for the traditional final trial and that's when Phil Blakeway came in at tight-head. I remember telling him that I would pack down behind him and so, whatever happened, I wanted him to stay rock-steady. I needn't have bothered because Phil, who had returned to the game after suffering a broken neck, proved to be a fantastically strong scrummager and became the cornerstone of the pack that season. He was in when the side was announced for the opening game against Ireland at Twickenham; John Carleton, Nick Preston, Tony Bond and Mike Slemen retaining their places in the three-quarter line, with Dusty Hare at full-back and Johnny Horton recalled to partner Steve Smith at half-back. Fran, Peter Wheeler and Phil Blakeway formed the front row and I teamed up with Nigel Horton in the second row because Maurice Colclough was injured. Roger Uttley was restored to the back row alongside John Scott and Tony Neary, and the die was cast for a Grand Slam season.

I still felt guilty that Peter Squires wasn't involved – an omission that effectively ended his top-class career. There was no place for Jim Syddall either. He had played very well against the All Blacks for the North but was something of an enigma. I always felt he could have done more with his rugby. Although he took over briefly in the England side when I was forced into retirement, Jim never quite fulfilled his potential.

He had better hands than Maurice Colclough, although Maurice was more athletic and a far better player, in a different league. Ireland brought in a newcomer at fly-half called Ollie Campbell and I remember thinking that he had to be one hell of a player to keep Tony Ward out of the side. They were also strongly fancied for the title, having won a Test series in Australia the previous summer but I felt we now had players who were good enough to win and we finished with a morale-boosting 24–9 victory. Kevin O'Brien was making his debut at full-back for Ireland and, while he knew most of us better than he knew his own team-mates, we also knew Kevin's strengths and weaknesses. I felt for him in the end because he had a real baptism of fire. In the opening minute he tried to find touch but it ended up as a cross-kick that put his side under pressure and, while Ollie had given Ireland a 9–3 lead with some precision kicking, Kevin failed to gather a kick, tried to side-foot it into touch, but missed and Mike Slemen was on it to score. If that was a nightmare for one of the victorious North team, it was later in the game to be so for another when the region's two-try hero from Otley, Tony Bond, broke his leg in a tackle. Bondy was probably playing right at the top of his game. He was incredibly brave, a strong tackler and as good an inside centre as there was around at the time, and he would have done very well in the modern game. I know it is hard to believe, but despite the noise made by around 60,000 spectators I heard the crack of his leg, it reverberating round the stadium like a gunshot. It was a bad break and a tragedy for Bondy. He was never quite the same player after that, and one look at his leg, once it had been repaired, left you wondering how he managed to come back at all. But Bondy was one of the game's most dedicated trainers and despite his handicap he actually made it back into the England side for one game two years later. I went to see him in hospital the morning after the injury and he was gutted. What made it worse for him was having to sit back and watch England play extremely well without him.

The injury did see another young centre coming on to make his debut. Welcome Clive Woodward. He arrived in time to see John Scott – who had earlier been given a bollocking by Tony Neary for messing up a planned manoeuvre – score from a back-row move. Alongside the new we had experienced players who could run things for me. In fact, as I pondered in the dressing room afterwards, many of that side had been around for a long time but had never been picked together. I felt that at last we had a team with a good blend of youth and experience.

Even in victory there are disappointments. Nigel Horton was almost in tears when Budge Rogers told him that Maurice, who was playing his rugby in Angoulême, would be brought back for our next game against France in Paris. Nigel was a tough bloke, both mentally and physically, and I questioned whether Budge was doing the right thing, pointing out that we had just had a good win, Nigel had played well for England and particularly so against the French in the past. But Budge wouldn't move on the issue and Maurice linked up with us in Paris when we arrived on the Thursday before the game.

None of us had ever won in Paris and when we looked at the French side we realised we were in for a very demanding afternoon. One or two familiar faces were missing but Jean-Pierre Rives was captain, and their pack included such characters as Philippe Dintrans, the hooker from Tarbes, Manuel Carpentier at number eight and Robert Paparemborde at prop. Jerome Gallion was at scrum-half and Serge Gabernet at full-back. We were soon in arrears. France did a switch move in midfield and Rives went over for a try. I was dismayed, Paris being the last place where you want to fall behind. Once French tails are up you have your hands full; it's far better if they are trailing and starting to fall out with one another. Dusty kicked a penalty to reduce their lead but they responded with one of their own after Fran had been penalised. He was up against Paparemborde, who was probably as good a tighthead as there was around at the time, but he had a habit of boring in a lot at the scrums. Clive Norling, the Welshman, was the referee and he awarded us a penalty only to reverse it when Fran stood up and lashed out at his opposite number. I knew why Fran had done it but we couldn't afford to keep giving away points so when I got a chance I had a quiet word in his ear to suggest it hadn't been such a good idea. Fran, who wasn't known for taking prisoners, retorted, 'Well, he didn't do it again, did he!'

We got back into the game and Johnny Horton dropped a goal either side of half-time. Then Nick Preston got over for a try and John Carleton scored his first international try when he finished off a back row move. John Scott picked up and passed to Smithy, who moved it on to Maurice Colclough. Maurice passed to me and I fed it back to Smithy, who sent JC racing for the corner. It still wasn't all over. Roger Uttley had to go off for stitches so we were down to 14 men with just four points separating the two sides at that stage. We had a scrum close to our line and France took the heel against the head when Peter Wheeler kicked it through. I really thanked Wheelbrace for that one because we had to endure a very interesting last five minutes!

French tails were up, which was the last thing we wanted, and that's when Phil Blakeway sacrificed himself for me. I had to go down on a loose ball as the French pack charged in but Phil recognised the danger and dived in front of me, taking a hefty size-twelve boot in his ribs for his pains. The impact actually broke a rib but he played on and even battled through the rest of the campaign. They breed tough boys in the West Country.

Our forwards proved the most disciplined and we hung on to win 17–13. What followed was one of the biggest sessions I have ever been involved in and I ended up with Dusty Hare, Maurice Colclough and two French players at six o'clock the next morning trying to get into a restaurant for a meal. The staff immediately slammed the shutters down but I waved a credit card and they then let us in. In the past we had always travelled back to Heathrow on a 10 a.m. flight but the northern lads had decided to fly back to Manchester on the Sunday evening. Instead of resting in bed we got into another session at our hotel and I arrived back at Manchester airport feeling absolutely dreadful, not through my endeavours in the game but through booze and a complete lack of sleep.

We were at the half-way stage in the championship, and, with Wales next up at Twickenham – rather than at our perpetual graveyard in Cardiff – a Grand Slam had suddenly become a distinct possibility. Although international sides still only met up on the Thursday before the game, Wales had set the trend of having extra training sessions – Gareth Edwards and company used to spend Sundays practising on the beach – and we had got into the habit of training on a Monday at Stourbridge. On the Monday before the Welsh game we turned up to find a big crowd there to watch us go through our paces so it looked as though our fans also sensed that this might be the year for a little overdue glory.

Sadly, the exuberance of the fans wasn't matched by the media. In the build-up to the game newspapers carried a series of totally unfounded stories about rival players who were going to sort each other out. Fran Cotton and Graham Price had played together all over the world and had tremendous respect for each other. But not if you read certain publications. It also appeared that Geoff Wheel and I had scores to settle, and that John Scott, an Englishman playing his club rugby for Cardiff, was going to let the Welsh know that he was the roughest, toughest thing around. At the same time we were being blamed for the closure of coal mines in Wales, and some Welsh newspapers even raked up alleged bad feeling over our only victory in the previous 16 years because, according to reports, that win had been handed to us by bad refereeing decisions. If we had also been blamed for the weather and the price of bread I wouldn't have been in the least surprised. It was all absolute nonsense and I spent much of our final training sessions attempting to psyche the lads up for the game while also attempting to cool them down and telling them not to believe anything they either read or heard.

I had never been on a winning side against Wales; in fact only three players in the side had experienced that pleasure, back in 1974 at Twickenham: Roger Uttley, Tony Neary and Dusty Hare. Steve Smith should have played in that game but had to pull out through injury and Jan Webster had taken over. Peter Wheeler sat on the bench that day because hooker John Pullin was also captain of the side. Wales still had great players but key men like JPR Williams, Phil Bennett and Gareth Edwards had gone. They were in a transitional phase and I was confident that we could beat them. We had made a change when Nick Preston pulled out through injury and I think the inclusion of Leicester's Paul Dodge actually strengthened the side. There was also anxiety concerning Phil Blakeway's ribs. As mentioned earlier, one of them was broken, but an X-ray didn't reveal this at the time and Phil insisted on having a pain-killing injection and playing, even though he must have been in great discomfort.

The usual happy atmosphere you associate with rugby internationals was missing that weekend, and the theme of poor, oppressed Wales having to take on the English bully-boys was very much in evidence. Much of that, I deduced, was down to the fact that Welsh journalists realised that, for a change, we had a side capable of beating Wales, even if they didn't like our style. It is hardly surprising then that it was an absolutely awful game from the first minute, with the Welsh fans booing English players and our fans doing the same whenever a Welsh player was on the ball. All kinds of things were going on, but we were more sinned against than sinners, and I was pleased with the way my players kept their cool. Geoff Wheel, a player I greatly respected, was after me all the time and saying things like, 'So you think you're going to be the Lions captain do you,' but I just ignored it and tried to get on with my job. I felt really sorry for Dave Burnett, the Irish referee, who had the difficult task of trying to keep the peace.

There were cheap shots going in all the time and Dusty Hare was the victim of a blatantly late tackle quite early in the game. Sadly, that was a foretaste of what was to come. Scrums were going down on a regular basis but it was little wonder considering the way the front rows were charging at each other like rutting stags. It was certainly no place for the faint-hearted. For all the problems Dave Burnett had to contend with, I think he could have refereed the scrums rather better and that might have reduced the temperature a touch. I have played in a few roughhouse games in my time but that one really took the biscuit, with players on both sides behaving totally out of character. That is always a problem when people hype up a game too much. At the end of the day, it is still only a game and not a declaration of war.

Dave had to take me and Jeff Squire, the Welsh captain, to one side and read the riot act to us after just ten minutes. He made it perfectly clear that the next player guilty of any act of foul play would be taking a very early bath. I asked the referee if I could take time out to convey that message properly to my players and gathered them around me. I told them what the consequences would be, not just for the team but also for our title chances. It was a time for showing discipline in the face of provocation and they took note of what I had said. It wasn't long before the red card was being waved at Welsh flanker Paul Ringer, who had clearly encountered a little of the famous red mist. Our fly-half Johnny Horton, probably the smallest guy on the pitch, had just kicked the ball downfield when he was caught with a late tackle from Ringer. I have seen later tackles and I have seen higher tackles but his sense of timing couldn't have been worse and Dave Burnett had no option other than to wave him off the field. The incident was one from which Ringer never recovered and it cost him a place on that summer's British Lions tour to South Africa.

That left Wales down to 14 men and should have given us an advantage but the effect was that they became even more united than they had been before. Although Dusty Hare kicked the penalty awarded for the late tackle, we were playing poorly and Wales took the lead when we lost control at a scrum close to our own line. The scrum wheeled and Jeff Squire snatched it up to score, putting his side ahead, and we suffered another setback just before the interval when Roger Uttley was kicked in the head. His nose had been split wide open, and there was blood pumping everywhere.

Mike Rafter went on as replacement and Dusty kicked

Like the hairstyle? Well it was 1975. This was the fresh-faced version as I turned out for my only club, Fylde, before being called into the international arena.

The 1977 British Lions tour to New Zealand was the wettest on record but that didn't deter my great pal, the late Gordon Brown, and myself from getting in as many rounds of golf as possible.

Jet-lagged and weary after returning from my first Lions tour to New Zealand in 1977, Hilary treated me to tea in bed.

Here I am in action against the All Blacks in 1979, when the North beat the tourists by a record score for a provincial side. Keeping a watchful eye on me are Peter Dixon (left) and Roger Uttley.

As a region the North always seemed to have a stronger sense of identity than other parts of the country and that was reflected in games against touring sides. The 1979 victory over the All Blacks by this group was labelled the finest ever by an English side.

Holding the County Championship Trophy aloft after Lancashire had beaten Gloucestershire in the 1980 final at Vale of Lune, Lancaster. I felt as though I had led a team of mudlarks because the game was played in torrential rain.

Squaring up to Welsh second row Geoff Wheel during the 'battle' between England and Wales at Twickenham in 1980.

Steve Smith took time out from chattering to find time to score a try against Ireland at Twickenham at the start of England's 1980 Grand Slam campaign.

Enjoying one of my little charges into opposing ranks during our Grand Slam victory over Scotland at Murrayfield in 1980, with Lancashire pals Steve Smith (left) and John Carleton in support.

After England had beaten Wales at Twickenham in 1980 I responded to calls from delighted fans by saluting them from the stand.

The team that performed the Grand Slam in 1980, a feat that hadn't been achieved for 23 years as England endured one of its worst periods in the history of the game.

With the England team that won the *Daily Express* team of the year award in 1980 for our heroics in clinching a first Grand Slam for 23 years. Back row (left to right): John Carleton, Tony Bond, Nick Preston, Mike Rafter, Maurice Colclough, Phil Blakeway, Paul Dodge, Robin Cowling, Johnny Horton, Roger Uttley, Dusty Hare, Peter Wheeler. Front row: Steve Mills, Bill Beaumont, Steve Smith, Tony Neary, Mike Slemen.

I always enjoyed being in the thick of the action. Here I am feeding the ball out of a ruck for the 1980 British Lions during our 32–12 victory over Transvaal at Johannesburg.

End of the road although I didn't realise it at the time. Flanked by Lancashire team doctor Noel Atkinson (left) and Lancashire coach Des Seabrook, I left the field suffering from another head injury during the 1982 County Championship final against North Midlands at Moseley.

Erica Roe displaying her charms during England's test against Australia at Twickenham in 1982. I couldn't understand why the players weren't concentrating on my team talk

My pride of Lions. Leading the British Lions in South Africa was the pinnacle of my career and, despite losing the series it, was a very happy tour.

Comrades in arms.
Bill McLaren and
myself enjoyed many
years of working
alongside each other
for the BBC. He was
a master at his trade.

Every cloud has a silver lining so, after
being 'professionalised' by the game I love,
I was able to involve myself in commercial
activities and a sponsored Rover car from a
local dealer was just the start.

Front rows don't come any better than this one. Welshman Graham Price (left),
Peter Wheeler (centre) and Fran Cotton played together for the British Lions and
would have matched any current front row trio.

Phil Bennett, who captained my first British Lions tour to New Zealand in 1977. It was sad to watch a great player lose confidence as results went against them on what was an unhappy tour.

Simply the best. That's my assessment of the great Welsh scrum half Gareth Edwards. I believe that Gareth would have been the star of any side, in any era.

another penalty to restore the lead. Leading 6–4 with full-time rapidly approaching, all I could think about was the referee blowing the final whistle. We managed to pressurise the Welsh, but we were generally playing a defensive game rather than taking it to them. I thought that if we could just play for territory we could hang on. Steve Smith drilled a ball down the left touchline to earn us a respite but when he tried the same thing again his trusted left peg let him down. He tried to get the ball behind Welsh wing Elgan Rees but hooker Alan Phillips charged down the kick and sent Elgan racing clear. He touched down half-way between the posts and the corner flag.

As we trudged back behind the posts we were absolutely gutted. We hadn't played well. In fact, we had played badly and felt that we had really blown our chance of a rare victory over Wales. I could envisage the newspaper headlines the following morning, telling the world how 14 brave Welshmen had beaten 15 Englishmen in their own backyard. As we waited for the conversion attempt I suddenly spotted Smithy, down on his haunches and all alone out by the corner flag. I had known the Sale scrum-half for a long time and you couldn't wish to meet a more ebullient character, but at that moment he looked as though he wanted the earth to open up and swallow him. I trudged across to him and hauled him to his feet. There have been numerous stories told about what I said to him and the most popular was that I said, 'You stupid bastard.' Hardly my style that. In truth I put my arm around his shoulder and, trying to appear more optimistic than I was feeling, said, 'Look, we've still got a chance, so forget it.'

Had we lost that game it would have been a permanent nightmare for Steve but Gareth Davies missed the conversion, leaving us within just one score as the game moved into injury time. Wales won the restart and Davies kicked the ball into touch. For some reason, and I can't for the life of me think why, I called a two-man line-out. I suppose I was thinking of breaking things up a bit. John Scott won Pete Wheeler's throw and tapped it down to Smithy. He threw me a pass around my ankles but I somehow managed to hang on to the ball and found Paul Dodge in support. He drove into the Welsh defence, their scrum-half Terry Holmes went in and killed the ball and Dave Burnett signalled a penalty. I went to give the ball to Dusty and remember thinking that he seemed the coolest bloke in the stadium. It was a horrible, murky day and the kick was on his wrong side of the field, but he wobbled up and stroked the ball straight between the posts. 'Thank God!' I thought. The game continued for another minute and then we managed to get the ball into touch and the referee blew his whistle for the end of the game. There was more of a feeling of relief and elation than in any other game I have played and the dressing room resembled an army field hospital.

Budge Rogers came in and said, 'Look, there's going to be a lot of flak flying around from the Press after that game so let's be very sensible about what we say at the press conference.' I did something that wasn't normal practice for me, and went to the Welsh dressing room. I got a muted reception, but then they were understandably gutted to have battled so well with just 14 men and then been beaten in injury time. I had been looking for Geoff Wheel because he had run off the pitch at the end and I hadn't had a chance to shake his hand. He wasn't in the dressing room either so I just said, 'Look guys. It was a shit game, bloody awful, so let's all forget about it.' If anything they looked even more brassed off after that but it was a sincere gesture on my part. I had toured and played with some of those guys. I regarded them as friends and I just wanted the whole episode put behind us.

When I got back to the England dressing room, one of the committee arrived to say that the crowd was on the field and chanting my name. I went out on to the balcony to be confronted by a sea of chanting faces and I wasn't sure what to do. I am a quiet sort of bloke really and this was a totally new experience for me. A more confident skipper would probably have milked it for all he was worth but I just gave them the thumbs-up. Despite the terrible game, I was delighted for them because we hadn't beaten Wales for years and there was a massive feeling of jubilation in the ground.

We were all pretty battered and bruised at the dinner that evening and I sought out Paul Ringer to say that I was sorry over what had happened to him, anxious to build a few bridges. After all, in those days it was a major scandal to be sent off in an international match and the stigma stayed with him. Players generally have the capacity to leave what happens on the field where it belongs – on the field.

England supporters had been devoid of real success for a very long time but, after the Welsh game, they could sense a Grand Slam in the offing, and if the reaction of the crowd after the game hadn't convinced us of that, the northern contingent was in no doubt when we called in at a pub near Rugby on the way home the following afternoon. I walked in with Smithy, Fran and Mike Slemen, and we were given a standing ovation. Everybody wanted to buy us a drink, and goodness knows what condition we would have ended up in if we hadn't reminded ourselves that we still had to drive home.

Not surprisingly, we all wished we could play our final game, against Scotland at Murrayfield, the following week but we had to kick our heels for a month, so, prompted by the lads, I asked for a full-blown squad session on the weekend when the other four nations were playing. It was possible in those days, because, as amateurs, we were not tied to our clubs and there were no such things to worry about as league tables, promotion and relegation. Nowadays, understandably, the clubs do their best to limit the number of occasions that their players are taken away on international duty.

When the big day finally dawned, Andy Irvine was captaining Scotland for the first time and, after the toss, he looked at me, grinned and said, 'And the loser has to leave the country,' a reference to the Lions tour in 1977 when, with the dreadful weather and little else to occupy ourselves, we would sit watching awful wrestling and boxing on television and use that same expression.

I was confident about our chances, Scotland having been beaten in Cardiff two weeks earlier in a tame game. We planned to attack the Scottish pack, to limit the chances for players of the calibre of Irvine, Jim Renwick and John

Rutherford to have a run at our defence. As a result, we annihilated them in the first half, taking a 19–3 lead by the interval. A superb break by Clive Woodward put John Carleton in for the first of his three tries and the maverick centre did a similar favour for Mike Slemen on the other wing before JC grabbed his second. By mid-way through the second half we were coasting, 23–6, following a try by Steve Smith.

All credit to the Scots. They decided that if they were going down then they weren't doing so without a fight, and they came back at us with tries by Rutherford and second row Alan Tomes. But we were never going to let our moment of glory slip away. Dusty Hare popped over another goal with his usual aplomb and JC dived over to complete his hat-trick. Both Roger Uttley and Phil Blakeway should have gone off because they were struggling with injuries but I kept them on the field. They had been with us all the way and I wanted them to be there at the end.

The English fans went crazy when the final whistle sounded and I was chaired off the field by Fran and Peter Wheeler. My opposite number, Alan Tomes, asked if he could make the fairly traditional jersey swap but I said that if he didn't mind I wanted to hang on to that one. The occasion meant so much to me but it was almost an anticlimax as we sat in the dressing room and took on board the reality of what we had achieved. I looked around at some of the more experienced members of the side, aware that, like me, they had endured hammerings in Cardiff and Paris and defeats in Dublin. They deserved their moment. I also had a particularly pleasant duty to perform. We had realised only two days before the game that Tony Neary would be setting a new record number of appearances for England. Somehow, the lads had managed to buy a tankard and get it engraved in time so that I could present it to Nero in the dressing room.

We all had hangovers the following morning as we had embarked on a 'last-man-standing' session once the formal part of the evening was over. I was approached at the hotel by a large number of South African journalists who had flown in to watch the match and then stayed on for the announcement of the Lions squad to tour their country that summer. Those Lions selectors who had not been at the game had flown in from Dublin, where Ireland had been playing, and were due to deliberate on the Sunday afternoon. The press boys wanted to know if I was going to be captain but, although I knew the answer to that question, I pretended that I hadn't a clue and said that like the rest of the leading players in the four countries, I had to await the official announcement.

Public reaction to winning the Grand Slam was fantastic and, for a few days at least, rugby took over from soccer as the main talking point in sport. The news was all over the front pages of the newspapers on both Sunday and Monday, and when John Carleton and I called in at a motorway service area with our wives the following day on the way home, the place was packed with English supporters who had been at the game, and they all stood and cheered. JC and I subsequently spent quite a long time signing autographs as we tackled a meal aimed as 'blotting paper' for the excesses of the previous evening. We didn't linger too long with our fans on the motorway because we were keen to get home in time to watch the game's highlights on *Rugby Special*, a Sunday ritual.

The one great disappointment of the weekend was that my father hadn't been there to share my triumph. He was a great supporter and it was one of the few games he missed during the whole of my career. Whether I was playing for England or Fylde's sixth team, he would always be there, invariably in the background because he wasn't the sort of guy who sought the reflected glory. I loved and respected him for that. He missed the game because my cousin was getting married. I had told her when she announced the date that I wouldn't be able to attend due to the Scotland fixture in Edinburgh, and I had wanted Dad to be there too, to watch the game, but he went to the wedding instead. I deeply regretted that he wasn't a part of our day because he had such a love of rugby, but no doubt he received regular score updates, most of the wedding guests being eager to know how we were faring at Murrayfield.

Even my mother had started to warm to rugby and went on a supporters' tour to South Africa when I captained the Lions. She would also travel down to Twickenham with Hilary and Dad, the three of them lunching in the car park. Fran would look out of the team-coach window as we arrived at the ground, and say, 'I see the mill-owners are down from Chorley', much to my mother's amusement.

After our win in Scotland everyone seemed to be delighted for us except the Welsh who, knowing they had had the beating of us a month earlier, were still bitter about the result and also about Paul Ringer's dismissal. But the bitterness didn't become personal and there was one very pleasant Welsh interlude. At the start of that season a Welshman had approached me asking if he could compile a scrapbook for me of the season. Perhaps he had a premonition that it would be England's year. Anyway, I sent him programmes, dinner menus and the formal invitations we used to receive from the RFU telling us that we had been selected for the team. For his part he collected all the cuttings from newspapers and magazines and invited me down to Cardiff to receive the finished article. By coincidence I had been invited to play for the Barbarians in Cardiff, so I took the opportunity to call in at his club and was given a marvellous welcome. He presented me with a beautiful, leather-bound scrapbook that is now one of the most treasured possessions from that period of my career.

I often wonder how that Grand Slam team would have compared with the present England side. If pressed, I would say that, with the same advantages the modern professional player enjoys, we could probably have matched it. We will never know, of course, but there were some great players in the side of 1980 and they did their country proud.

CHAPTER SIX

Leader of the pride

Simply becoming a British Lion in 1977 was for me the pinnacle of my rugby career although, with hindsight, it should have been a far more memorable interlude in my life. In many respects that tour was something of an anticlimax because I had been expecting something special and that wasn't how it had turned out. I assumed a Lions tour would involve the best players, best coaching, best possible organisation and facilities of the highest standard.

When I was asked to lead the 1980 Lions on their politically sensitive visit to South Africa I determined that things were going to be very different than they had been three years earlier. For a start, I resolved to make certain that it was a united tour, knowing how lonely an experience touring can be otherwise, especially if things aren't going well on the field. You end up with cliques, certain guys sticking together all the time rather than integrating fully with everyone else. I read afterwards with interest, and a little sadness, in the auto-biography of South Africa's black wing Chester Williams how black players in the Springbok side had been ostracised by their team-mates. Chester and the other black players would never go into the dining room first because they knew that if they were sitting at a table then the white players would deliberately go to sit elsewhere. That sort of behaviour was totally unacceptable and, hopefully, things have changed in that respect. I had witnessed something similar with the Welsh-speaking players on the 1977 tour to New Zealand and, so far as I was concerned, there would be no repetition. Whatever my feelings about that 1977 tour, being invited to captain the Lions in South Africa was a tremendous honour. Only a few players in each generation achieve Lions status, and just a handful are handed the captaincy. It was not, in my book, a responsibility to be taken lightly.

I had felt very confident of securing a place in the Lions party and knew that being captain of England would make me an automatic candidate for the captaincy on tour. Fergus Slattery was another obvious candidate who sprang to mind but – as with a number of other senior players I would have loved to have had on board – he had other commitments and was unable to join us. As it was, I knew of the selectors' decision regarding the captaincy both before the announce-ment of the Lions party and before leading England to the Grand Slam. The Irish duo of Syd Millar and Noel Murphy had already been named as manager and coach respectively, and it was at the dinner following the infamous battle between

England and Wales at Twickenham that Syd had taken me to one side to say he wanted me to captain the side.

Had Fergus been available, it would have produced an all-Irish management team, which, regardless of the individual merits of the trio concerned, would probably have been bad for morale. In selecting a Lions squad it is important to strike a fine balance between the four different home nations and, wherever possible, to avoid demonstrating a strong bias towards players from a particular country. It is a difficult balancing act that requires skill on the part of the selectors, because a player in a dominant side can look better than he actually is because of the calibre of the players around him. Selectors have to assess how a player in a struggling side might perform given the advantage of team-mates better equipped to provide the platform he requires truly to express himself.

Having been approached by Syd about the captaincy I was then sworn to secrecy, although there was the inevitable speculation in the media. Fergus seemed to be the front-runner, with Jeff Squire, the Welsh captain, and I also in the chase. Andy Irvine had only just taken over as captain of Scotland, so probably wasn't as high in the pecking order. My lips were sealed and the only person I told was Hilary. Chalking off victories in the Five Nations Championship all helped fuel the speculation because there had been a trend of appointing the captain from the most successful side in that competition. This happened in 1983 when Ireland won the title, selectors mistakenly appointing Ciaran Fitzgerald in the hope that he would repeat his Irish success at the helm of the Lions side.

Willie-John McBride managed the party, with Jim Telfer as coach – two men who, in their own way, have earned their place in Lions folklore. Yet Ciaran's inclusion as captain had kept Scottish hooker Colin Deans out of the Test side, and I was not alone in deeming Colin the better player. It caused a lot of controversy at the time, but it wasn't Ciaran's fault and the guy certainly wasn't done any favours by the selection.

I remember something similar happened in 1966 when Mike Campbell-Lamerton captained the Lions. Nobody had expected him to be given the job, and he ended up even dropping himself for one Test. I was determined that, if I were going to lead the Lions, then I would have to guarantee my place in the Test team, which is one reason why I embarked on the most serious training regime I had ever undertaken. Things are very different in this professional era, but in my day the captain was responsible for things like the pre-match warm-up and would often take full training sessions, so I knew I couldn't afford to show any weakness. I could hardly put the players through drills I was unable to do myself.

No player, not even the captain, should have a place in any team by right. He has to be put under pressure from other members of the squad but he has to be able to respond to that challenge and stamp his authority where it matters most – on the field. People have to believe you are worth your place in the side. A leader shouldn't be there just because he can make speeches, be nice to people, open village fêtes and speak at the local Rotary Club meeting. He has to perform in the arena and that's why Leicester's Martin Johnson was chosen to lead the last two Lions tours. The first of those produced a series win against the odds in South Africa and although the Test series in the second was lost in Australia, this was in no way down to Martin's leadership.

After the initial approach from Syd Millar I had no further communication until the touring party was announced two days after our Grand Slam victory over Scotland in Edinburgh. Hilary and I drove back home on the Sunday with John Carleton and his wife, and our thoughts, amid all the euphoria of what we had just achieved, turned to the Lions tour, the staging of which had, at one time, looked doubtful because of the politics involved. Even then I kept quiet about the approach made to me, having not even told my best mates, because I wanted to see it in black and white. Until that happened I wasn't exposing my backside just to get it kicked!

There was still no word from Syd, but confirmation of my captaincy and of the final squad was broken to me at work on the Monday morning by the usual source, Terry Cooper of the Press Association. Like myself, Terry is mad about cricket and, as he knew all about my Uncle Joe, he would always start his conversations with, 'Right Blackledge. Do you want to know the team?' Terry reeled off the squad and, apart from the English contingent, I knew a few of the lads from the previous tour, but many were unknown to me apart from the odd 80 minutes we had spent in opposition in the Five Nations Championship. One thing I quickly realised was that we were a little short on experience in one or two areas, the most glaring deficiency being in the crucial open-side flanker position. Slattery was a class act but unavailable and I was particularly disappointed that my Lancashire and England pal Tony Neary had decided not to tour.

A week before England's Grand Slam game against Scotland I had played for Fylde against Tony's club, Broughton Park. After the game we were sitting in the bath together and I posed the question about South Africa. Tony told me he wasn't going because of pressure at work and I couldn't persuade him to have a change of heart. I still believe 'Nero' was the key component we lacked in the squad, for we were left without a top-class number seven. I had genuinely believed he would move heaven and earth to tour because he hadn't achieved what he should have on his two previous Lions tours. He had been a fixture in the England side for a decade, but apart from successes in New Zealand and South Africa it had only been in that season that he had won anything tangible. It is ironic that he played in just one Test on his two Lions tours; had he held his form, he would certainly have played in all four Tests in South Africa.

The withdrawal of 'Slats' and 'Nero' clearly posed a problem for the selectors, especially as they apparently didn't consider the claims of Paul Ringer, the Welsh flanker who had been sent off during the England versus Wales fracas that winter. The decision not to take him to South Africa was wrong. Paul had served his punishment for letting the red mist take over, and, provided he was considered good enough, he should have gone. The other player they should have looked at was Mike Rafter, who had been kept out of the England side by 'Nero' but was a fine player who would have done a good job for us.

To what extent we needed a player of their calibre quickly became apparent when the tour started, because the outstanding Springbok was open-side Rob Louw. Erroneously, we hadn't thought much of him until he played against us and then we realised that he was likely to be a perpetual thorn in our side. So it turned out, Rob undoubtedly proved their player of the series. So much for him being a soft touch – our pre-tour assessment. We tried every means possible to get into him but simply didn't have the firepower to do so, for although our back row had plenty of power, physical presence and skill we simply didn't have the pace to ensure first arrival at breakdown time.

The Springboks were decent guys and we would often share a few beers with Rob and the two Zimbabweans, Ray Mordt and David Smith, in particular. Rob and Ray later moved to England to play rugby league and I went along many times to Central Park to watch Rob in action for Wigan and to have a drink and chew the fat afterwards.

In the end the only specialist open-side in the touring party was Stuart Lane, who had taken over from Ringer in the Welsh side. He lacked the experience of the others and, sadly for him and the Lions, he was injured in the opening minute of the first game against Eastern Province at Port Elizabeth and took no further part in the tour.

I had had no involvement in selecting the squad so was keen to discover who my travelling companions would be. Not unnaturally I looked first at the second-row selections and was surprised to find that there was no place for Ireland's Moss Keane, whose place I had taken on the previous tour, or Geoff Wheel from Wales. Moss worked for the government in Ireland and, considering the stance taken by many countries towards South Africa's system of apartheid, he was refused permission to take part in the tour unless, of course, he was prepared to give up his job – which is what my Lancashire colleague John Carleton did when placed in the same situation by the local education authority in Wigan where he was working as a teacher. I had assumed that Wheel would be selected and had spent some time pondering the interesting challenge to my position this would have presented me with because he was a very tough customer and an extremely difficult opponent. Neither travelled, so my second-row companions were Allan Martin from Wales, Alan Tomes the tall Scot and my England partner Maurice Colclough, who had been playing so well that I had been fully confident he would make the 30.

The two full-backs were Bruce Hay, who had been on the tour to New Zealand, and Ireland's Rodney O'Donnell, a nice lad who turned out to be the most superstitious character I have ever come across. Most players, of course, have their little foibles. For example, as mentioned earlier, when not precluded from doing so because of the captaincy, I always liked to take the field last. Other players have a ritual about which sock goes on first or such like. Few though take it to Rodney's extremes. Among other things, he had a phobia about keeping pictures absolutely straight in hotel bedrooms and had to touch the bottom sheet first when getting into bed. I hadn't realised just how bad he was until we were walking towards the spot where a team photograph was to be taken and I heard Irish scrum-half Colin Patterson call him a stupid idiot. Not wanting acrimony in my camp I asked what the problem was and Colin explained that Rodney was mincing his way down the pavement because superstition meant that he couldn't step on a crack! As you can imagine, the lads had a lot of fun during the tour at Rodney's expense – especially on Friday the 13th when they taped lines all over the hotel corridor and moved all the pictures on the walls so that they were crooked. Even during matches he had the strange ritual of fielding opposition penalties and conversions and then throwing the ball back over the crossbar before kicking it downfield so that the game could restart. Sadly, his luck ran out because he dislocated his neck during the tour, and although he rejoined us after being discharged from hospital he never played again. In typical Rodney style he put his injury down to wearing the wrong shorts!

The wings were my Lancashire and England team-mates, John Carleton and Mike Slemen, along with Andy Irvine. The rest of the back line was made up of Welsh centres David Richards and Ray Gravell, a lovely guy for whom I have enormous respect, Jim Renwick from Scotland and two players with the versatility to play in a number of positions: current England head coach Clive Woodward and Peter Morgan, from Llanelli, who, at 21, was the youngest member of the squad.

We looked strong at half-back with Ollie Campbell and

Gareth Davies to battle it out for the number ten shirt and Terry Holmes and Colin Patterson to scrap for the scrum-half berth. Physically, you would have been hard pressed to find two more different scrum-halves, anywhere. Colin was razor-sharp and a gutsy little player, with better hands than Terry but not as strong. Terry was a big guy who could play like an extra forward when circumstances called for it and a really nice lad. In the opening game against Eastern Province, one of their forwards peeled from a line-out on the short side and I remembered thinking that they would probably score. But I was forgetting about Terry covering the channel and he promptly put the guy into the second row of the stand. Terry, I thought, you'll do for me! Unfortunately, he never had the best of luck with injuries – a jinx that followed him into rugby league when he later signed up with Bradford Northern Bulls – and, not for the first time in his career, his tour was cut short. After my enforced retirement I went to the dinner after the England versus Wales game at Twickenham and Terry came up for a chat, asking if he would have made the Test team if he hadn't been injured. I told him that not only would he have been in the side but we would also have won the series. That's no disrespect to Colin but Terry could ask so many questions of the opposition because of his enormous strength.

I felt we had genuine experience in the front row with the selectors having gone for the Welsh trio of Clive Williams, Alan Phillips and Graham Price and their English counter-parts Fran Cotton, Peter Wheeler and Phil Blakeway. As I have already said, I was concerned about the back row and the lack of a top class open-side flanker, but the surprise package was Colm Tucker who had only ever appeared for Ireland as a replacement. The other flankers were Stuart Lane, Jeff Squire and Ireland's John O'Driscoll, who was from Manchester and had played for Lancashire. The number eights were Scotland's John Beattie and Derek Quinnell from Llanelli. I was delighted to see Derek on board. I was going to need experienced players around me that I knew I could be rely on and he fell readily into that category.

The one thing I was determined to do was make certain it was a happy ship, especially in view of all the bad feeling that the fractious England versus Wales game had engendered. I had stopped playing a month before the tour was due to depart but had turned out for the Barbarians against Cardiff in the traditional Easter fixture and had been booed on to the pitch. Fair play to the players though, including the Welsh boys in the Barbarians team. Their attitude was to shut them up by playing some great rugby and I never had any problem with the Welsh players after the 1980 international. Derek Quinnell hadn't played in that game. Had he done so, I believe he could have been in the running for the captaincy. On that 1980 tour he gave me nothing less than 100 per cent support right to the end. It made no difference when we dropped him before the second Test; he was still just as supportive. When I approached him following the selection meeting he said he knew what I was going to say. He even agreed we should drop him but he continued to train just as hard as everyone else.

The build-up to the tour was extremely low key. We met up

quietly at our hotel close to Heathrow Airport and left without any fanfare. The reason was quite simple. The tour had been something of a hot potato due to the issue of apartheid, a number of countries having decided to discourage sporting links. For a long time it looked as though there wouldn't be a tour but the rugby authorities here, believing that things were changing in South Africa, took the decision that it should go ahead after all. Several club and divisional sides, including North West Counties, had been to South Africa and played against multi-racial sides but that clearly didn't convince everybody and there were threats of a boycott of the Olympic Games in Moscow if the Lions undertook the tour. A decision was also made to allow the South African Barbarians to tour over here. Those opposed to the South African regime, however, saw the equal mix of whites, blacks and coloureds as a purely cosmetic exercise that bore no relation to what was happening back home. Irish pressure meant that the Barbarians didn't play on the Emerald Isle but, although there were protests throughout the UK, the demonstrations were nothing like those that marred the previous Springboks tour in 1969 and led to an end to full international tours to these shores by South Africa for two decades. I had been studying at Salford Technical College at the time, and had witnessed demonstrations when I went to watch the South Africans play against the North West at White City Stadium in Manchester, but these were not as serious as they were at some venues.

Were I to be asked to lead a tour in such circumstances now, with the benefit of the years, I would be far more aware of the difficulties and issues involved, but, as a young man, all I wanted to do was to play rugby against the best. I knew, deep down, that the political situation in South Africa stank, but, like other players, I tried to put that to one side, imagining that I could go to play sport over there without in any way legitimising their regime. Far from feeling any guilt at the time my main concern was that I might end up on a United Nations blacklist. As a sportsman, you want to compete at the top level, and political issues become secondary. It was the same with the Olympic Games in Moscow that year. The fact that athletes took part in those games did not mean that they agreed with what was, at that time, a very hard-line Communist regime any more than that we supported apartheid. As an amateur you are free to play against whoever you wish, when and where you like, but I respect those who wouldn't play in countries like South Africa because of their strong beliefs. John Taylor, the former Wales flanker, was a case in point when he refused to tour in 1974.

Although we played against multi-racial teams, except for in Test matches, the sad aspects of the regime were brought home to us in little ways. In Johannesburg I gave a pair of trainers to one of the chambermaids and she said I would have to write a note to that effect on the hotel's notepaper, other-wise she would be suspected of stealing them. A similar thing happened when I had a few days' holiday in Zimbabwe on my way back from the Lions tour to South Africa in 1997. You would have thought, by then, that things would have been different, especially in a country like Zimbabwe that had its independence and was run by the indigenous population rather than a colonial regime.

During the tour I met 'Cheeky' Watson, a guy who had played for Eastern Province and been a Springbok trialist. He was a well-publicised opponent of apartheid and as a demonstration of his feelings had started to play for a black team in a township. I met him and his brother after the third Test in Port Elizabeth and they agreed to take me and one or two of the other Lions to see where he was now playing his rugby. When we arrived, however, we found the place locked up, and gained the strong impression that the authorities had decided to prevent us from going in. I was then torn between making a bit of a fuss or keeping quiet. Quite simply, although I had been keen to see the conditions under which these local youngsters were playing the game, I didn't want to get involved in politics, or stir up any controversy for the Lions. It was something of a dilemma. As Lions captain I could have made representations to the authorities about not being allowed in but I opted to keep my head down. In the same situation today, I would probably have taken a totally different attitude but that's something that, in hindsight, you put down to experience. Apartheid was an abhorrent and indefensible system, but as a young sportsman you are so wrapped up in the challenges the game offers that you don't necessarily see the bigger picture.

Once the squad had been announced, and the world at large was fully aware that we were going ahead with the tour, I remember wondering what sort of reaction there would be from the public. Not everyone was happy that we were going and I half expected to be targeted with letters and telephone calls by people from the anti-tour brigade. Surprisingly, I received very little mail on the topic and of the letters I received 90 per cent were in support of the tour taking place.

We all arrived in dribs and drabs during the Friday evening at the Holiday Inn at Heathrow, there being nothing in those days of the week of preparation and bonding that modern Lions parties enjoy. We even had the traditional team photograph taken in the car park!

For one member of the party it was not a day to remember. Andy Irvine had been nursing a hamstring injury that he had sustained at the Hong Kong Sevens, but he was hopeful that even if he weren't 100 per cent fit at the start he would be okay two weeks into the tour. When the tour doctor, former Welsh centre Jack Matthews, examined him however, he felt that Andy wouldn't be fit to play until three weeks at the earliest. As a result Syd Millar took the decision to pull him out of the tour, much to Andy's annoyance. Given the length of the tour ahead of us, Andy believed he should have been allowed to travel and continue treatment. The bricks didn't exactly come out of the pram, because Andy wasn't that sort of person, but we all knew how he felt about the decision. Happily, he was to be reunited with us later in the tour, because of all the injuries we suffered, and he proved a much-needed asset.

Andy had been selected as a wing rather than a full-back so we needed to find another wing quickly and I suddenly realised there was one almost on the doorstep. Wales were travelling to the United States and Canada and were staying at a hotel just down the road. I suggested Elgan Rees, who had toured New Zealand with the 1977 Lions, playing in one Test and ending the tour as third-top try-scorer. So a rather surprised Elgan found himself suddenly switching into Lions livery and waving goodbye to his Welsh colleagues. Not that he will have felt homesick, because his inclusion brought our Welsh contingent up to thirteen, which was by far the biggest national group. England had eight in the thirty-two-strong party, Ireland five, and with Andy's withdrawal the Scots had been reduced to just four.

In my preparation for the tour I had done a lot of sprint training on the road because I knew from previous experience that you end up with sore calves due to the very hard grounds in South Africa. I gave the neighbours something to think about as I hurtled up and down the street but at least the old legs grew accustomed to hard surfaces. In order to maintain my tough training regime, I went out before breakfast for two circuits of a golf course alongside the hotel. When Derek Quinnell joined me at breakfast later and told me he'd barely managed just one circuit of the golf course, I didn't like to tell him I'd done it twice, but then training wasn't Derek's favourite pastime!

Syd Millar and Noel Murphy had occasion to let everyone know exactly who was in charge before we left the hotel at Heathrow to board the flight to Johannesburg. Some of the lads had shared a few bottles of wine at dinner the previous evening and 'disappeared' to their rooms before the bill arrived. Syd came up with a very effective way of covering the debt. He said the tallest member of the party would have to pay the bill himself and then it was up to him how he recovered his losses. That just happened to be Allan Martin, who subsequently spent the early part of the tour trying to extract the money from those who had been imbibing!

We spent the long, overnight flight to Johannesburg in economy class. Modern Lions, of course, fly business class and have even been known to travel in the front of the bus. I had experienced first-hand the difference between the two when, on a trip to South Africa with North West Counties after a muddle with bookings, Hilary and I had been transferred to first class. On all my other rugby journeys the players were crammed into the rear of the aircraft, but this suited some because, in those days, that was the only place where you were allowed to smoke. Since it was impossible for the big forwards to cram their frames into the narrow seats and get any sleep, we would get stuck into a few beers instead – a good way of getting to know your travelling companions. On arrival we went to our hotel at Vanderbijlpark, home of South Africa's petrochemical industry, about an hour's drive from the airport and definitely not the prettiest spot in what is generally a beautiful country. After dropping our bags, it was straight on to the training field. Noel immediately endeared himself at the warm-up by telling us that the best way to do a particular exercise was to 'spread out in a bunch'. There's nothing like a little Irish humour, intended or otherwise, to break the ice.

These days we would have travelled with a string of coaches

specialising in every aspect of the game, from scrummaging to line-outs, back drills to defence, and there would even be a coach to concentrate on kicking skills. There were no such for us and, in terms of coaching, we were rather top-heavy in the forward department. Syd had been an outstanding prop, and had coached the 1974 Lions side that stormed undefeated through South Africa. Noel played in Ireland's back row for many years and held the record number of caps for the position until overtaken by Fergus Slattery. As captain I had to help out with the coaching so, as a second row, we had considerable experience for each row of the scrum but not much else. Of the three of us, I suppose I was best qualified to coach the backs. After all, I had played much of my early rugby as a fly-half! However, whenever Noel concentrated on the backs I would take the forwards, which proved useful in helping me to identify the ball players.

Many players on tour benefit from being taken away from their comfort zone for the first time and that's why some, like I did three years earlier, return with reputations enhanced. I may have been sixth choice when I was called out to New Zealand but I felt I was better than Moss Keane, who had played in the first Test. Because of my competitive instinct I wasn't going to be beaten. My attitude on that tour had been that if I couldn't get into the Test side I would at least make selection difficult. I had occasion to use that experience to advantage during the 1980 tour when Alan Tomes told me that, because I was there, he didn't expect to make the Test side. I assured him that if I played like a drain and he was playing well then I would be big enough to drop myself and pick him in my place.

Players very often get picked for a Lions tour because they happen to be playing in a good national side rather than because they are better players. Iain Balshaw is a prime example. He looked good playing in a strong England team but his experience in Australia in 2001 was such that he hasn't looked anything like the same player since. On the other side of the coin you had someone like John O'Driscoll in South Africa. He really shone in such exalted company and we were all able to see just what a good player he was.

I have a high regard for Robert Howley who played in an indifferent Welsh side for a number of years. Behind a great pack, like the one England had at the time, he would have been incredible. The same could have been said about fellow Welshman Robert Jones, while one can only dream about what Jonathan Davies might have achieved had he been in Rob Andrew's position behind a dominant England pack.

The last-minute withdrawal of Andy Irvine should have been taken as an omen of what was to come in terms of injury and illness because, quite apart from the blisters on our feet from racing around on the rock-hard training ground during that first week, players started dropping out for one reason or another. Ollie Campbell tweaked a hamstring during kicking practice and missed the first two games. Before the week was out we then received the tragic news that David Richards' father had died at home in Wales, so David flew back for the funeral, leaving us without two midfield players for the opening game against Eastern Counties at the Boet Erasmus Stadium in Port Elizabeth.

As captain I felt it was important that I played in the tour opener, and I was paired with Allan Martin. I hadn't wanted Maurice Colclough in straightaway, even though I was fairly confident we would continue our England partnership once the Tests came around. I wanted him to prove to everyone else just how good a player he was, which he most certainly did in our second game on tour. With Campbell and Richards both out of the picture, we chose the Welsh pairing of Terry Holmes and Gareth Davies at half-back.

We won the match and were to go on to equal the record set by the 1974 Lions of never losing a provincial game. It was just in the Tests that our luck ran out and that was hardly surprising considering the injury problems we experienced. That first game was less than a minute old when Stuart Lane damaged his knee ligaments so badly that not only was he out of the match, he was also out of the tour. It was a tragedy for him, and we will never know whether or not he would have been able to make the spot his own and challenge the threat of Louw in the Tests. Worse was to follow when Gareth Davies damaged his shoulder as he put in Mike Slemen for the opening try of the tour. As a result, he was out of action for a month.

'Doc' Matthews was certainly kept very busy and at times John O'Driscoll, who was a doctor, had to help out. The Lions didn't travel with a physiotherapist in those days and, while the Doc was great if you needed something for a headache, you had to rely on local practitioners for the usual injuries you invariably pick up either in games or on the training field. It would be a case of speaking to the local liaison guy and asking him to ring around physiotherapists in the area to see if one of them was prepared to treat a few wounded Lions. The injured players would then clamber into a taxi and hope the driver could find the right address.

The previous summer England had toured the Far East with a travelling physio in the shape of Don Gatherer. Unfortunately for us, Don had a practice to run back home and had to return before we moved on from Japan to play Tonga and Fiji. However, he very kindly left his ultrasound machine with us, and our hooker, John Raphael, who was training to be a doctor, was handed the responsibility of trying to sort out our injuries. Using that machine, we to a large extent treated ourselves, but we were in for a surprise. When Don returned, he discovered that the machine had fused, so there we were telling all and sundry how bloody good it had been when, in reality, it hadn't been doing anything for us at all. Which just goes to show how much recovery from injury can be in the mind.

Times have certainly changed. When I was playing for England there was only one small room at Twickenham where Dr Leon Walkden would stitch up our wounds before sending us back into the fray. Now, it's more like walking into a hospital, with fancy machines everywhere. There is even a dental facility, which is not a bad idea when you consider how many times you take a whack in the mouth. Some might say they go too far these days but you have to remember that this is now a professional game and there is no reason, in a stadium as modern as the one that has been created at HQ, that the players shouldn't have the best available facilities in order to aid their recovery and deal promptly with injuries that would, previously, have required a trip to hospital.

Although we didn't have anything like the back-up that the modern Lion enjoys – they even measure the beds these days when they check out the hotels, and carefully inspect training grounds to assess their condition and facilities – I have to say that we were treated throughout like professional sportsmen. The South Africans had been starved of international rugby and looked after us very well. Perhaps the best thing they did was to provide us with a liaison officer in the shape of Choet Visser. What a character he turned out to be. Choet was a real Mr Fixit and our financial situation in particular was eased somewhat by his presence. Unlike the fees today's tourists receive, our daily allowance was £3, which doesn't go very far, even in a country as inexpensive as South Africa. Quite apart from handling the sale of our allowance of match tickets, Choet also arranged commercial deals, including personal appearances at a supermarket chain. As amateurs we weren't really allowed to get involved in that type of venture but nobody seemed to take any notice and the money went into the players' fund. On one occasion some of the Welsh lads were walking past the supermarket of a different chain to the one we were involved with and were invited in by the manager. He told them to help themselves from the goods on display in return for posing for a photograph.

We all ended up with jerseys sponsored by Life, a South

African cigarette company. The fact that we didn't smoke the product didn't seem to matter, and the money once again went into the kitty, which is all rather farcical when you consider what happened to me when I had the temerity to benefit financially from an autobiography when I had ceased to be a player. I can imagine what those in the corridors of power at Twickenham would have thought about it all but so far as the players were concerned we regarded Choet as a top guy.

The second game on tour was against a multi-racial South African Rugby Association Invitation side just down the coast at East London, and our injury problems were compounded when Phil Blakeway, the prop who had recovered from a broken neck to play such a crucial role in England's Grand Slam side, further damaged the ribs that he had broken during that campaign in the game against France. So, there we were, two games into an 18-match tour and already we were sending for replacements. Stuart Lane and Phil were replaced by flanker Gareth Williams and prop Ian Stephens, who were both on the Welsh tour to North America. On a brighter note, Ollie Campbell did get through the 21–15 victory over Natal at King's Park, Durban, although he handed over some of the kicking duties to Allan Martin and Mike Slemen.

It was back to altitude for the game against a South African Invitation XV, and we were intrigued to see the way the South Africans were using some of these fixtures almost as trials, including several Test hopefuls in the Invitation side. They had been forced to reassess their strengths and weaknesses after the Argentinian Pumas – called Jaguars in those days – had almost beaten them in two Tests, and as a consequence had made wholesale changes by the time they lined up against us in the first Test. Had they not made those changes there is no doubt in my mind that we would have won the series. For our part, David Richards was at fly-half in the absence of Ollie Campbell, whose hamstring was playing up sufficiently for the management to send for Ireland's Tony Ward. The airlines were doing a roaring trade in moving rugby players backwards and forwards, on occasions injured players travelling back to the UK in little groups! It looked in that game as though we might suffer our first defeat. With time running out, the lead having changed hands several times, our hosts were ahead by a slender margin. I wasn't playing in that fixture, so I sat watching anxiously until the boys suddenly produced what has been dubbed the longest try in the history of the game to win the contest in dramatic fashion. John O'Driscoll stole their ball at the tail of a line-out and Colin Patterson released David Richards. The move was halted by the home defence on a number of occasions but each time the boys recycled it well and away they want again. Patterson and Richards – understandably, considering their half-back partnership – were involved in the move several times, even when the ball went to ground and the home side hacked downfield. Richards was on hand to keep the move going and, after a staggering one-minute-and-36 seconds, Bruce Hay put Mike Slemen over. The ball had passed through 32 pairs of hands, and the standing ovation from the crowd lasted for some considerable time. I have seen some great tries in my time but that was rather special and I'm only sorry I wasn't a part of it.

We may have had our injury problems but at least those gave us the opportunity to ring the changes in the side. I had been determined that everyone would get a fair crack to prove themselves before the first Test, not wanting a scenario like Graham Mourie's Grand Slam tour of the northern hemisphere when one guy only got to play in two of the 25 games. The poor sod had to get up every morning to spend his day holding tackle shields. I didn't want anyone to come back to me afterwards to say they had never been given a chance.

I genuinely wanted everyone in the squad to compete for a Test place but, as I said earlier, I wanted to play well enough to ensure that Allan Martin and the others challenging for my position had no chance of wresting it from me. I certainly had deficiencies. I wasn't the biggest second row around by any stretch of the imagination but I made up for that in other ways. To survive in the line-out I had to learn how to cheat, to push and to shove. Through hard work I became good at receiving kick-offs and restarts, and regularly out-jumped taller opponents. Having said that, I did have Fran Cotton to lift me – even though in those days, unlike now, it wasn't permitted – and had Peter Wheeler to throw the ball in to me. Wheelbrace was the best hooker I ever played with, by a mile. In the modern game he would have been a fantastic player because he had great hands.

As captain I was involved in selection and it would have been easy to press the claims of my England team-mates but you couldn't look at players in terms of nationality. Once you pull on that red shirt you should be as one. Willie-John McBride, I remember, told me the story of how a Welshman had turned up at the team hotel during the 1974 tour and asked if he could get the autographs of all the Welsh Lions. Willie told him there was no such thing as a Welsh Lion. They were, he said, all just Lions, and looking back on my own experience I can appreciate what he meant. A Lions tour is unusual in that players of different nationalities come together to pool ideas and experience. Then, six months later, they are back knocking seven bells out of each other.

One privilege of captaincy is being afforded your own room. Others weren't given that luxury and one of my tasks was to help draw up hotel rooming lists, which proved a good way to ensure that the different nationalities integrated. There was rarely a problem, except that nobody wanted to share a room with Fran Cotton who, like Gordon Brown on the previous Lions tour, snored like you wouldn't believe. Not many wanted to share with Rodney O'Donnell either, not just because of his strange rituals and paranoia over whether or not pictures were lined up symmetrically but also because, just like my old Lancashire team-mate Richard Trickey, he always wanted to keep the windows wide open to allow in plenty of fresh air. You always try to break things up in the first weeks of a tour but, after a time, you find players who pal up and enjoy sharing a room.

The injury nightmare continued. Tony Ward had just arrived to cover for Ollie Campbell and Syd sent for a second Irish scrum-half, John Robbie (who just happened to be playing for the Goshawks touring party in neighbouring Zimbabwe), to do the same for Terry Holmes who had injured his shoulder playing against Orange Free State. Another problem was about to hit us; one that we should perhaps have seen coming because Fran Cotton had seemed out of sorts for a while, laid up with the recurrence of a condition that had laid him low during the previous season back home. His leg would become inflamed and he would have to take to his bed with flu-like symptoms. That eventually brought a fantastic career to a close the following season. Indeed, he played just one more game for England, against Wales in Cardiff. He left the field that afternoon suffering from a hamstring strain but missed out on the post-match dinner because the old flu symptoms had returned and he was forced to take to his bed at the team's hotel. Fran knew then that his career was over.

With the first Test fast approaching, we were going to have to make a decision, especially as Clive Williams had played well on the loose-head. He was playing better than Fran and it was a close call but I had an inherent loyalty to a guy I considered my best rugby pal. I had played all my rugby with him for Lancashire, the North, England and the Lions, and knew him to be a better rugby player than Clive. But Clive – a plasterer from Porthcawl with no delusions of grandeur – was very fit, a good scrummager and a thoroughly nice guy.

We decided to give Fran the chance to prove his fitness at Stellenbosch against an invitation side called the Proteas, four days before the first Test in Cape Town. Clive had played well against South Africa's Test prop Martiens le Roux and, even though he was feeling out of sorts, I suspect Fran felt he had to play well to be sure of playing in the Test.

It was a poor contest that was marred by dirty play and we were happy just to maintain our 100 per cent record. But I didn't see the finish. Fran had complained of chest pains to Allan Martin and a quick word with the bench saw him being led from the field. He was holding his chest and looked dreadful so, sensing that something was very wrong, I made my way to the dressing room. The medics were so concerned that they whisked him off to hospital, and I followed by car. The first indications were that he had suffered a heart attack and I set about trying to track down his wife Pat. I eventually reached her at her parents' home in the North East. By then, although I wasn't able to say exactly what the problem was, it seemed fairly certain that it wasn't a heart attack.

Fran was later transferred to the Groote Schuur Hospital in Cape Town made famous by Dr Christiaan Barnard, who had pioneered heart-transplant surgery. Peter Wheeler and I went to visit him, and found him lying in a hospital bed with wires coming out all over the place. Dr Barnard had actually been to see him and joked that he would fix him up with a new heart should he need one. Wheelbrace said it would have to be a bloody big one! Fortunately, it turned out to be a viral infection of the heart wall rather than a heart attack, and Fran was up and about within a few days. But it was not the sort of distraction you wanted in the build-up to a Test match. Fran was an extremely popular guy and everyone was hugely concerned for his welfare. He was one of the elder statesmen in the party and an automatic choice for a senior players' committee that we set up at the outset of the tour to deal with any grumbles within the camp. Previous Lions like Bruce Hay and Derek Quinnell were members, and we ensured that each of the four countries was represented.

We lost the first Test 26–22, due in no small part to the South Africans having softened us up in the weeks prior to the game. They repeatedly packed sides with invitation players who were invariably in line for Test appearances, a ploy that I recall Noel Murphy getting very angry about. Instead of the sides being truly representative, the 'Boks were beefing them up and using them almost as trials. We got a bit emotional about it at the time but, with hindsight, it was clear what they were up to. They were introducing big forwards to knock lumps out of us, such that at kick-off and restart time you would be watching for the ball dropping down from out of the sun while simultaneously trying to keep a wary eye on players like the massive 'Moaner' Van Heerden who would be bearing down on you like a rampaging bull elephant.

The Test proved what we had known all along: our forwards were better than theirs but we lacked pace in the backs and at loose-forward. Furthermore, our planning had been disrupted by so many injuries that in the crucial half-back positions we took the field with our fifth different combination in just seven games. Terry Holmes, Ollie Campbell and Gareth Davies had all been ruled out and Tony Ward found himself partnering fellow-Irishman Colin Patterson in only his second tour match. In fact, with the arrival of John Robbie, we had four Irish half-backs in the camp at that stage.

The game was only a few minutes old when Derek Quinnell smacked Springbok skipper Mornie du Plessis when he was offside at a maul – an aspect of the game we were to dominate throughout the tour. Mornie just accepted it and got on with the contest. I increasingly grew to like and respect the guy as time went by. Afrikaners are, by nature, aggressive, tough characters but he was charming: a true sportsman in every sense of the word. He was under massive pressure to produce victories but he struck me as someone above those around him. He certainly never gloated when the Springboks won.

He demonstrated his qualities when we travelled to Bloemfontein for the second Test. On the day of the game the Springbok manager, Butch Lochner, had been quoted in the press as saying that his side played its rugby hard and clean, which, he added, was more than could be said for the Lions. Syd Millar went bananas and, although he didn't mention Lochner by name, he referred to the comment in his speech at the reception following the Test. To his credit, Mornie responded by saying he hoped the South Africans could learn from the example set by the Lions. They would have achieved something, he continued, if they could be as gracious in victory as we had been in defeat, adding finally that he hoped the morning's comment in the press would be withdrawn. His country, he said, owed the Lions a great deal. It took a lot of courage for him to stand up in public and criticise one of his own selectors, and after that speech we invited him back to our team room to join in a Fran Cotton-led singsong. I liked the guy and have always been pleased to run into him – except on the occasion when I was hardly an advertisement for sartorial elegance as we bumped into each other at the Sun City resort between the semi-final and final of the World Cup in 1995. I was there with a few pals from Fylde rugby club. We had planned to play golf but, for some reason, it wasn't possible and somebody suggested we play tennis instead. The trouble was that I didn't have any suitable kit with me, but I resolved that problem because Graham Price was also staying there and I persuaded him to lend me whatever he could spare – mainly from his laundry basket. So, there I was, walking down the road looking a proper scruff and who should be marching towards me, resplendent in his attire as manager of the Springboks, but Mornie. I looked as though I had been out on the ale all week but we still went for a pint together, and have continued occasionally to meet up in the UK when he comes here on business.

Not that we had much to sing about after that Test or the one that had taken place two weeks earlier at Newlands in Cape Town. Life becomes tough when you lose your first Test and I felt we had deserved better from that game, especially considering the way we came back after drifting into arrears. Tony Ward had kept us in touch with his pin-point goal-kicking, and a drop-goal gave us the lead for the first time after the forwards had well and truly piled on the pressure. Unfortunately, his kicking out of hand wasn't always quite so precise and one misdirected effort was run back at us for Springbok wing Gerrie Germishuys to score. All credit to Tony, he did then pull us level again with his fifth successful penalty which, added to his drop-goal, handed him the individual points-scoring record for a Test in South Africa. We should have held out after taking the lead but we didn't and they punished us in injury time with their fifth try of the game. It was hardly the way we had planned to start the Test series and I remember repeating in the dressing room afterwards the exact words coach John Dawes had used after the first Test on the previous tour to New Zealand, to the effect that this was only the first of four Tests and that we could still win the series. At a time like that you have to look for positives and I had been pleased with the way we had fought back, especially up front, after being on the ropes. Physically, the South Africans were a lot bigger than us but we were far superior technically, and there was one spell of 20 minutes in the second half when we absolutely murdered them.

It was in that South Africa game, in particular, that everyone came to appreciate just how good Maurice Colclough was. He was pretty good at organising our 'Sunday school' too, although I don't recall religion coming into it! Unless we were due to be involved in a Test match the following weekend, we would travel to our next port of call on a Monday morning, thus leaving Sunday free for recreational pursuits. Syd Millar, one of the old school of tourists who would be puzzled by the modern culture of rehab in a gymnasium rather than in a bar, thought we needed to let our hair down. Maurice, whose

appetite for drink was matched only by his appetite for food –
he would be in the first division if there were a league table –
would take charge. The idea, so far as I could make out, was for
everyone to drink until they dropped and I, as captain, felt I
ought to be there to drink with the lads and accept, with good
grace, all the stick I invariably got. The favoured tipple was
Depth Charge, which comprised a pint of beer with a Crème
de Menthe base. Noel Murphy didn't drink but would join us
in a sort of bonding exercise, and would sit sipping his orange
juice. I wonder if he realised how many Vodkas would be
tipped into it when he wasn't looking! Some of the lads retired
earlier than the rest but Maurice was usually last to leave. I
remember seeing him wandering off down the corridor one
Sunday evening carrying a crate of beer after everyone else
had retired hurt. A larger-than-life character who knew how
to party, he was also a great guy to have alongside you in the
scrum. I'm not too sure hotel managers saw him in quite
the same light, especially when he started playing Frisbee with
the dinner plates (former Rugby Football League supremo
David Oxley was his headmaster at Dover College and he tells
me that Maurice was a better-than-average discus thrower)!
On the odd occasion a member of the management would
approach me to say there was a little problem involving one of
the Lions. My first question was always to ascertain whether
or not he was big and had red hair!

The joker in the pack, so to speak, was David Richards who
had a habit of telephoning players in their room and pretend-
ing to be a journalist anxious to write a feature about them.

I have to admit that he caught me out on one occasion, until I finally cottoned on. Mike Slemen fell for it hook, line and sinker and agreed wholeheartedly with the 'journalist' when it was suggested that he had been the best back during the opening weeks of the tour. In fact Slem had played well, and I was sorry to lose him when he withdrew from the tour after the first Test. His wife Eileen was expecting and hadn't been too well. Also, his son Richard was missing him, so Mike had made up his mind before the first Test that he was returning home to be with them both.

John Carleton, our other wing and Mike's Lancashire colleague, popped a rib in that first Test, so he was out of action too. The original squad was changing almost daily. Slem, Phil Blakeway and Stuart Lane flew out together bound for Heathrow, while Andy Irvine flew in at last, hot on the heels of Irish prop Phil Orr, who had toured New Zealand with the 1977 Lions.

We continued our habit of winning the non-Test games and there is no doubt that Andy Irvine gave our back division a new impetus. His first appearance was against Transvaal, where he helped us to a 32–12 victory, with a little assistance from Clive Woodward, the current England head coach, who was playing on the wing. I have a lot of time for Woody. As a player he was a real maverick who could win a game or just as easily lose it for you depending on whether or not the ploy he attempted was successful. A very talented sportsman, he would spend most of his time on tour playing soccer, much preferring that to training. On the field, he was a bit of a drifter who always wanted the ball. The only problem was that you were never too sure what he was going to do with it. Sometimes you would want to hug the guy and then, the next minute, to kick his backside. He has to take a lot of credit though for moulding England into the team it is now. I always enjoy talking to him, and remember how he telephoned me recently for my opinion on the protective gloves that players had suddenly started wearing. He thought they might be useful for this year's World Cup because of the heavy dew you can get in countries like Australia. I told him I thought they were just for nancy boys! His next tack was to tell me that he didn't like the use of a drop-kick for every restart, though he liked to start every game with a high ball. I pointed out that that was all right for him because he wasn't the guy standing there waiting for it to come down. 'I never saw you queuing up behind me to catch the ball,' I observed, drawing an appreciative chuckle.

On that tour Woody played in the same back line as Ray Gravell and you couldn't have had two more different characters. Woody, rather like Jason Robinson, would go off on his weaving runs not altogether sure where he was going – so what chance did defenders have! 'Gravs' on the other hand preferred the direct route, just like my Lancashire team-mate Tony Bond, and, while he wasn't the best handler in the game, he was incredibly enthusiastic and a real handful in both attack and defence. Woody was pretty laid back about things whereas Ray was a worrier needing to have his confidence boosted all the time. At the end of a game he desperately wanted to know how you thought he had played. 'Did I play all right?' he would ask and I would always tell him, 'Yes'. You would never tell him he had had a crap game, even in jest, because he would stay up all night worrying about it. Rugby is a funny game in that you only see guys for 80 minutes in a match and probably think they are pillocks until you go on tour with them and realise they are not just great guys but also very loyal too. Ray is someone I got to know well, and we have remained good pals ever since.

Tours were different in those days in a number of ways, not least in the relationship with the media. They are generally kept at arms' length these days, apart from scheduled press conferences and one-to-one sessions, which probably reflects the game's higher profile and the fact that interest now extends beyond that of the long-serving rugby writers who were keen not to abuse the privilege of being allowed into the inner sanctum. A sign of how much things have changed was the Lawrence Dallaglio incident when, as England captain, he allegedly confessed to drug use. I was unhappy over the treatment he was subjected to, finding it is hugely distasteful that a newspaper should set out, in what they apparently call a 'Honeytrap', to embarrass someone, engineering salacious and damaging headlines in order to further sales. Whatever their sphere of life, people should be confident that discussions in private will remain private, especially when there is no way of knowing whether or not comments are made in all seriousness. Lawrence is still a popular guy and I have a lot of time for him. It was a very difficult time for him, made even more traumatic by a knee injury that kept him sidelined for a lengthy spell, but he behaved in a dignified way throughout the whole episode.

When I toured I had a good working relationship with the press boys, typically travelling around with the likes of Terry O'Connor from the *Daily Mail*, Tony Bodley (*The Express*), John Reason (*Sunday Telegraph*), John Mason (*The Daily Telegraph*), David Frost (*Guardian*), Clem Thomas (*The Observer*), Norman Mair (*The Scotsman*), Ned van Esbeck (*Irish Times*), Karl Johnston (*Irish Press*), Sean Diffley (*Irish Independent*), Chris Lander (*The Mirror*) and Ian Todd (*The Sun*). But times change and I suppose the intrusive aspect of journalism is a downside of rugby union going professional. The press guys I had to deal with had a genuine love for the game and we had respect for one another, having travelled many thousands of miles together and shared a few pints along the way. We may not always have agreed in our assessment of games, but they were entitled to their opinion and we didn't have to worry about them trying to dig up stories simply to titillate their readers.

On the 1980 tour they were very supportive, understanding what we were trying to achieve and taking into account the terrible catalogue of injuries. And that list just got longer and longer. Between the first and second Tests we lost both David Richards and Terry Holmes through injury. Neither took any further part in the tour, flying back instead to the UK with Fran.

With Mike Slemen's departure, I suggested we call up Peter Squires, who was on tour in Zimbabwe with Public School Wanderers. I felt he should have been on the tour from the start, and even when I bump into him today I have a massive guilt complex over this. Pete had been with the Lions in New Zealand in 1977, and had played well for England, but he was probably a victim of Lancashire's success in the 1979–80 season. We were very much the dominant northern county and he wasn't exactly getting much ball playing for Yorkshire. He was in the squad when the North enjoyed its historic victory over the All Blacks at Otley in 1979, but John Carleton got into that team ahead of him and carried his success through to the England side, where he vindicated his selection with a try against France and a hat-trick at the expense of Scotland. Peter never got back in, but with Slem returning home I thought I had found a way for him to be part of the tour. We telephoned, asking him to join us, but fate stepped in, Peter suffering an injury in his last game for the Public School Wanderers, the day before he was due to cross the border into South Africa.

Another player who also missed out on that tour was Alan Old, who should have been awarded many more caps by England. He was as good a footballer as I have seen. Defence wasn't his strongest attribute, but in that era not many fly-halves played like Jonny Wilkinson. Even the best Welsh fly-halves regarded tackling as a job for back rows!

Talking of fly-halves, after the second Test we were down in that position too, Gareth Davies damaging his medial ligaments in a tackle by Naas Botha, South Africa's much-vaunted goal-kicker. That was the tour over for him and, by that stage, we had been joined by our seventh replacement, England centre Paul Dodge, who arrived in time to watch us lose that Test 26–19 at Bloemfontein. Despite the fact that we staged another of our determined revivals I have to say that we were beaten fair and square. On that occasion, if not on the others, the Springboks were the better side.

'Dodgey' made his debut against the Junior Springboks, a match that saw yet another injury, Rodney O'Donnell being the unlucky Lion stretchered off on that occasion. We seemed unable to get through 80 minutes unscathed. He dislocated his neck and underwent surgery the following day, expressing gratitude to referee Steve Strydom who had heard a click as the Irishman tackled Springbok centre Danie Gerber and told people not to move him. Thanks went also to John O'Driscoll, who as a qualified doctor, was on hand to issue instructions as to how Rodney should eventually be carried off.

The third Test was a do-or-die affair. We had to win in order to have a chance of saving the series and were greeted by driving rain at Port Elizabeth. The pitch was really wet and we dominated the first half to such a degree that by the interval our half of the field looked in pristine condition while that which the Springboks had been defending resembled a ploughed field. That man Rob Louw had scored the opening try in each of the first two Tests but, for once, we scored first when Ollie Campbell kicked a penalty, and we led 7–3 at half-time after Bruce Hay had scored in the corner, gathering a poor clearance by Springbok scrum-half Danie Serfontein. We were all over them but our backs put down passes when tries were on offer and a four-point lead was scant reward for the effort the forwards had put in. Even when we faced the elements in the second half we still put our hosts under tremendous pressure, and there seemed to be no way we could lose. Unfortunately, Clive Woodward slipped into his 'drifting' mode when Naas Botha kicked to his wing, just side-footing the ball into touch instead of booting it into the back row of the stand. Gerrie Germishuys was thinking on his feet and raced to pick up the ball, threw in quickly to an equally alert Theuns Stofberg, the Springbok flanker, and then took the return pass to score a soft try. That brought the sides level but Botha kicked the conversion to give South Africa a 12–10 lead, and there was almost an air of inevitability about things when Ollie Campbell missed a last-ditch penalty chance. To say that the forwards were absolutely gutted would be an understatement. It was the worst possible feeling walking from the pitch knowing that you had lost a series you had dominated.

We still had two weeks to go, with three tough games ahead of the fourth and final Test in Pretoria. Sides like Western Province and Griqualand West were not going to be a picnic and my concern was that heads would go down, concentration be lost and our 100 per cent record in the non-Test games be blown away too. We beat the South African Barbarians in a fairly relaxed game in Durban and, the following day, I remember sitting at the front of the team coach and sensing from both the general mood and the body language that the players weren't concentrating on rugby, so I did something I had never done before. I grabbed the microphone and, putting on my best shop-floor voice, told them, 'I don't care what you did last night but we have three more games to play. We are going to win them all and then piss off home.' That must have had the desired effect because we hammered Western Province 37–6, the forwards in awesome form that day and Ollie in great shape with the boot, adding two drop-goals to his four successful penalties and two conversions. I'd been a little anxious when we took the field and saw that Western Province had a second row who looked about seven feet tall (it was Hennie Bekker, who turned up in England later to play for Waterloo), especially when, having expected him to jump against Maurice Colclough, he lined up instead against me who, even on a good day, was only six-feet-four inches tall. At the first line-out Peter Wheeler, who was about to throw in, walked over to me and said it looked as though I was standing in a hole. Thankfully, however, it is one thing being built like a giraffe but something else being able to play rugby. He turned out to be pretty useless as a line-out forward, and I beat him easily.

Our penultimate game in Kimberley against Griqualand West saw us become only the second Lions side to win all its provincial games in South Africa but that record came at a cost, Colin Patterson becoming our latest injury victim. He tore ligaments in his right knee in a tackle, and after transferring with the squad to Johannesburg the following morning had an operation that day. That left us without a scrum-half replacement for John Robbie, himself a replacement on tour, for the final Test. A number of names were bandied about as possibilities until I suggested sending for my old pal Steve Smith. I told Syd and Noel to leave it to me and got on the telephone to Steve, urging him to get over to Johannesburg pretty smartish because we needed a scrum-half on the bench in Pretoria. He arrived two days before the game and, typical Smithy, was immediately chipping in with his views on how things should be done. In the end I had to shut him up, saying, 'Smithy, you've been here ten minutes but we've been here ten weeks and we do know what we are doing.' We intended to engineer something during the game to get him on the pitch for a time but in the end it wasn't possible so he became something of a statistic at the time as a Lion who never got on to the field. Three years later, in New Zealand, he was called up as a replacement for the Lions when Nigel Melville injured his neck. By that stage Smithy had been discarded by England so it made a truly remarkable story when, for his first game as a Lion, he was appointed skipper, leading the side to a 25–19 victory over Hawkes Bay in Napier thus ensuring he would feature in many a sporting quiz as the player who captained the Lions on his debut – on his second Lions tour! Even though he had been rather short of match practice, Smithy performed well in the closing days of the New Zealand tour and there were many who felt he should have been picked for the final Test ahead of Scotland's Roy Laidlaw, who was pretty battle-weary by that stage.

In the build-up to the final Test I repeatedly asked the players how they would feel if they returned home having suffered a whitewash in the series, emphasising that they were too good to carry that tag with them. I certainly didn't want to be remembered as a whitewash captain, well aware that, irrespective of success in provincial games, you are judged by Test results. The Ellis Park Stadium was being rebuilt, so the game was played at Loftus Versfeld in Pretoria – much to my pleasure, since I had twice been on a winning side there, against Northern Transvaal for the Lions and for North West Counties.

The last few days of a Lions tour are difficult. You know you will be heading home 24 hours after the final Test and are desperate to see your wife and family again, but you also have this amazing bonding with the squad and, until you get back into the swing of things, returning home is a massive anti-climax. On tour you get used to a routine and that becomes a way of life – the humour, the piss-taking and the sense of camaraderie. I'm told that it was often difficult for soldiers to settle back into civilian life after returning from the war and I suspect rugby touring is similar, although obviously not on the same scale.

All I wanted to do was to win that final Test and I didn't care too much how we achieved it. As in the previous game, the forwards took the battle to the enemy and completely dominated the Springbok pack. We scored the opening try when Andy Irvine ran the ball out of defence and linked with Ollie Campbell and John O'Driscoll. They combined to put prop Clive Williams over but Ollie missed several kicks and, for all our dominance up front, it was the South Africans who clawed their way into the lead after Gysie Pienaar had taken over the kicking duties from an out-of-sorts Naas Botha. The great kicking exponent was given stick by his own fans that afternoon.

I couldn't believe what was happening and started to fear the worst, convinced we were going to lose this one too but the backs finally started to play with real purpose and Andy Irvine, who I would have loved to have had with us throughout the tour, got over when he supported a break by Bruce Hay. Andy was indirectly involved in the final try too. He should have given the ball to John Carleton, who was unmarked as we opened up the Springbok defence, but he held on to the ball and was tackled short of the line. Still, we got a scrum and Ray Gravell, who had an excellent game, worked with Campbell to send John O'Driscoll over. Ollie's conversion gave us a 17–13 victory.

It was fantastic to go back to the dressing room having won the game, but a little galling to see that the Springboks didn't look the least gutted. They hadn't performed their own Grand Slam but they had won the series and that was what really mattered. As a forward, though, you can at least take some satisfaction from a game, even when you lose, providing you have won the battle up front, and we had achieved that distinction in every one of the Tests. We had literally taken the 'Boks apart in that department but had lacked the necessary cutting edge to make it count. They had guys who could score from a long way out, whereas we didn't. Our cause would have been helped had we had the likes of Andy Irvine, Terry Holmes, Gareth Davies and Ollie Campbell available to us throughout but, due to injuries, we never had a settled team and that cost us dear. Even so, it was an experience I wouldn't have missed for the world.

CHAPTER SEVEN

A brain discovered . . . and damaged!

Without being conceited, I think I returned from the 1980 Lions tour with my reputation intact and, in some respects, probably enhanced because we had performed pretty well despite a horrendous catalogue of injuries. We hadn't won the Test series but were undefeated in all other games and, as a result of winning the final Test, we hadn't returned empty-handed. My ambition at the time was to continue leading England for three or four more years and then retire from the international scene after, hopefully, becoming the first player to captain two Lions tours – a distinction deservedly achieved later by Martin Johnson. England were also scheduled to tour South Africa in 1984 and I felt that would provide a perfect swan-song. After that, the plan was to continue playing for Fylde, hopefully as skipper, finally realising that ambition a good many years after I had first been invited to take the reins. Perhaps my one regret is that I never achieved that goal of captaining my club.

At the start of the 1980–81 season we had the Welsh Centenary game at Cardiff, which was an opportunity for all the Lions to get together again. After that it was down to the serious business of trying to lift the Five Nations title for a second successive year. As we had performed a long-awaited Grand Slam the previous season, there was a belief that England had a very good side but the true sign of a good team and good management is being able to perform successfully at the highest level week in and week out, or, internationally, on an annual basis. In other words, to do what Manchester United manager Sir Alex Ferguson succeeded in doing for over a decade.

England hadn't reached the same stage in its development as Manchester United at their peak, and the loss of three key players had its effect. Tony Neary and Roger Uttley retired from international rugby and, although we didn't realise it when we set off for our opening Five Nations game against Wales in Cardiff, Fran Cotton's retirement was also just hours away. He had just helped Peter Wheeler following a line-out close to the Welsh line when he was forced to limp out of the action after pulling a hamstring. That evening he was taken ill at the team's hotel and had to retire to bed. As mentioned earlier, Fran had a problem with one of his legs becoming infected whenever he suffered a cut or scratch, being laid low with flu-like symptoms if that happened, but it wasn't until he saw a specialist after the Cardiff incident that he finally got to the root of the problem. Any dirt in a wound, he was told, would lead to a recurrence of the condition, so, knowing that it is impossible to play rugby at any level without picking up a few cuts and scratches, Fran decided it was time to hang up his boots.

You can't remove three players of such calibre from a team and expect to perform to quite the same high standard. That's no criticism of those who came in to replace them, just a simple statement of fact. In sport, qualities like youthful enthusiasm and endeavour are hugely important but there is never any substitute for experience. Fran's place when we played Scotland in our next game was taken by Newport's Colin Smart, and the replacements for Neary and Uttley when we played Wales were David Cooke, from Harlequins, and Mike Rafter, a player I had long admired.

England hadn't won in Cardiff since 1963 and it had become my quest to lead England to victory there. We should have walked that 1981 game because we were the better team. Indeed, I thought we had it in the bag as we led by one point late in the game. Wales had the put-in at a scrum about 30 metres from our line and the Welsh scrum-half, Brynmor Williams, did something that has since been outlawed. He dummied his pick-up out of the back row and pretended to pass what was a non-existent ball. Clive Woodward, who was playing in the centre, started to move forward in anticipation, Brynmor alerted referee Brian Anderson and a penalty was awarded under our posts. Steve Fenwick, who captained Wales that day, stroked the ball over to give Wales a 21–19 victory.

As that game had moved into injury time we were awarded a

penalty 45 metres out from the Welsh posts and I started to wonder if lightning really could strike twice. I gave the ball to Dusty Hare and thought back 12 months to the moment when Dusty's last-ditch kick at Twickenham had saved England's bacon after my old pal Steve Smith had given away a try. This time Smithy walked past me and said, 'He's not going to kick this one.' He was right and I remember walking off the field feeling completely gutted. Not only had we lost the game; I also felt I hadn't played particularly well or captained the side well either. I just don't think we were sufficiently focused on the game. We had thought we were the bee's knees but, clearly, we weren't and all hope of back-to-back Grand Slams had been blown right out of the window.

Our next game was against Scotland at Twickenham and, with Johnny Horton injured, Huw Davies, the Cambridge University fly-half, was brought in for his first cap, with Moseley's Nick Jeavons making his debut at blind-side in place of Mike Rafter. We won in the end, thanks to a good try from Mike Slemen, but Dusty had a bit of an off day at full-back and was dropped for our next game against Ireland in Dublin.

The Scottish match was really the start of the problem that finally brought about my retirement a year later. I took a mighty whack on the head during the game and, although I knew what was going on around me, my vision had gone. I knew Peter Wheeler was throwing the ball into the line-out and also knew the score but everything else seemed hazy. Nick Jeavons had already gone off, I think to have an eyelash repaired – he was a good lad but a bit of a film star – so I decided I would have to stay on because our only back-five replacement, Bob Hesford, was already on the field. I told Smithy to captain the side and asked Peter Wheeler to take charge of the forwards.

Gradually, my vision was restored and I started to feel better but I should have done the sensible thing and taken a couple of weeks off. Instead I turned out for Fylde the following weekend and then led England to a narrow victory over Ireland in Dublin a week later. Phil Blakeway went off injured so, while we were waiting for Gloucester's Gordon Sargent to come on as a replacement to win his only cap, I told Peter Wheeler that I would go to tight-head. I was up against Phil Orr, who I had toured with four years earlier with the Lions, and I must have been affected by the bang on the head in the Scottish game because at the second scrum we were engaged in I decided to wind him up asking, 'Is this the best you can do then?'

'Shut up you daft bastard!' exploded Wheelbrace, as our scrum was immediately shoved backwards at a million miles an hour.

In international rugby, even though it is so hugely competitive, players build up an enormous respect for one another and that was brought home to me during that match in Ireland. I went down to kill what was Ireland's ball under our posts and looked up to see Irish second row Moss Keane. He was in the perfect position to give me a really good shoeing, which I deserved because I was cheating, but he just gave me a knowing look. I got the message and didn't do it again. Sometimes that is all it needs when players have mutual respect such as

Moss and I enjoyed. I had taken his place in the Test team on the Lions tour to New Zealand in 1977 but he had been fine about that and, as fellow second rows, we enjoyed a few drinking sessions together. If we made a decision on anything he would spit into his palm, clench his fist and say, 'Right!' – a tradition we always followed when we lined up against each other in matches.

That Ireland game afforded another very enjoyable Dublin weekend, the only disappointment in those days being that wives and girlfriends weren't included in the trip as they are now. One year Hilary travelled across on the overnight ferry from Holyhead with my father and a few friends. They had a bite to eat before the game and then set off back the same evening. You can imagine what the journey was like for her in the middle of winter with a rough sea and hundreds of beer-swilling rugby fans as her travelling companions. We couldn't even get together after the game for a cup of tea, because she wasn't allowed in, the best we could do being to snatch a few words together through the bars of a locked gate. At the time we were in the middle of moving house, so it wasn't too tactful of me to stomp into the house at teatime on the Sunday to tell Hilary what a fantastic weekend it had been!

Playing for England in my day was like encountering the old feudal system. Although we were the guys entertaining the masses we lived in fear of officials and selectors and were made to feel as though we ought to feel bloody lucky to be invited to play. Officials carried too much power, and if you upset one you could very quickly find yourself dropped from the team. It was very much a 'them and us' scenario; a case of keeping your nose clean and 'three bags full, Sir'.

With France finishing off the campaign with a visit to Twickenham we were still in with a chance of sharing the title. The fact that they were on for a Grand Slam gave the fixture added spice, and they had beefed up their side with a few heavyweights like second row Jean-Francois Imbernon, and, of course, Fran Cotton's old pal Robert Paparemborde, who was still at tight-head – a pleasure for Colin Smart to look forward to! We lost that game 16–12 and didn't play terribly well but France only won thanks to a controversial try just before half-time that didn't exactly endear me to referee Allan Hosie, with whom I was destined to break bread years later to prevent England's banishment from the Five Nations Championship. Our full-back, Marcus Rose, had cleared the ball into touch, so far into touch, in fact, that it almost ended up in the Royal Box – I'm told the ball landed in the lap of former England scrum-half and RFU President, Dickie Jeeps. We started to walk towards the touchline for the line-out but Pierre Berbizier, the French scrum-half, took another ball from a ball-boy, threw it in quickly, and France went over unopposed in the corner. We were all aware that France had used the wrong ball but Allan hadn't worked that one out. Nor had his fellow Scottish referee Brian Anderson who was running touch on that side of the field. As we gathered behind the posts I said to Anderson, 'Go tell your mate Hosie that I know, we all know and, more importantly, he knows that that try shouldn't have been allowed because the French used the wrong ball.' I was furious but I joke about it with him now, although he has, to this day, never admitted that it was the wrong ball.

Looking back at that season I think we had become used to winning and expected to win every time we took the field. That was the major difference between that side and the one I first played in back in 1975. After years as losers, England had discovered how to win international games and we went off confidently to Argentina later that summer to become the first European side to win a Test series there. Only New Zealand had ever won there previously. A couple of the lads had been to Argentina before and the country had a bit of a reputation as not such a great place to visit. Some of the players decided not to travel and others were unable to do so because of other commitments, their number including Mike Slemen, Marcus Rose, Maurice Colclough, Peter Wheeler and Phil Blakeway, all of which made for an inexperienced squad.

Despite what we had been told about Argentina, I found it a fascinating place with strong British connections. Our culture was very evident, a lot of private schools being run on the English system and the many municipal authorities and services, such as railways and electricity, being managed by Brits. Apart from the high cost of living, I thoroughly enjoyed the tour – once we had sorted out our accommodation. One of the English 'blazers' who knew the country had suggested that we stay at the Hindu Club (we renamed it the Voodoo Club), a country club well away from civilisation. It was a massive place spread over a wide area, with the accommodation in individual apartments owned by Argentinian families, the standard varying according to whose apartment you happened to be in. It was pouring down as we arrived, there was nothing to do, and we were hopelessly scattered around the complex. We stayed for one night but the players were so disgruntled that we called a team meeting and said we weren't prepared to stay there any longer. Derek Morgan was managing the tour and he had us all transferred to the Sheraton in Buenos Aires.

When we got down to the rugby, I knew it would be tough because I had previously played against the Argentinians for a combined North and Midlands side. One thing the game taught me is that those boys can scrummage. Their hooker never once struck for the ball when it was their own put-in. The scrum-half simply rolled the ball into the scrum and their forwards drove over it – a tactic the South Africans also used to good effect at times. During that time in Argentina they put out a formidable pack of forwards, but that didn't stop us returning undefeated, even though we were somewhat lucky to draw the first Test 19–19. That was one tough, hard game in which we struggled as they put us on the rack. But we showed character and clawed our way back into the contest when it was starting to look pretty desperate. I hadn't been included in the selection process before we left for Buenos Aires but once on tour I was brought into the equation.

It had been important to get the balance of the side right and one of the hardest choices had been at open-side flanker. David Cooke had played there during the Five Nations but Mike Rafter was playing some fantastic rugby so we dropped Dave to bring 'The Grafter' back in. Without Peter Wheeler, the hooking job was between Andy Simpson, from Sale, who had spent two years growing calluses on the England bench without getting on the field to win a cap, and Gloucester's Steve Mills. I knew the lads got on a lot better with Steve so, for the only time in my career, went along with the players' preference as to who should be in the team. The choice of a second row partner for myself was another key decision and the choice was between Steve Bainbridge and John Fidler, both of who had been drafted into the squad. I felt I needed a grafting type of player alongside me, in view of the opposition, so John got the vote. Another newcomer to the side was wing Tony Swift, who had been playing for Swansea but had previously played with me at Fylde, being the son of a Preston butcher. The other wing in contention was David Trick, from Bath, who was like the proverbial 'off a shovel'. I would like to have seen him in action but we were hardly playing expansive rugby so he never got a chance to show what he could do – at least, not on the field. Off the field was another matter. We were having a few beers one evening after a game and ended up betting on whether or not David could beat one of their players in a sprint in the street outside. Afterwards, so David tells the story, our coach Mike Davis called him up to his room and, expression stern, exploded, 'I'm really surprised at you. It's your first international tour and you're not even in the team. We'll have to call a disciplinary meeting and, in all probability, you'll be sent home.' The tension crackled, until Mike, unable to contain himself any longer, burst out laughing and asked, 'Did you win?' He had done of course, and we went on to win the second Test and take the series.

I really wanted that win because English sport was crap at the time. We had lost at soccer and cricket and I urgently wanted to put a W alongside England's name. I gathered the players before we went out on to the pitch and said, 'As a sporting nation we are losing at everything. Let's stand tall and go out there to give the English something to cheer.' In the end we were hanging on the ropes but we survived. It was a good night after that victory!

There wasn't a lot to do in Argentina and what there was proved to be ridiculously expensive. Mind you, the steaks were absolutely wonderful. The 'Sumos' – guys like Colin Smart, Gary Pearce, Clint McGregor and John Fidler – really enjoyed themselves in that department, and must have returned home considerably heavier. Although beer cost an arm and a leg we did indulge after the second Test win, and it was a very hung-over, bedraggled bunch that presented itself at the British Ambassador's home in Buenos Aires for drinks on the way to the airport for the flight home. It had been a tough place to go and a totally different environment to what we were used to. The Argentines were very passionate about their rugby, but there was an atmosphere of detachment about the place. The country, of course, was ruled by a military dictatorship, and Anglo-Argentinian relations were rather sensitive, culminating in the attempted capture of the Falkland Islands less than a year later.

When I returned home I discovered that Lancashire had

organised a pre-season tour to southern France. It was the county's centenary, and John Burgess, having taken over as president, was keen to celebrate the occasion by winning the County Championship. I had played just about non-stop rugby for as long as I could remember and really wanted a complete break for what remained of the summer, but, although I explained this to county officials, I still received a call from Burge saying they had a problem because he had sold the tour to the French on the basis that I would be in the party. 'John', I said, 'I'm not travelling to France because I've had enough.' Instead, Hilary and I went away for a holiday with friends in Corfu, and I thought no more about the Lancashire tour until I was lying in bed one Saturday morning and Burge telephoned to suggest that I fly out on the following Friday, play a game and return home in time for work on the Monday morning. He could be a very persuasive character and I finally agreed. Steve Smith had likewise been persuaded to play, and it was decided that we would fly out together but that he would then stay on for the remainder of the tour. It wasn't a fun journey. We had to fly from Manchester to Gatwick, then take a flight to Toulouse, and then hire a car and drive to a small ski resort in the Pyrenees where the opposition, Agen, had assembled for their pre-season training. Being driven by Smithy for a mile was quite enough. After that I made him pull over so that I could take the wheel instead. I wanted to be sure we arrived in one piece because I knew that, playing in France, we'd pick up more than our fair share of injuries on the field. So it proved. Mike Dixon, the

Fylde hooker, needed stitches almost from the start and I remember saying to him, 'Whatever you do, don't go down. Don't show them that it hurts. Get it taped up and carry on.'

After the game on Sunday I drove myself back to Toulouse, arriving at midnight to discover that there was no room booked for me at the hotel where I was supposed to be staying. I eventually got myself a room and grabbed a couple of hours sleep before having to get to the airport by 6 a.m. I arrived home absolutely knackered and went straight to work. So you can imagine my reaction when the telephone rang the next day and it was Burge begging me to go back to France because he had also sold the final game in Béziers on the basis that I would be playing. I said that if I kept flying backwards and forwards the authorities would think I was running drugs! But, once again, I weakened and agreed to travel provided that Hilary went with me so that we could make a weekend of it and meet up with our friend Michel Palmie, the French second row.

We flew out again on the Friday and I trained with the squad the following morning in preparation for that evening's game against a Languedoc provincial side. We played quite well and were leading as the game headed towards injury time. They restarted after a score and I remember going up for the ball, but the next thing I recall was waking up on the ground and wondering where I was. That was the second knock on the head, and it was much worse than the bang I had taken in the game against Scotland. I still don't know what happened but I like to think it wasn't a case of dirty play, simply that I had the misfortune to be caught by someone's knee or a misdirected boot. To cap it all we lost the game and I felt bloody awful. I sat in the dungeon-like dressing room and Michel Palmie and Hilary came in to see how I was. It was obvious that I wasn't at all well and off we went in an ambulance to hospital where they took X-rays. The doctor told me that I had the neck of a 60-year-old, and expressed concern about my continuing to play rugby. I shared his anxiety for I was experiencing symptoms I had never experienced before, including impaired vision, slurred speech, pins and needles and a tingling tongue. Those seemed to indicate I had a real problem, but when you are an otherwise fit young man you like to believe any injury is only temporary and will go away. I discharged myself in the early hours of the Sunday morning and returned to the hotel, where I continued to feel pretty lousy. Hilary and I flew home and the first thing I did was arrange to see a specialist in Liverpool, who, much to my relief, said I had a slight problem with my neck but that it was all right to continue playing.

I did start to feel better too and, like a fool, played in Fylde's first game of the new season when it would have made a lot more sense to rest until just before the County Championship campaign got under way. As England captain I could even have afforded myself the luxury of missing out on the early stages of that competition but Lancashire meant so much to me that I wanted to lead them to the title in their centenary year. After all, John Burgess had been a great influence on me both as a person and as a rugby player and I really felt I owed it to him to help secure the silverware. That's why I'd twice gone over to France, at great inconvenience, when had anyone else called I would have told them to get lost.

Lancashire won through to the county final but I injured my shoulder playing against Cumbria at Vale of Lune and should have taken a couple of weeks off. Once again my desire to play overruled my common sense and I played for the North against Australia a week later, with the result that I felt rotten and had to undergo six weeks of fairly intensive physiotherapy to get back into shape. Although Lancashire were beaten by Yorkshire at Headingley, the Tykes were subsequently beaten by Durham, so we scraped through to the county semi-finals and, having played poorly all through the campaign, we managed to beat Gloucestershire at Kingsholm. I even scored a try right in front of 'The Shed' after a 20-metre trundle.

Having helped Lancashire to reach their target I was able to concentrate on leading England against Australia at Twickenham on the day after New Year's Day. We won the game 15–11, that scoreline not really reflecting our superiority. Three incidents relating to that game stand out in my memory. First, when I arrived at the Petersham Hotel at Richmond, where we were staying, I was greeted by a champagne celebration because news had leaked out that I had been awarded the OBE in the New Year's Honours List. Then, during the game itself, the referee missed an offside so blatant that I asked him how he could possibly not have picked up on it. I believe he realised his mistake because I met one of the touch judges later and he told me that at half-time the ref had said, 'I made a real balls up of that and Beaumont gave me a right bollocking.'

Didn't sound like me! The final incident is one that everyone in the stadium picked up on, because that match saw the moment when Erica Roe achieved her moment of fame, or notoriety, by pulling off her top and running on to the pitch to display her enormous charms. Her picture appeared in every newspaper and she was quite a celebrity for a time. It happened at half-time and I was delivering my usual boring team talk when I realised the players had stopped paying attention and were more interested in something going on behind my back. I continued my dirge until Peter Wheeler chipped in and said, 'Bill, you are going to have to look at this. Some bird has run on to the pitch with your arse on her chest.' That, as you might imagine, was the end of the team talk, as everybody fell about laughing . . . although still managing to keep their eyes firmly fixed on the young lady's attributes. The reference to the shape of my backside stems from comments made by Steve Smith, who always referred to my posterior as an outboard motor. For years he would walk past, give it a pat regardless of where we were, and ask, 'How's the outboard motor today?' As for my health, I felt fit and played pretty well that afternoon, though not as well as my partner Maurice Colclough, who was simply outstanding.

The tourists were next due to play the Barbarians in what used to be the traditional finale of an incoming tour, and I was picked to play. However, when we opened the bedroom curtains at Cardiff's Royal Hotel on the Friday morning, there was a blizzard blowing and we looked out on to a white world. The game was called off, so I rang Peter Makin, Fylde's secretary, and offered to play for the club at Nuneaton, as it was virtually on my way home, but by the Saturday morning we were completely snowed in. I remember having to sit around watching darts on television because there was no other live sport able to be played. Nobody could leave the hotel, nor could anyone get in to us, so we did what all self-respecting rugby players do in such circumstances and retired to the bar, where we sank a few beers and a couple of bottles of wine. David Richards, the Welsh international, lived only down the road in Porthcawl but he was stranded at the hotel until Tuesday. Peter Wheeler and I decided to chance it and followed one another very gingerly down the M4 motorway only to discover, when we crossed the Severn Bridge, that hardly any snow had fallen in England.

Two weeks later I was in Edinburgh for the start of the Five Nations, but it was so cold and icy we couldn't find anywhere to train. The Scots wouldn't let us use Murrayfield, so we ended up at the Hibernian soccer ground, where they had under-soil heating. I was feeling pretty confident that England would have a good season but the night before the game I was terribly sick and at 2 a.m. I rang Mike Davis and Budge Rogers, who told me to spend the morning in bed. Budge said they really needed me to play and urged me not to let anyone know how sick I was feeling. I was throwing up and suffering from diarrhoea, but somehow I got myself ready and travelled to the ground on the team coach.

Once on the field I think adrenalin carried me through but we had to settle for a draw, which is just about the most frustrating outcome of an opening game in the Five Nations. You haven't been beaten but you know you can't do the Grand Slam. We were winning 9–6 in injury time when the referee awarded England a penalty at a scrum on the halfway line, but our prop, Colin Smart, pushed one of the Scottish players out of the way and the ref reversed his decision. Up stepped Andy Irvine to kick the goal. Colin's push hadn't been violent or malicious, and it didn't seem right that a game should turn on such a trivial incident. Mike Davis came up to me in the dressing room and thanked me for playing, and by the following Saturday I was ready to take on North Midlands at Moseley to help Lancashire to another county title. I was on a treadmill and I didn't know how to get off. North Midlands, captained by Les Cusworth, weren't a strong side but Lancashire made heavy weather of beating them. I ended up watching the end of the game from the players' tunnel, not realising that I had just played my last game of rugby.

I hadn't even made it through to half-time. Midway inside a scrappy first half I ended up at the bottom of a ruck and a stray knee caught me in the back of the head. I carried on with the game but realised my vision was going when I joined a line-out, so I called on our physiotherapist, Kevin Murphy. I told him I couldn't distinguish distance properly but said I would carry on for a few minutes to see if it cleared. It didn't, and I trooped off feeling very dizzy and nauseous. Hilary left her seat in the stand and came down to the dressing room. I told her I felt really ill and just wanted to go home. Billy Wood, who was my GP at home, also came to the dressing room. Since I'd been to him many times over the years suffering from concussion he was aware of my medical history and said I needed a full neurological examination. Noel Atkinson, the Lancashire team doctor, arrived to confirm that opinion and told me there was no way I would be leading England against Ireland the following weekend. I thought differently, of course.

Hilary and I stayed on until the final whistle and presentation of the County Championship Trophy, and then set off back up the motorway. On the Monday I was seen at Preston Royal Infirmary by the neurologist, Dr Sarosh Vakil, after which I had to run the gauntlet of journalists and photographers eager to find out how serious the injury was. I did everything in my power, without telling outright lies, to assure Dr Vakil that I was all right, because I desperately wanted to play against Ireland. I did hold back information relating to the number of times I had experienced a problem but Dr Vakil wasn't fooled and told me that I shouldn't play in the international. The brain scan had shown a dark patch that needed further investigation, but I was quietly confident I would be playing for Fylde against Orrell a week after the Irish game. However, Dr Vakil had unearthed reports of two visits to a neurologist some years earlier after I had suffered similar symptoms, and by the time I was seen by Dr Ray Lascelles, the consultant neurologist at Manchester Royal Infirmary, just two days after I had watched England beaten by Ireland at Twickenham, the die was cast. I sat in his office, listened to his advice that I risked possible paralysis or brain damage if I took another whack on the back of the head, and was forced to concur with the medics' conclusion: I had to retire. I would have travelled anywhere to find a specialist prepared to say I could continue playing, but I knew that just wasn't going to happen. I felt physically sick at the thought of having to give up what had become a hugely enjoyable and rewarding (in a non-monetary sense) way of life.

For two or three years afterwards I thought I had done the wrong thing in retiring – the injury must have affected my brain more than I thought! – but I eventually came to realise it would have been stupid to have risked serious repercussions by going against qualified medical advice. Even so, that didn't stop respected rugby journalist John Reason writing a totally irresponsible article in the *Sunday Telegraph* suggesting I had made the wrong decision and should carry on playing. It was ill informed and, in any case, it wasn't his neck on the block.

It was hard to come to terms with my situation. I had gone on as a replacement for Tony Neary in Australia in 1975 and then played 33 consecutive games for England, many of them as captain. As I drove home from Manchester I pulled into a motorway service area in order to telephone Hilary and break the news to her. She was as devastated as I was but, as ever, very supportive.

I had been due to attend an Anglo-American Sporting Club dinner in Manchester in honour of the Lancashire team that evening, so had to telephone team secretary Eddie Deasey to pull out, saying that something had cropped up. I couldn't tell him the truth because I still hadn't relayed the bad news to my parents, who were on holiday in Barbados, or to Twickenham, but I think he suspected the real reason. I tracked down my parents, relieved to be able to tell them personally because I didn't want them hearing the news on the radio or reading it in a newspaper before I had had a chance to talk to them. I also telephoned Budge Rogers, still chairman of the England selectors, who felt I had made the only sensible decision. My next call was to coach Mike Davis, who had become a good friend, and we talked for more than an hour. We were very much on the same wavelength, and he proved an important crutch at that difficult time.

The following day the world was told the news and the *Lancashire Evening Post* carried a 'Beaumont Quits Rugby!' headline across the top of the front page. I knew it would be manic and I endured a succession of interviews at a time when I just wanted to be at home with Hilary trying to get my head around what retirement would mean. I told the media that there had been no discussion when I was given the 'you must quit' advice from the doctors. I wasn't bitter, I said, having had a good run in the game, and at least I was free to take part in other sporting activities that didn't involve putting my head where it hurts. It would of course be hard watching England from the comfort of a seat in the stand, but I had to bite the bullet and accept this in future would be my only participation in the game.

There were requests to film me watching my club Fylde playing at Orrell that weekend but I said I felt that would be a touch macabre and, with me as the centre of media attention, would detract from what the two sides were doing on the field. I had always been open and honest with the media and we had enjoyed a good relationship. On that occasion they respected my wishes and stayed away, which I really appreciated, and I was able to learn without distraction my new role as a spectator – not a very good one according to Hilary! Orrell had a good side in those days but Fylde played really well that afternoon and came away with a surprise win. I was quite emotional as I walked into the dressing room afterwards to congratulate them. Micky Weir, who was still skipper after all those years, told me it was the players' way of saying, 'Thanks for the memory.' The club has always meant a great deal to me and I am sad that, like a great many wonderful clubs up and down the country, they have struggled since the advent of professionalism, concerning which I will have more to say a little later.

Steve Smith was handed the captaincy of England and I was delighted for him because we had been great pals for a long time. He was a bit of a Jack the Lad and a typical chippy scrum-half but he was a good player, for all his cheesy grins and smart quips; a tremendous competitor who loved playing for his country. He should have played for England more often than he did but suffered from bad selection and, for a time, a lack of fitness until his sidekick Fran Cotton took charge. Fran, who didn't like to see talent wasted was determined to do something about it, and, as Smithy used to say, when Fran gets you out of bed at the crack of dawn to tell you that you are going for a run then . . . you are going for a run! I gave Steve a call to wish him all the best and, typical Smithy, he was all sympathy. 'Christ Bill, you shouldn't complain,' he said. 'After five hours of tests the doctors have proved that you do have a tiny brain inside that big, dull head of yours. Who would have believed it? Mind you, having found a brain, you've gone and damaged it.'

Tributes poured in from people in all walks of life, and it gave me enormous help in coping with the desolation of retirement to know that I had been valued. Robert Atkins, the Preston North MP, even tabled a motion in the House of Commons regretting my retirement and paying tribute to my 'distinguished services'. The late John Burgess very kindly, and in his usual emotional way, said that, as a man and a player, I had been the best thing to have happened to rugby in Lancashire and England for as long as he could remember. I don't know about that but they were nice sentiments and all I will say is that I did my best and had wanted nothing more from my playing career than the respect of my peers.

Nothing goes on forever and Steve Smith, in his more serious mode, encouraged me to look back at what had been achieved in the previous ten years – great victories for Lancashire and the North, a Grand Slam, and captaincy of both England and the British Lions. He was right. Nobody could take those memories away from me, and it was time to move on.

CHAPTER EIGHT

Banished

One of the hardest decisions I have ever had to make in my life was the one I knew would lead to my banishment from the game I loved. From being a well-respected former England captain I was to become a pariah overnight, barred from having any involvement in rugby union at any level, and all because I had the temerity to accept the monetary rewards from writing my autobiography. I had devoted my life to rugby, had given nothing less than my best on the field of play, whether for my club's sixth team or the British Lions, and had asked nothing in return. The joy of playing the game and the honour of leading my country was sufficient. Yet I knew that the archaic amateur laws precluded me from receiving any sort of payment even after I had been forced to retire from the game through injury.

Despite the fact that many players succeeded in circumventing the strict amateur code by arranging for brown envelopes (not empty ones either) to be left in boots or by accepting jobs that had more to do with their ability on the rugby field than their skills in the workplace, my inherent honesty prevented me from joining the 'sham-amateurs'. If I had wanted to be deceitful it wouldn't have been too difficult because I could have claimed that my work for the family business was on a consultancy basis and that my main occupation was as a journalist – I was having articles ghosted for the local newspaper and my involvement as a broadcaster was increasing. I have always, though, tried to be honest and I simply couldn't have taken part in what I, and probably the authorities, would have known to be a complete charade. Even when I was still playing I had received a number of approaches from publishers wanting me to write an autobiography, but I had told them I wouldn't consider it until my playing days were over. That situation, of course, came about rather more suddenly than I had anticipated. In February I had still been an international player, captain of my country and looking forward to completing the Five Nations Championship as well as leading England's tour to the US and Canada. The following month I was a former player who had retired on health grounds, and my interest in a book was rekindled by the realisation that I would never play again. The dilemma remained, however, because I was aware of the consequences unless I was prepared to give all the proceeds to the Rugby Football Union, to a charity, or to both. I had happily handed over all the fees I had received for my involvement as a team captain on the BBC television programme *A Question of Sport* but I was married with a family and, in all honesty, knew the money would come in useful. Rather than toy with the problem indefinitely I decided to seek wiser counsel and went to see my grandfather, William Blackledge. His advice, as I had expected it would be, was to the point and helped me to reach my decision. He asked, 'If, ten years hence, your backside is hanging out of your trousers, would the RFU buy you a new pair?' I knew the answer to that without even having to think about it and, through the broadcaster Ian Robertson, who was then also rugby correspondent of *The Sunday Times*, the book went ahead. All that was required was for me to travel to London to sign the contract, and I put that off until after a charity game between Lancashire and an International XV at Fylde, which the Diners Club had organised in my honour. That was a wonderful occasion on a sunny afternoon in April, Fergus Slattery skippering my International XV, which included team-mates from England such as Dusty Hare, Tony Swift, Johnny Horton, Phil Blakeway, Clive Woodward, Paul Dodge and Peter Squires, and guys like Moss Keane, Clive Williams, Graham Price, Allan Martin, John O'Driscoll and Jeff Squire, who had been fellow Lions tourists.

The publishers were ready to issue a press release about the book, called *Thanks To Rugby*, but I asked if they would leave it to me to make the announcement when I felt the time was right. After all, I had one or two niceties to deal with, such as informing the RFU. I wrote to the late Bob Weighill, who was secretary of the RFU at the time and a thoroughly decent man, and I also spoke to him on the telephone. I explained that I knew the implications of what I was doing and said that whilst I disagreed with the rules, which I thought belonged to another age, I fully understood that I was placing myself in contravention of them and would therefore become *persona non grata* so far as rugby union was concerned. He confirmed that that was indeed the case but he was never funny with me about it, in fact turning up as a guest when I sent him an invitation to the eventual book launch. I was delighted to see him, fully aware that it wasn't his fault I had been banished from the game. He was simply doing his job.

All my close friends in the game fully supported what I was doing and I was just as welcome at Fylde rugby club as I had ever been. I also had the complete backing of my family but I very quickly realised I had crossed the Rubicon because my life changed completely, almost overnight. I can't say that I ever encountered open hostility but the attitude of some people in the corridors of power changed towards me. From having been, in their eyes, the best thing since sliced bread when I was leading England, I was a dirty professional who had demeaned himself by taking the money.

I wasn't alone, of course. Others like Phil Bennett, Mike Burton, Gareth Edwards and my old pal Gordon Brown had crossed the same line and Fran Cotton was to follow soon afterwards. When I rationalised the thing I told myself that I had achieved just about everything possible in the game as a player and was being presented with the opportunity, after years of sacrifice in terms of both time and money, to make a few quid. There were times when I wondered if those in authority, who stuck rigidly to the amateur principles, realised just how much time top-class players had to devote to ensuring they stayed at the peak of their game, not to mention the money that was spent on travel, food and kit or lost through time taken off work. Rugby league grew from the old broken-time row when the rugby union authorities refused to allow players who worked in the mines and factories of the industrial North to be compensated for the wages they lost through taking time off on a Saturday in order to play the game. The top-class players of my generation had to work for a living and many made enormous sacrifices, including loss of employment in some cases, in order to tour with their national side or the British Lions.

Until my banishment I had always played by the rules. The only time I ended up putting money in my pocket was through the sale of match tickets while on tour and that was common practice, going some way towards buying presents or a few drinks when you felt like getting away from the team room at the hotel. It didn't apply at home because the international tickets I received, or was able to purchase, were always needed for family and friends.

While still England captain I received a fee of £2100 from the BBC for each series of *A Question of Sport* and all the money was handed over. Half would go to the RFU Charitable Trust and the balance to Fylde rugby club. I was working on the quiz show when the ban took effect and Mike Adderley, the producer, asked if I wanted the fee paid to me instead. He said that, as I was no longer an amateur, I was free to keep the money, but I told him that I was a man of principle and, for that series, wanted the fee to be paid to the RFU and Fylde as I had agreed.

It took a long time to adjust to being a professional. There was still a stigma attached to it in the circles in which I moved and, while I was welcomed at Fylde with open arms, I still kept glancing over my shoulder when I got involved with coaching. Technically, it wasn't permitted and club officials would have had their knuckles rapped if it had become common knowledge. There have been times when I have wondered if certain people at Twickenham knew what was going on but, because of my previous association with them, had decided to turn a blind eye. I like to think that they were starting to realise the stupidity of banning players for writing books once their playing days were over. Around that era a succession of players, who had served their countries and the game at large with distinction, had been lost to rugby union. The tragedy is that we all had so much to offer on a coaching front because of our vast experience. Fortunately, the game is now benefiting from the transition that top-class players are making into coaching and administration.

I am often asked why I didn't go into coaching and I have to explain that I simply wasn't allowed to get involved. Having said that, I did help out surreptitiously from time to time but I never felt comfortable about it. I was always concerned that I might get the players or organisation involved into trouble with the authorities. I recall going to a coaching course at St Mary's College in London to prepare a book on coaching, with the assistance of Peter Wheeler. We ended up buying the students a load of beer to keep them happy. We didn't want them complaining that they had been coached by a dirty old professional!

Don Rutherford was a very senior employee at Twickenham and he had asked me, while I was still playing, if I would present the prizes at his son's school speech day. Someone else at Twickenham asked if he was still happy with that bearing in mind that I was out of the loop but, all credit to Don, the invitation still stood, the professional tag never allowed to stand in the way of friendship. Dudley Wood took over from Bob Weighill as RFU Secretary, and he was a top man. We would often meet up for a coffee or a beer when I was in London, even though I was banned from the game and occasionally people would approach me for my autograph. It was all because of *A Question of Sport*, I told him, nothing to do with rugby, which led him to observe that, with so many better things to do, he couldn't understand why I wanted to get back into the game. When I see him now, with all the game's political shenanigans that have gone on since, I sometimes wish I had taken his advice and stayed away!

In some respects I was fortunate because I was invited to work for the BBC as a summariser at international games, which meant I still virtually had the freedom of Twickenham when England were playing at home. I remember Fran Cotton being asked to leave the dressing room corridor when, after he had been banned, he went to wish his former colleagues well, but I had access through my BBC work. I was also able to wander around the car park, chatting to old friends but, daft as it may sound now, the feeling of guilt stayed with me; the feeling of being an outsider wouldn't go away.

The players treated me just as they always had but I also felt an outsider in the team camp, although that had nothing to do with feelings of guilt about being a professional. Before I had even taken that step I had gone to Paris with Hilary to watch England play France, which was Steve Smith's second game as captain after taking over the reins from me. That was the evening when Colin Smart failed to live up to his name and was conned into drinking some aftershave by my old sidekick Maurice Colclough, with fairly disastrous results. The players wanted me to go out on the town with them afterwards but I ducked out because it somehow didn't feel right. I was conscious that things are different when you are no longer captain and no longer playing the game.

My behind-the-scenes coaching continued at Fylde, and members and players just took it for granted that I would be around as usual. So far as they were concerned nothing had changed.

Another issue at that time relating to amateur regulations was, of course, that of players who had switched rugby codes. At Fylde the door was always open to them, although the great rugby league player and coach Alex Murphy was once asked to leave when on a scouting mission. One of the players who took his fancy was centre David Stephenson, who was a very talented youngster and had been an outstanding prospect when he played for England Schoolboys. Stephenson tele-

phoned me when he was just 19 to say that Alex had offered
him a contract to join Salford. Dave seemed keen to go and
I suspect he was a bit fed up because he hadn't been picked
to play for Lancashire when many, including him, felt he
should have been. I tried to persuade him to stay in our game
and offered to introduce him to a top London club, such as
Harlequins, where, if he had been successful and got into the
England team, he would probably have ended up with a job for
life. As it was he worked for Guardian Insurance, where quite a
few Fylde players ended up, that becoming a full-time career.

One of the anomalies of the amateur regulations was that
you couldn't receive a penny for playing the game but that
many top-class players ended up with well-paid jobs that may
not have been available to them had they not been performing
at a high level. Eric Evans, that great Lancastrian who had been
the last captain to lead England to a Grand Slam before I
achieved it in 1980, followed a pattern by working for Shell;
after joining Harlequins, England flanker Peter Winterbottom
switched from farming to Euro Bond dealing; and David
Pears, the fly-half, made a similar switch from his job as a
joiner. Many players gained employment through being international rugby players. I don't blame any of them for taking up
a secure job but you had to wonder just where the line was
drawn between professionalism and amateurism. I could, so
very easily, have lied about my occupation and carried on in
the game after I had been forced to retire from playing. Some
did pull the wool over the eyes of those in authority and I don't
blame them for doing so but that wouldn't have rested easily

with me. I'm glad the game did eventually go open, although I have strong views, to be expressed later, as to just how open it should have become. At least it stopped all the nonsense that had been going on, even if the decision then sparked nonsense of another kind.

It wasn't easy adjusting to enforced retirement, especially as I wasn't allowed to coach or have any other official involvement in the game, but there was a pleasant distraction in that Hilary was pregnant, leading to our first son Daniel arriving on the scene. That kept me occupied, something other than rugby taking precedence in my life for a change, and I was also able to throw myself more fully into helping run the family business. Furthermore, I decided that if I was to be deemed a professional then I might as well behave like one, so with the help of Ian Robertson, I found myself an agent. John Hockey and his assistant Jane Morgan were to play a major supporting role as I launched into after-dinner speaking and product endorsement. One of my first ventures was a job advertising Gordon's Gin, following which, I suppose on the assumption that rugby forwards eat a great deal, I was asked to munch my way through Holland's pies and McDonald's burgers for the cameras. I enjoy a Big Mac but they did 36 takes and there is a limit to my appetite! I had to take a huge bite out of each one and, much as I like them, my waistline didn't. Heinz baked beans and Tetley's Bitter – a fearsome combination – were also endorsed.

I quickly came to realise that you have to be very professional when you are being paid to do something. As England captain I had to make speeches at post-match functions and would be asked to speak at various functions, mainly rugby club dinners. That was something I can't say I particularly enjoyed at the time. I had never been the type of bloke who relished the opportunity to leap on to a soapbox to pontificate, and I found it a daunting experience. Very often I probably talked gibberish but as England captain it didn't really matter because they were just glad that you were there and of course you weren't being paid anyway. I remember one occasion when I spoke at the Halifax rugby club dinner. It was in the period between two internationals and I remember wondering, as I drove through snow and sleet, what on earth I was doing there. Quite apart from anything else it was my birthday! When people are actually paying you to speak the expectation level is far greater and you have to do a professional job. Not through choice, I had become a professional so I worked at a routine and rehearsed it. Naturally, the more often you speak the more accomplished you become, and I must confess it has changed from being a terrible chore to something I enjoy, especially if it is well received.

I did a lot of motivational seminars for Humphrey Walters of the MAST Organisation and appeared with sporting personalities such as swimmer Duncan Goodhew, cricketer Geoff Boycott and runner Seb Coe. I would talk about the management and leadership skills required as captain of a national side, and would often chat with Humphrey, who taught me a great deal about the art of public speaking. I felt much more confident as a result of the time I spent with Humphrey but, professional or not, I did draw the line at appearing on stage.

Ian Botham, who was the rival captain on *A Question of Sport*, had got into the habit of doing pantomime every winter and I was invited to join him. That wasn't something I relished so I turned it down. I suspect we would have been cast as the Ugly Sisters in *Cinderella*!

Through my work for the BBC as a commentator and my appearances on *A Question of Sport* I had acquired a fairly high profile, higher in fact than I had ever enjoyed as England captain. More people today relate to me through the popular quiz show than through rugby, although I got the impression that some rugby officials were jealous of the profile I was enjoying as someone cast off from their game. No open hostility, just undercurrents. The resulting tension could prove quite embarrassing, because my opinion would be sought on rugby-related issues; a case in point being the fracas in Cardiff in 1987 when Wade Dooley broke Phil Davies's cheekbone during a mass brawl in England's game against Wales. That became a big media story with talk of possible criminal proceedings against Wade, who I knew well because he had left his club Preston Grasshoppers to team up with another England second row, Steve Bainbridge at Fylde. The BBC rang me at work and asked me to provide an RFU view of the incident, really putting me in a difficult situation. For a start I didn't want the thing to be inflamed out of all proportion, Wade and Phil having already made their peace over the incident. Furthermore, I could hardly present the views of an organisation I was banned from having anything to do with. In the event I telephoned Twickenham and explained my dilemma. They told me to go ahead, and although I was on the other side of the fence I felt from that point on that they respected me as a person. Perhaps they realised my love for England and for the game was equally as strong as theirs, and that I would never do anything to embarrass them. At no stage in my exile did I ever feel like hurling the bricks out of the pram. Instead I quietly got on with my new life as a businessman, after-dinner speaker, broadcaster and television personality while enjoying family life in a way that would have been impossible had I been chasing around the country playing rugby and spending at least part of every summer on tour. Throughout the years when the boys have been growing up, the one thing I have always fiercely protected has been the family holiday every summer. I also continued to help out behind the scenes at Fylde and quietly assisted the Lancashire coaches. Playing rugby for the red rose county had afforded me so much pleasure that I willingly gave of my time to help prepare young players, in the way that I had been groomed by experienced coaches whose advice I had always valued. My only concern was that my Lancashire friends would be found guilty by association if it were known that I was involved in this way but I think a blind eye was being turned again.

Common sense concerning amateur status usually prevailed if it was left to the players. If a playing colleague went off to play rugby league, which was a reasonably common occurrence in our part of the world, he was still a mate even if the 'blazers' didn't see it that way. I never quite understood the animosity that some people in rugby union have shown towards the other code over all these years. Much of it, I think, was from the Midlands and farther south where, because they didn't know any better, rugby league players were regarded as aliens and no attempt made to understand the game or glean ideas from it. Thankfully, barriers have broken down now but so many years have been wasted when the two codes could have worked side by side and learned from each other. I have always got on well with rugby league players. I have great respect for their athleticism and skills, and northern rugby union players were frequently seen on the terraces at grounds like Central Park, Wigan, in the days of the great divide. I would even go so far as to suggest that youngsters should play rugby league before attempting to take on board the more intricate laws of our game. By playing the 13-a-side code youngsters would spend a good deal more time learning the basics of both games – passing, catching and tackling. No matter how good you may be at scrummaging, jumping at the line-out, rucking and mauling, you will be a far more rounded player if you have safe hands and rarely miss a tackle. It is interesting to see so many former rugby league players being drafted into rugby union to act as defensive coaches. Anyone who understands both games will tell you that while you might get away with a missed tackle in rugby union you can't afford that luxury in the other code because there are no flankers roaming around picking up the pieces.

You need a certain amount of intelligence to play sport and you can learn from experience. Some things, however, are pure instinct, such as knowing when it is right to hang on to the ball or to pass it. Rugby league players are good at that but you can't coach it and we haven't reached that same high standard yet in rugby union. If you watch a decent rugby league side, and the players get into a three-on-two situation, then you know they will score. In rugby union you can't be sure, even at the higher levels of the game, but I still think union is the better game.

Although my exile was a painful experience it did enable me to do so many other things that would have been out of the question had I continued as a player or, on retirement, got heavily involved in coaching and adminstration. My involvement with A *Question of Sport* increased and I had many very enjoyable years as a team captain. I was also recruited to broadcast for the BBC at major games alongside Ian Robertson and Chris Rea on radio and with the incomparable Bill McLaren on television.

As England captain I had frequently been interviewed but, just days after announcing my retirement, I found myself in Paris commentating on the France versus England international with Nigel Starmer-Smith. Bill Taylor, the BBC producer, had telephoned to ask if I was prepared to fly to Paris to work with Nigel, and he picked up Hilary and myself at Charles de Gaulle airport, drove us into the city for lunch at a restaurant, and then took us in a limo to Parc des Princes, where France played in those days. I remember thinking to myself that I could get used to that life! The commentary position at the stadium was way up in the gods and I spent my afternoon squinting at a little monitor and trying to make intelligent contributions about what I thought I was seeing. Although nobody complained, I thought my earliest attempts at being a television summariser were pretty shocking. Like most things in life, however, the more often you do them the better you become and I quickly learned not to gabble and to use just one word if that would suffice. On that first occasion, though, it was all very new to me and goodness knows what it sounded like, especially as we also had to work with a French producer.

I enjoyed working with both 'Starmers' and Bill McLaren because they would let me have my say. Having said that, the role of a summariser is to enhance the work of the commentator, not the other way around, and each role should be clearly defined. Some commentators not only want to relate what is happening on the field but also like to play the role of expert at the same time. They start questioning things that are going on, especially decisions taken by the referee. It should be left to the summariser to question and interpret decisions.

Of the current crop I think that Stuart Barnes and Miles Harrison do a good job at Sky, but then Miles came from a BBC radio background, which I believe has traditionally been the best proving ground. Ironically, BBC coverage today has slipped from the very high standard that was set by the likes of Starmers and Bill, though even they had their critics. People took the mickey out of Starmers but that was probably because he had a double-barrelled name and played for Harlequins, which, although a fine club with great traditions, many saw as reserved for 'toffs'. The critics would also say that Bill made the most simple rugby act sound absolutely sensational – they would be proud of him in Hawick for that – but they need to consider what a great job he did building up the game with the viewing public. He took rugby commentary to a new level and was never remotely biased, even when England were giving his Scottish boys a hard time! Bill is a true gentleman and, although he hadn't been too keen on working with a summariser, he did say on one occasion that of all the people he had worked with on air he always felt most comfortable with me alongside him; something I took as a huge compliment, but then I was aware of my role. He was part of the establishment and the voice of rugby, and I wasn't going to start contradicting him on air or trying to hog the limelight as some summarisers do.

I had got to know Bill when I was England captain, because he would attend the training sessions to familiarise himself with any new players in the squad. He always used to have some mints with him called Hawick Balls, and during breaks in training I would shuffle across to the touchline and ask him for a couple, one for me and one for Fran Cotton. He would often pop into the dressing room before a game to offer these sweets around, saying, 'Here, these will make you play better.' What with him being such a nice man, we didn't have to worry if they'd been doctored! Actually, I found his Hawick Balls rather tame so I got into the habit of taking him a tin of Uncle Joe's Mint Balls, which carried rather more firepower.

When the BBC lost the Five Nations contract in 1996 I was gutted because I had been involved for the best part of

15 years and, although the financial rewards from the BBC wouldn't pay the mortgage, I got a real buzz out of covering the games. So I was pleased to get a call from Martin Turner, who was Sky's rugby producer, asking if I would like to be in their studio for an England versus New Zealand game at Twickenham. I couldn't resist asking why they wanted me and he replied, 'Well, the grannies like you.' He did add that he felt I could do a good job for them. In the event, that job lasted for several years. I was impressed with Sky's professionalism, even though they had a different way of presenting the sport. They were rather more outspoken. The BBC liked you to play it straight down the middle but I always felt that Sky wanted you to be more controversial. They certainly didn't want you to be bland, and I respected their enthusiasm.

My stint came to an end because the Six Nations went back to the BBC last season. It has always been felt by many in the game that rugby union, in so far as attracting people to the game is concerned, is best served by England's games being seen on terrestrial television. Having said that, I think Sky has been good for the BBC because its excellent coverage has forced our national institution to significantly sharpen up its act. Complacency had set in, but we have moved on now since the days when the Beeb got every major sporting event almost automatically. For a start there is far more sport on television than when I was growing up. It was more a case then of the FA Cup Final, the occasional England soccer international, Test Match cricket, Wimbledon and very little else. Then the Beeb lost cricket to Channel Four and Sky, while soccer is now almost exclusively the preserve of Sky and ITV. The only rugby games seen in the old days were those in the old Five Nations Championship and a few snatches of other important games on *Rugby Special*.

My long association with the world of broadcasting enabled me to continue my involvement in the game after I had been cast into the wilderness, and the high profile that the England captaincy and my appearances on *A Question of Sport* gave me meant that my life seemed fuller and more active than when I was playing the game. I may have been persona non grata with the rugby authorities but that didn't stop the invitations to attend a whole range of events dropping on the doormat.

On a couple of occasions Hilary and I were invited into the Royal Box at Wimbledon, which proved a very enjoyable experience, even though it rained all day the first time we went. Kim Hughes, the Aussie cricket captain, was so cold that he sat wrapped up in rugs but Sir Douglas Bader, the former wartime flying ace, thought that everyone was being a bit soft and suggested that he and I go out to play a few sets (he had an infectious enthusiasm, was definitely up for it). Now that would have been quite a spectacle! That first invitation to Wimbledon arrived when I was England captain but it was nice to be invited back after I had been professionalised. Fergus Slattery was a guest on the second occasion and Hilary, who enjoys tennis, busied herself collecting autographs. As she didn't have anything else for players to write on she used the Royal Box souvenir programme and Bjorn Borg told her they didn't get too many of those to sign. She also received strange looks from Jimmy Connors and John McEnroe, who probably wondered which minor royal she was. The company was always excellent and we met up with former Liberal leader David Steel and racing driver Jackie Stewart who, in later years, invited me to test my aim by taking part in his annual Celebrity Challenge in aid of charity. Throughout we were charmingly hosted by the Duke and Duchess of Kent.

Now, meeting a duke and duchess in the relaxed atmosphere of a sporting occasion is one thing but taking lunch with the Queen at Buckingham Palace is a very different kettle of fish, yet that's what happened to me. It was during the Five Nations in 1981 that I answered the telephone at home and the caller announced himself as one of the Queen's private secretaries. When you had been involved in a leg-pulling world like rugby as long as I had then, in a situation like that, you started to smell a rat. I wracked my brain trying to work out which of my team-mates would pull such a stunt and even asked, 'Are you straight up or taking the mickey?' I'm not too sure if Her Majesty's secretaries are accustomed to being asked such questions but I rather gathered from his tone that it wasn't the first time. He replied that it wasn't a wind-up and I would receive the formal invitation in the next day's post as proof. That set me into panic mode and my first thought was that the luncheon was scheduled for the Thursday before we were due to play Scotland at Twickenham, the day the squad would be meeting for a training session. I immediately telephoned Budge Rogers, who was chairman of selectors, and explained my dilemma.

'Look Budge,' I said, 'I know the rugby comes first but

I've had this invitation, so what on earth do I do?' 'Bill', he answered, 'you have to go to the Palace. Don't worry about it and just join us when you can.' The next call was to Harry Miller, a tailor in Chorley, because I thought I had better get myself a new suit. He asked why I needed one so quickly, and when I told him I was responding to a summons from my sovereign he promised to have one ready in double-quick time. It felt very strange jumping into a taxi in London and saying to the cabbie, 'Buckingham Palace please.' He just answered, 'Right Bill,' but then I suppose it's not that unusual a request for a London cab driver.

It really was a daunting experience. I remember waiting in an anteroom feeling absolutely petrified. There were only about a dozen of us for lunch, the other guests included Dame Josephine Barnes, a past president of the British Medical Association, who I found myself seated next to at the table; Sir Tasker Watkins VC, an eminent judge and currently President of the Welsh RFU and Terry Duffy, who was leader of the General Engineering Union. Terry was a nice chap, and a couple of years later I was approached by his son, who introduced himself and said Terry often had a laugh about the day he and I had lunch with the Queen. Sir Tasker told me how he was president of Glamorgan Wanderers rugby club and asked how one of their former players, a young flanker called Tony Simpson, was faring at Fylde. 'Simpo' was highly amused when I told him I had been discussing his playing career over lunch with Sir Tasker Watkins and the Queen and Prince Philip at the palace.

The Queen's arrival was heralded by several corgis running into the room ahead of her and then it was a case of moving around and circulating in turn so that the Queen and Prince Philip could chat to individuals. Fortunately, the Queen started chatting to me about attending the Welsh Centenary match in Cardiff, when I had played for a combined England and Wales side against a team representing Scotland and Ireland. I was a bundle of nerves but at least we were able to talk about something I knew about, so I was able to relax a little until we sat down for luncheon and I found myself being invited to take my own seafood pancake from a silver salver without spilling the cheese sauce all over myself, the table or, even worse, Dame Josephine Barnes. I was so convinced that I would make a complete mess of things that I opted to forgo the sauce, scraping it off my pancake before removing it from the salver.

Needless to say, I was given a terrible ribbing when I finally turned up at England's training camp.

I was privileged subsequently to meet the Queen and other members of the royal family on a number of occasions and I was back at Buckingham Palace later that year to attend a garden party. The invitation was also extended to Hilary and we really enjoyed ourselves, although she had to meet her own expenses. Mine were met by the RFU because I was deemed to be on their business; another example of how wives tended to be discounted. Eleven years later Hilary and I were there again for another garden party as guests of the Central Council of Physical Recreation, and a red-letter day was 2 March 1982, shortly after my retirement, when I was at Buckingham Palace to receive the OBE from the Queen. Once again she had done her homework, because she said she hoped the award would help to make up for my disappointment at having to give up the game. My mother accompanied Hilary and I for the ceremony. Little did I know then that 20 years later I would be attending another investiture to witness my mother receiving the MBE for her services to education. She had been chairman of governors at one of our local schools for many years, doing a really good job, and it was nice that her efforts had been recognised.

The Queen also entertained the 1980 Grand Slam team, and Hilary and I were in attendance when she held a reception for people who been champions of their sport during her reign. We had been to a luncheon first, and Frank Bruno and his wife gave us a lift to the palace. He was driving this enormous Mercedes, and when we reached Hyde Park Corner he wound down his window and waved his arm to halt the rest of the traffic, thus allowing us to proceed unhindered towards our destination. London cabbies are not known for giving way but on that occasion they simply waved him through, yelling, 'Good on yer Frank.' He was then allowed to park right outside the palace.

Perhaps the most amazing event I have ever attended was a Celebration of Achievement luncheon hosted by the Queen and the Duke of Edinburgh at London's Mansion House. Nominations had been sought from across the country and a selection panel had drawn up a guest list of 400 people, from all walks of life and every field of endeavour, to celebrate their achievements throughout the last century. The list they came up with was mind-blowing. I found myself sitting on the top table just six places removed from the Queen and between comedian Ronnie Barker and fashion designer Vivienne Westwood, and almost opposite Dame Vera Lynn. Sir Bobby Charlton sat nearby and further along were Henry Cooper, Lord Andrew Lloyd-Webber, John Major, Sir Robin Day, Lord Richard Attenborough, Baroness Thatcher, Colin Jackson, Matthew Pinsent, Dame Diana Rigg, David Bailey, General Sir Peter de la Billiere and surgeon Professor, Sir Magdi Yacoub. Sir Tasker Watkins, who had been a luncheon guest on my first visit to Buckingham Palace, was also there along with Martin Offiah, the former high-scoring rugby league wing.

One member of the royal family that I met more often than most was the Princess Royal. While I would never have cut much of a figure on a horse, we did at least have rugby in common, as she is very knowledgeable on the subject. When I went to the palace to receive the Queen's Export Award on behalf of my company I recall that we talked more about rugby than business, as we did when we met at a variety of textile factories (at which I was present because of textiles being my line of business and the Princess Royal as a patron of the Textile Manufacturers Association). She is a marvellous sportsperson and I have an enormous amount of respect for her. You don't win medals at the Olympic Games unless you are at the very top of your field, and certainly not because of who you are. You have to go out and prove yourself a winner against the very best in your chosen sport, and she did just that in a sport that requires guts, strength and a good deal of self-belief. Having met her on a number of occasions I am never surprised to learn that she is the hardest working member of the royal family, yet one who quietly gets on with the job in hand and with the minimum degree of fuss.

The spin-offs from being perceived as a personality are enormous and I found myself taking part in events I would never have thought of getting involved in. My prowess with a shotgun was put to the test when I was invited to take part in the Jackie Stewart Celebrity Challenge at Gleneagles, an event the former motor-racing champion organises to raise money for charity. The teams are made up of people from all walks of life, with members of the royal family pitting their skills against broadcasters, sports stars, lords and ladies of the realm, entertainers and successful businessmen. One year I was teamed up with Derek Bell, Kenny Dalglish and former world motor-racing champion Nigel Mansell, who I got to know quite well. He was living in the Isle of Man and would fly over by helicopter, after which we would all pile into the car and drive up to Scotland. On another occasion I again teamed up with Kenny, along with Tessa Sanderson and jockey Peter Scudamore. Film-maker Steven Spielberg took part, along with the likes of Billy Connolly, Sean Connery, Michael Parkinson, Captain Mark Phillips, Prince Edward, the Duke of Kent, Michael Winner, Dame Kiri Te Kanawa, Imran Khan, Selina Scott, Martin Brundle and any number of dukes and duchesses.

Pro-celebrity golf also started to feature in my life and I began to wish I had taken lessons at an early age, even more so now as my 11-year-old son Josh puts me to shame. I'm a big guy who can hit a ball a long way if I connect properly, but I wouldn't win any prizes for style. On one occasion I had to play in a competition at Turnberry that was being filmed for television. Some of the competitors, such as enthusiast Bruce Forsyth, had spent a week there practising but I arrived at the last minute from a family holiday in Portugal. Knowing that I was due to take part on my return I had taken the clubs with me and had a few practice rounds. The more I practised the more I played like an absolute drain. I travelled to Turnberry with Hilary and the kids and we were well looked after by the sponsors, Famous Grouse, but the moment of truth was approaching. I managed to squeeze in a practice round with Bernard Cribbins before the main event, in which I was partnering Sandy Lyle, with Lee Trevino playing with Terry Wogan to make up the foursome. To say that I was bricking myself would be a massive understatement. It is bad enough lining up alongside great golfers like Sandy and Lee but much worse when you have a cameraman standing next to you and you can't play your shot until he is ready to start filming, not to mention the crowd of knowledgeable golfing spectators packed around the tees and greens. Terry sensed my nerves and told me that he had played in a lot of these competitions, urging me just to relax and not worry if I made a mistake. We played a Texas Scramble, which means each pair plays the best drive, and in our case that was invariably Sandy's, so I would

pick up my ball and drop it next to his. On the approach
to one hole Sandy reckoned that even though his shot had
landed in a bunker it was a better shot to play than the one
I had managed farther back down the fairway. Pessimistically,
I decided that this was where I would make a complete fool
of myself, envisaging the green being buried in sand as I desperately tried to dig my way out. I surprised myself by not
only getting out at the first attempt but also actually playing
a reasonable shot. Sadly, those were few and far between.
I played appallingly, while Terry, although he started out just
as badly, improved as the round progressed while my game
deteriorated further.

Terry is a great character and it was interesting to discover
that he is just the same affable chap off-screen as he is on it.
Emlyn Hughes and I were invited on to his television show,
and that proved great fun because he is very good at helping
you relax on air. He is also a rugby fan – a regular at international games, especially when the Irish are playing – so we
had quite a bit in common.

One of my more interesting assignments was to appear as a
guest on the Russell Harty Show. I was first on and we chatted
about the injury that had ended my playing career. Oliver
Reed was the next guest and he made a dramatic appearance,
decked out in a blood-covered headband similar to the one I
used to wear. He said he wanted to meet one of his heroes
and clearly loved rugby. Not unnaturally, Oliver had had one
or two drinks and was very funny. I'm not sure that Russell
knew how to handle him but I felt Oliver and I had something

in common; in time, I reckon, we could have turned him into a decent third-team prop!

I had an enormous amount of fun over the years but I wasn't going to make a living out of my occasional broadcasting and after-dinner speaking, so, throughout, I had to keep an eye on the business. After all I had a wife and a growing family to provide for and, in any case, I had always been involved in the family firm. It had been good to me, because I doubt any other employer would have been quite so understanding about the amount of time I needed to take off to fulfil all my rugby commitments. Initially I joined the business more out of convenience than anything else, but I grew to enjoy it, even though my uncle Joe Blackledge and my father were tough taskmasters and I had to work twice as hard as anyone else. I suppose that stemmed from a fear of the rest of the workforce thinking that family members weren't pulling their weight. We manufactured largely industrial fabrics for the rubber trade, which would be used in the production of green wellies, tents, canvases and tarpaulins. Interestingly, considering the image rugby union has in some quarters, we also supplied materials for Barbour jackets.

No business can afford to stand still and I felt we needed a change of direction. I was only one of a number of family shareholders, so I couldn't do as I pleased as far as the business was concerned. However, two of my three cousins, who also owned shares, didn't want to work in the business so, a few years ago, I bought them out and set up Bill Beaumont Textiles as a subsidiary of Blackledge's. In 2003 the Blackledge name disappeared and I am now the sole owner of the company, but I am very proud of the Blackledge heritage.

The business keeps me very busy although I suppose you shouldn't be driving it forward when you are my age. It should have been done earlier but I suppose we became a little complacent, only to suddenly realise, with competition from around the world, that the future didn't look as secure as it always had done. The demands on the company increased, and if we hadn't responded then we wouldn't be in business today. But I diversified into household textiles and upholstery, and that business has grown. We changed direction through a good friend from Spain, Salvadore Monllor, who ran a textile business in Preston. When I asked him what the market was like he told me there was room in it for someone with my business background, even though it was a different branch of the textile industry, and, while we are technically competitors he has been an invaluable help. The whole industry is developing and has certainly been helped by television programmes like *Changing Rooms*. At one time people only changed a lounge, for instance, when the sofa finally gave up the ghost. Now, people will change their home decor as frequently as every two years.

Although it is a very competitive sector I have been helped by competitors and, at the moment, there is still a massive UK manufacturing and retail side. Not too much is done overseas but that situation will change, as it has in other areas of business, so we can't afford to rest on our laurels. We resource textiles very competitively for our customers, looking after things like quality control, and I believe we offer an extremely good service. This is now a global industry and I do a lot of business in places like Germany, France, Turkey, China and other parts of the Far East.

As a person I am very competitive and like to succeed in what I do. If the business isn't successful then I will not just be disappointed but will also take it personally. Of course, when dealing with fabric, it is good that I have Hilary's help. She has a very good eye for design and I greatly value her expertise. In particular, she travels throughout Europe attending trade shows, it being better that *she* goes rather than me because she can see what is needed and is a far better judge of what designs, colours and fabrics are likely to come into fashion. Hilary has come fully into the business as a partner, which means it is more a partnership now than it had been previously, the two of us working together to develop and expand the business. She has always supported me in all things, and now that the children are growing up it's nice that she is able to work alongside me. In a way it brings us even closer together, and it is our hope that in time our three boys will join us, although I would like them to have a spell in business in a country like Australia or America first to gain experience.

CHAPTER NINE

Battle stations

The wind of change finally swept through rugby's corridors of power and, in April 1989, the International Rugby Board took the decision to reinstate players like Fran Cotton and I, who had retained the proceeds of their autobiographies. At the same time they also opened the door to 11 rugby league players who had formerly played rugby union. I heard the news from England's IRB representative, John Jeavons-Fellowes, who told me that we were free to get involved in coaching and selection at club, county and provincial level. It was made pretty plain that we wouldn't be allowed to get involved in a similar capacity with the national side but, so far as coaching was concerned, we had been away from the game too long anyway.

I was immediately given the title of team manager at Fylde, partly because I didn't want the responsibility of coaching because of all my other interests. In any case, I wasn't conceited enough to think I knew it all and felt it would be better simply to head a team of five coaches. At the time the club was in the process of finishing third from the bottom of Division Three and the aim the following season was to turn things around and gain promotion, which is what we achieved. Not that I was inclined to get carried away, because we were relegated 12 months later, and when the game went open it became an uphill struggle – an experience that helped to formulate my ideas on the future of the game, which I will deal with later in this book.

For his part, Fran took over as coach at Sale (now called Sharks) but things didn't work out for him, partly I think, due to the fact that we had been away too long suddenly to pick up the coaching reins. Our experience could be used in other ways, however: we both became North of England selectors and I was chairman of selectors when Lancashire collected another of their County Championship trophies. It was just like old times, because the North, as ever, fared well in the oft-maligned Divisional Championship. Despite county rivalries, especially those between Lancashire and Yorkshire, the North has always succeeded in burying hostilities for a common cause whereas divisions like the South West always suffered from the rivalry between the big three clubs of Bath, Bristol and Gloucester; London and the South East somehow lacked a clear identity; and club rugby always seemed to take precedence over county or divisional interests in the Midlands.

Although neither Fran nor I had actually gone away from the game during our enforced exile, we were happy to be back, legitimately involved and able to contribute to a game we both loved. The fact that we were told we couldn't progress farther than provincial level didn't bother me because I was happy with the new arrangement. For me, the important thing was that the stigma attached to professionalism had been removed. The next olive branch was waved in the summer of 1995, the year the game went open. The RFU decided to create two new positions on the Council, with the title of National Member. Jeff Probyn, who had served England well at prop for many years, was invited to fill one of the positions and I was asked to fill the other post. We were to represent ourselves and nobody else.

The call had come completely out of the blue from a good friend, Malcolm Phillips, who was one of Lancashire's two representatives on the RFU. I had known Malcolm for a long time because he had been a playing member at Fylde, before my time, and was a Lancashire and England selector when I graduated to the red rose side. My respect for him knows no bounds because he has done everything in the game yet is one of those quiet, unassuming guys who just gets on with the task ahead of him. He was a very talented centre, partnering Jeff Butterfield in the England side, and went into rugby administration as soon as his playing days were over. A selector for Lancashire, the North and England, he is also a member of the International Rugby Board, a director of the World Cup, and due to take over as England President in 2004. I can't think of anyone more fitted for the honour because the amount of time he devotes to the game is absolutely amazing. For years he gave up his holidays because of the time he had to take off from work in order to fulfil his rugby commitments. He even took early retirement to concentrate on helping to run a game that wasn't always appreciative of the unselfish and unpaid work done by quiet people behind the scenes. His wife Margaret has helped him throughout, assuming the role of unpaid secretary.

The idea was that Jeff and I would represent an open view on the game. Unlike some people, we had no axe to grind, but Jeff and I had been around the game for a long time and, having played at the top level, we probably had a better understanding than most on the Council of the problems being encountered on both sides of what was destined to become a great divide between the RFU and the new breed of professional club owners. Not to mention the barriers building between the RFU and the Celtic nations.

In many respects I had gone full circle from being England captain, to banishment and then to a place in the holy of holies. There certainly had been a wind of change, and this was to rise in velocity fairly quickly because I barely had my feet under the table at Twickenham before the great amateur game came to an abrupt end; rather ironic considering that it had been to protect the amateur ethos that I had been shown the door some years earlier. I was appointed to the Council in July and my first meeting was in September. In the intervening month the decision had been taken by the International Rugby Board to make the game open. In other words you could remain an amateur if you wished but there would no longer be any stigma attached to receiving money for playing rugby union.

The England representatives at that meeting in Paris were the late Peter Brook and John Jeavons-Fellowes. They had received no mandate from the Council to support such a historic decision and there was some unjustified criticism that they hadn't fought against it. While many felt it almost inevitable that the top end of the game would go professional one day because of the environment and economic climate in which it was being played, I doubt if any in the England camp had realised it might happen so quickly. Having talked to many people about the events at that meeting in Paris I firmly believe that it was a *fait accompli* and that objections by England's representatives wouldn't have changed a thing.

After the success that summer of the World Cup in South Africa there had been almost an air of inevitability about it. Such a move had already been mooted in the southern hemisphere, with Australia, South Africa and New Zealand driving the whole thing. Support from the northern hemisphere nations was clearly more guarded but they went along with it in the end and, with hindsight, I believe it was a great move. The only problem was that we in England were ill prepared for it and were rather caught with our trousers down.

Those who were determined to retain the game's almost unique amateur ethos were really backing a loser, because of rugby union's success. It was no longer a game played purely for recreation. Events like the World Cup, increased television coverage and massive media interest had raised its profile to such an extent that the opportunities for making serious money out of the game seemed limitless.

Not surprisingly, the players were soon negotiating with the RFU for a slice of the action. I don't think players have actually changed too much in some respects: like myself they enjoy playing the game and the massive kudos that goes with doing so at the highest level. So, you might ask, why didn't they simply settle for that? I have to say I could see the issue from a player's point of view. They saw the money that was being generated by the World Cup and made the point that they were expected to devote every free minute of their time to the cause while remaining amateurs. They had Brian Moore as their negotiator and wanted us to look at the question of setting up trusts, with payments set aside until they had finished their playing careers. The players would, I think, have welcomed such a system with open arms but subsequent events meant that this eminently sensible approach came to nothing.

The truth of the matter is that it could have been managed so much better. The International Rugby Board did introduce a 12-month moratorium with the aim of providing a cooling-off period, in the hope that we could proceed to a professional game in a structured way. But that wasn't to be. In England the senior clubs, an increasing number of which were suddenly owned by entrepreneurial businessmen, weren't prepared to wait, and once a few clubs started paying players the floodgates simply opened because nobody wanted to get left behind.

Although I firmly believe that professionalism has brought massive improvements to our game, there has also been a downside because we have ended up with a seamless game in which anybody can be paid to play. That may be all very

Clive Woodward celebrating another England victory, but the best was yet to come – winning the World Cup in Australia. I was one of those instrumental in bringing about Clive's appointment as England's coach. I never had any regrets and certainly don't now!

The moment when we knew it was finally all over. Jonny Wilkinson creating a major slice of rugby union history by dropping the winning goal in the dying seconds of extra time at the end of the 2003 World Cup Final in Sydney.

The unbridled joy of the England players, replacements, coaches and backroom staff moments after receiving their World Cup winning medals in Sydney. How we would all love to have experienced that magical moment as one of the participants.

Jason Leonard. The Harlequins and England prop-forward whose longevity and professional approach have always impressed me.

Jason Robinson (right) goes in support of England's powerful young wing Ben Cohen. With my knowledge of rugby league I never had any doubt that Robinson would make a successful switch of codes and force people to sit up and take notice.

With my rival *A Question of Sport* captain Ian Botham, flanking question master David Coleman – the man who truly 'was the show'.

Terry Wogan and I smiling for the birdie we wish we could have achieved when we faced each other in a pro-am tournament at Turnberry.

The appearance of The Princess Royal was a highlight of my years on *A Question of Sport*. The Royal contestant is seated with question master David Coleman with (behind and left to right) Scottish rugby international John Rutherford, team captain Emlyn Hughes, racing driver Nigel Mansell, myself and sprinter Linford Christie.

Twenty years after receiving my OBE, I was back at Buckingham Palace to watch my mother receive the MBE for her services to education. I am pictured, left to right, with my sister Alison, mother and brother Joe.

Posing with my parents and Hilary outside Buckingham Palace in 1982 before going inside to receive the OBE.

All in a good cause. I tried my hand at synchronised swimming as
my contribution to Red Nose Day.

Spot the celebrities. A highlight of the year on a number of occasions was former
World Racing Driver Jackie Stewart's annual shooting tournament when I was given
the chance to pit my aim against members of the Royal Family, leading sportsmen
and women and show-business personalities.

Here I am pictured among the academics at Manchester University after being awarded one of two honorary degrees, the other being presented by the University of Central Lancashire.

Former Prime Minister John Major and I share a passion for cricket and that dominates the conversation whenever we meet. Hilary, who thinks cricket is boring, puts on a brave face.

Chips off the old block. With my eldest sons Daniel and Sam when they were youngsters. They have both inherited my love of sport and, in particular, rugby and cricket.

Family life has always been very important for Hilary and myself and, now that Daniel is away at university, enjoy those times when we can all get together. Josh joins me on the settee with Hilary, Daniel (behind me) and Sam.

Cutting a dash through the waves. I have always been a keen water skier and even campaigned against the imposition of speed limits on Lake Windermere, where we have a holiday caravan.

Josh, the youngest member of the Beaumont family, gets into the spirit of the occasion during the 2001 British Lions tour to Australia.

The family head out to sea from our holiday home in Spain. I even took a navigation course to make sure we don't end up all at sea!

I felt greatly honoured to become only the second Englishman to be inducted into Sydney's Hall of Fame. The ceremony took place during the World Cup and the personalities inducted with me were, from left to right: Ian Kirkpatrick, Jo Maso, Syd Millar, myself, John Kirwan, Gavin Hastings and Michael Jones.

democratic but it has resulted in clubs wasting money they can ill afford on players of very indifferent quality, and in some cases I really do mean *very* indifferent. Clubs have frequently forked out large sums simply to avoid relegation because, especially in the case of the top clubs, the economic reality of taking the drop has been unthinkable.

I will discuss the issue or promotion and relegation later, when I look at how I think the game should be structured in the future, but suffice it to say at this stage that I was one of the few people on the RFU Council to vote against automatic relegation from the Zurich Premiership. Not that debate would be necessary if we had said at the outset that the game would only go professional down to a certain level – with the players funded by the Rugby Football Union rather than individual club owners. Below that level, the old amateur format would prevail. Too late for that now, of course, so money will do the talking.

That's how Sir John Hall secured success for Newcastle Falcons. They went from bottom to top of National One (which is effectively the game's second division) and took the Premiership title just 12 months later. He achieved that by buying experienced players like Rob Andrew, Gary Armstrong, Doddie Weir, Va'aiga Tuigamala, Steve Bates, Dean Ryan and Pat Lam, proving that in a new professional sport such as rugby union it has become possible to buy success pretty quickly. If someone gave me £100,000 to spend at Fylde it wouldn't take long to start climbing the table in whatever division the club happened to be playing in at the time. I would simply buy a big pack of forwards and a decent goal-kicker. But success in rugby shouldn't be determined by the size of your wallet. The Premiership now operates a wage cap so, in principle, those clubs within it should be operating on a reasonably level playing field, which is hardly what is happening lower down the scale.

Meanwhile, battle-lines were being drawn between the Premiership clubs and the RFU over a number of issues but with control of the game as the central theme. There were clashes within the RFU hierarchy over who was actually in charge and making the decisions, and there were further skirmishes between the RFU and the Celtic nations over television deals. No wonder Dudley Wood had questioned why I wanted to get involved with the game again! Everyone wanted to have control while, in reality, the whole thing was sliding out of control and the benefits to be derived from professionalism were being lost in a morass of bitterness. A frequent threat from the top clubs was that they would break away, sign their own television deal and keep the money themselves. I had heard it all before, however. Soon after I was forced to retire from playing there were similar rumblings of a breakaway by the top international players from nations around the world, with a view to staging their own competitions.

The character trying to broker the deal was an Australian called David Lord and he toured the world signing up players on provisional contracts. He had a meeting with the England team and a number of backroom boys at a hotel at Wilmslow, Cheshire, close to Manchester Airport, and arranged to see me at a hotel in Edinburgh. As I no longer played the game I can only assume he wanted me to lend my weight to the venture. If so, he went away empty-handed. He told me that a Kerry-Packer-style circus was being put together – a reference to a similar failed scheme involving cricketers – and that England would travel around the world playing other rugby nations. Home games would probably be staged at Wembley Stadium (which, of course, was still standing in those days). The players were to be paid handsomely and I know quite a few were very tempted at the thought of a few years travelling around the world doing nothing but play rugby while boosting their bank balances. When they delved more deeply into the hare-brained scheme however, I think they found there wasn't any money guaranteed and it all fell through. I remember ringing Andrew Slack, the former Aussie captain, and asking what he thought about it. 'I like the song', he said, 'but I don't like the singer!'

Quite apart from anything else, I didn't want to jeopardise the career I was carving out for myself with the BBC through becoming involved. Just to be on the safe side I mentioned the approach to my agents and they told me to give the venture a wide berth. I took their advice and, as I say, the thing never materialised anyway. The whole idea was based on what I consider the misconception that people would flock to watch international games that, in reality, were just part of a 'circus' staged purely to raise money for those involved. They might have taken in the first two or three games because they would have had some novelty value, but they wouldn't have been anything like the real thing. The public want to see top inter-national games but they must have a purpose; something that was brought home to me in what was, before the inclusion of Italy a few years ago, the Five Nations Championship. England played some pretty dreadful stuff when I first joined the team in the '70s but there was always a full house at Twickenham. The games might not have been as entertaining as a circus, but they had a real purpose. Indeed both then, and now in the Six Nations format, they comprise such a part of rugby's fabric that it is incredible to recall that, not too long ago, a number of people in the England camp thought we should pull out and concentrate instead on playing South Africa, Australia, New Zealand and France, to provide more meaningful competition. In recent seasons Ireland, Wales and Scotland have all demonstrated the idiocy of that thinking by halting our Grand Slam ambitions at the final hurdle and, while I don't think we are the arrogant bunch many nations claim we are, daft ideas like that only fuel the fire for those who think otherwise.

It would have been interesting to see if the top players, when push came to shove, would actually have broken away from the game had Mr Lord's scheme come to fruition. I personally doubt they would have done so. Despite more recent talk of the Premiership clubs breaking away, I don't think the modern professional player would want to do that. At the end of the day they want to test themselves against the best in the world and the only way to do that is on the international stage.

With all this going on, you can imagine what it was like for me back in September 1995 becoming a member of the RFU Council. It was like walking into a minefield, and the first meeting was spent debating how on earth we were going to manage professional rugby. A good many of the members said that they would have voted against the game going open had they been given an opportunity to do so, and it was clear that the four home countries would have favoured retaining the amateur ethos but felt swept along by the rest at the meeting in Paris and unable to stem the tide.

If they weren't ready for a sudden switch to professionalism, the RFU were equally unprepared for wealthy businessmen wanting to take over rugby clubs and involve themselves in the game. Nobody at HQ foresaw that happening. The thinking had been that the only money generated would be in international rugby, with clubs carrying on in the time-honoured fashion, run by their memberships. It came as something of a shock to be dealing with wealthy, successful and bright businessmen suddenly pumping vast amounts of new money into the game. They were at the sharp end of the commercial world and could see professional rugby almost rivalling soccer as a means of attracting spectators, a corporate hospitality market and television revenue.

As subsequent events have shown, their optimism has been somewhat misplaced because, while crowd figures have been on the increase in the Premiership, our game will always be secondary to soccer. As you drive around the country you only find occasional pockets where there are more than the occasional rugby posts on the playing fields and local recreation areas. Gloucester is an obvious area and so too are the Scottish borders, but soccer goalposts dominate elsewhere and it will be a long haul to achieve anything remotely like a soccer following in the Zurich Premiership.

So the new breed of rugby-club owners have had to dig deep into their own pockets to sustain top-class action, and I suspect that Leicester, Northampton and Gloucester are the only clubs generating sufficient cash through bums on seats. Basically, the game is very dependent on the money the national side generates and that's one of the major differences between rugby and soccer because more people will attend one Premiership soccer match than would attend the whole of rugby union's league programme on a particular Saturday. Top soccer sides like Manchester United, Liverpool, Newcastle and Arsenal are actually bigger than England, apart from when the national side is doing well in a World Cup or European Championship. Manchester United's following is incredible – the club so big that the release of players to a national squad can be an issue. In rugby, although I would never suggest it was perfect, we do have a better partnership between the top clubs and the national side when it comes down to player release. So far as the general public is concerned, rugby players are better known for playing for their country than for their club and the national side always gets phenomenal support, regardless of how well it is playing.

But, if running a top rugby union side is a more costly business than many had imagined, one has to admire those who have taken the plunge. Despite what some people in the game think about the 'money men', they have played their part in creating a strong England side and, even more importantly, a strong development structure that augurs well for the future of the game. I hold my hands up to people like Nigel Wray at Saracens, who had been a Saracen all his life and bought into the club because he wanted to see it succeed. On a number of occasions I have met Brian Kennedy, the Scot who owns Sale Sharks, and found him a very generous host. What he has done could be used as a blueprint for the game. Despite being a Scot, he has established quite a conveyor belt of homespun talent, working overtime, with England the beneficiary. I also found Tom Walkinshaw at Gloucester, with his vision of 15 Gloucester lads all playing for the side, a very challenging and interesting person to talk to. As an Englishman, that's just the kind of thing I want to see too. But, decent though these guys are, when you are dealing with 12 Premiership club owners you are also dealing with 12 egos. Each is used to fighting his own corner and they may have 12 different agendas, so maintaining a good dialogue with them is important even though they may be viewed with deep suspicion in some quarters. At the end of the day, the Zurich Premiership is a fantastic product and has given English rugby an advantage, so we must take our hats off to such people for their contribution.

Sadly, relationships with club owners have been fraught ever since the game went professional. They seem better at present, but I grew weary of attending meetings and thinking we had reached an accord on something . . . only to discover at the next meeting that everything had changed again. That is no way to run a business and, with the rank and file convinced that the game was being run for the benefit of a few rather than the game at large, we seemed to lurch from one crisis to the next. We were faced with a series of special meetings in Birmingham, called by disenchanted county representatives who believed that important decisions were being taken without the backing of the membership, and they found a champion in Cliff Brittle. A special meeting of the membership had been arranged in Birmingham for the purpose of changing the rules to allow the game to go professional. It was a formality that had to be undertaken even though, to all intent and purposes, clubs throughout the land had pre-empted a rule-change by hurling money at delighted players. The meeting however was largely hijacked by a power struggle caused by the death of RFU chairman Peter Bromage. The RFU committee nominee for the chairmanship was John Jeavons-Fellowes while Cliff Brittle was nominated by the membership. Cliff won the day so we were left with a situation akin to a leader in parliament who had been elected by the public but wasn't wanted by the MPs. This, not surprisingly, left him largely marginalised. It certainly didn't make for a united front at Twickenham at a time when unity was important in light of the unholy row that had erupted over the television deal England engineered with BskyB. Television coverage of the Five Nations Championship had always been negotiated as a joint deal by the four home unions, with France making their own arrangements.

I had only just become part of the RFU Committee, so knew little about the deal, but, as mentioned earlier, this resulted in the first occasion when the other home nations kicked us out of what was then the Five Nations Championship. I was an instigator in getting England back to the negotiating table, and an agreement was drawn up to pool resources. Unfortunately the whole thing erupted again back in 1999 and we were kicked out once more. On the first occasion the package on offer from BSkyB had amounted to £87.5 million, and the temptation felt by the England management to sign was understandable, if not exactly in the spirit of their relationship with Scotland, Wales and Ireland. Professional rugby had just started and the clubs, or more correctly their owners, wanted a bigger slice of the cake from headquarters to offset costs that were just as ridiculous as they were frightening. At the time, talk of a breakaway by the top clubs was occupying the sports pages although, despite their claim of the offer of lucrative deals to 'go it alone', I still couldn't see anyone putting substantial funds into something that precluded international rugby as we, and more importantly the general public, understood it.

So far as I was concerned it was absolutely imperative that all the English clubs, including those that had turned themselves into full-time professional organisations, remained beneath the umbrella of the RFU, but even that body had become divided, with factions pursuing different agendas. There were people who wanted to pull out of the Five Nations Championship anyway, arguing that a joint deal with the other three home countries didn't make any sense. Others felt that England were entitled to pull out of the traditional deal if they weren't allowed to have a much larger share of the financial cake. Then there were those like me, a newcomer to the political infighting, who couldn't understand why it wasn't possible for all sides to reach a mutually acceptable accord.

Just to make matters worse, the RFU and the clubs were involved in a tug-of-war over the players, which was to continue for many years. Had the RFU been on the ball then all the top players would have been contracted to the RFU when the game went professional, but instead they were technically the property of the top clubs and that gave these club owners a very strong bargaining tool. The main beneficiaries were the players, who had both England and their clubs throwing money at them, and a new breed of agents manipulating things in the middle. The result was that the wages being paid to players bore no relation to the money being obtained at the turnstiles, so unless club owners were happy to pump even more millions into the venture than they were doing already, they needed more money from HQ. The BSkyB deal was a means to that end.

Having just reinvented itself as a professional game, rugby union should have been enjoying a huge profile, but the profile we ended up with was not the one we wanted. On the field we were still failing to deliver the big prizes, at a time when success in a World Cup, given the failure of our footballers and cricketers on the world stage, might just have helped our game overcome some of the adverse publicity it was generating. Unquestionably, more than a few traditionalists, fed up with continual discord at a time when they were finding it difficult coming to terms with a rapidly changing rugby world, simply walked away from the game. To say that it was all very dispiriting would be a major understatement. Toss into that maelstrom international players threatening to go on strike and the other home countries pushing to get us kicked out of the Five Nations Championship and you have a recipe for complete disaster. It is a miracle that we have come through but all the nonsense has left its mark and I, for one, have felt the backlash of the undisguised distrust that our international rugby-playing neighbours have for us, the bad taste clearly still lingering so far as they are concerned.

It was bad enough that we seemed to be at war with our neighbours and our own top clubs, but that was nothing compared to the battle within the RFU caused by dislike of Cliff Brittle, even though he was something of a hero figure to the game's rank and file. Having seen off John Jeavons-Fellowes and, at the second special meeting in Birmingham, dealt in similar fashion with Bob Rogers for the position of chairman of a newly constructed management board, Cliff then found himself involved in another power struggle with Brian Baister, a former Chief Constable of Cheshire. From the outset I was a great Cliff supporter. I felt he had the game at heart and a lot of really good ideas but his style was such that he made too many enemies along the way. In the end I must admit I ran out of patience with him on one or two issues, feeling he could have tried to look more at the bigger picture. If you didn't agree with his views, he would get very annoyed; he saw issues as either right or wrong, with no middle ground.

To be fair to Cliff he did have a vision of the game, kept

his finger on the pulse and brought in checks and balances without which we could have ended up in serious difficulties. At least he prevented the game from moving out of the control of its elected representatives to just a few people running Premiership rugby. He devoted his life to the cause and was forever on the telephone discussing the many issues we were involved in. It reached the stage where, when the telephone rang at home, the kids would say, 'It's Cliff Brittle,' even before anyone had picked up the receiver. They were usually right!

It was an uphill struggle because, despite his support throughout the country and particularly from a hastily convened organisation called the Reform Group, of which Fran Cotton became president, he had difficulty carrying the game's managing body with him. I recall one vote that went against him by fifty votes to three, I being one of the three. I never had any involvement with the Reform Group, even though they were keen to get me on board; in fact, I even argued with Fran about it. I told him that while I had a lot of sympathy with the group's aims and objectives I felt the democratic way to fight for what they believed in was through the RFU Council.

Cliff was eventually replaced as chairman by Brian Baister, and it was a relief in many ways. Cliff hadn't read the tealeaves and believed he still carried much of the country with him. But he was not one to compromise and I think that people within the game had grown weary of the continual arguments and hoped for a period of stability under a new chairman. I had a major disagreement with his attitude when Peter Wheeler, who was a director of ERC (European Rugby Cup), was unable to attend a meeting in Dublin, and Graham Smith, who had been charged by the RFU to help find a solution to the difficulties between the RFU and the clubs – which led ultimately to the Mayfair Agreement – was asked to deputise. But initially Cliff wouldn't let him go into the meeting because he wasn't a director. Eventually however, he was admitted and allowed to address the meeting before being asked to leave. It was no fault of Brian's but there was more to come!

The other nations, as I say, had threatened to boot us out of the Five Nations Championship over the BSkyB deal and that concentrated the mind very quickly. England's bluff had been called but, with Cliff at the helm, we had finally reached a ten-year accord with the other countries and a tentative peace held things together for a time. But, almost on the eve of the start of the 1999 Five Nations Championship campaign we were not just threatened with removal from the cham-pionship, we were actually kicked out. Once more, money was at the heart of the matter, the other nations clearly having had enough of England disputing the amount of money they should be paid.

I outlined the events of the following days in the Prologue to this autobiography and see no purpose in going over old ground. Suffice it to say that the game against Scotland went ahead and, for all the bullish talk in some quarters at Twickenham about England's ability to pull out of the Five Nations Championship in order to pursue a competition ex-clusively with the southern hemisphere countries and France,

I believe there was general relief all round. It would be unthinkable for us not to be involved with our Celtic neighbours and I can perceive a pronounced change in England's attitude since that eleventh-hour reprieve. I was personally relieved because I have derived so much enjoyment from the Six Nations and there is no question that the general public takes great interest in the competition. The reasons for signing up with BskyB in the first place were purely financial and, while those involved in tying up that deal have come in for criticism, I believe they thought they were doing what was best for English rugby at the time. The longer-term implications hadn't been thought through, however, and it was clearly a mistake proceeding as they did without advising our Celtic partners.

Although the Premiership and European competitions have proved to be good products that have encouraged more people to turn out to watch rugby at top-club level, international rugby is the game's shop window and the BSkyB deal meant it was being watched by a smaller audience, although, as indicated earlier, I have to say that BSkyB are more professional, with excellent camera work. Viewing figures when the game is on terrestrial television are an indication of interest throughout the country. I know many people who don't otherwise involve themselves in our game but who like nothing better than settling down in front of the television on a cold, wet Saturday afternoon in February and watching England take on Wales, France and the rest of the countries in the Six Nations Championship. It is a marvellous competition; one that was so envied by the southern hemisphere countries that they modelled their own Tri-Nations tournament on it. Yet, for all the undoubted quality of rugby in New Zealand, Australia and South Africa, the Tri-Nations still lacks the drama of a competition that is so steeped in history that it is part of the very fabric of the game.

All this is not to say that England don't have a strong case for a greater share of the profits from any blanket television deal for coverage of the international game. Indeed, as a member of the Six Nations Committee, that is something I will always fight for. Naturally I don't want the other countries to be disadvantaged but England have to support financially far more players and clubs. If each nation received the same amount of money from the television pot then the smallest nations would benefit more than the larger nations, and if pay-per-view television was in operation then the television company would generate considerable more money from a country as heavily populated as England. Having been involved in this issue at the sharp end, and being left in no doubt about how our Celtic neighbours feel about it, I know how important it is that we operate within a genuine partnership. But it has to be a partnership that accurately reflects the roles of the different countries involved because, looking at it from a purely English perspective, we don't want to feel shafted because we aren't getting enough out of the deal. I want the Six Nations Championship to be the best competition in the world but, at the same time, I want England to be the best side in the world. Our domestic club system is now the envy of Europe and the other countries have some ground to make up.

Somehow, I didn't seem able to keep away from controversial issues, sampling more aggravation when I was appointed a director of the ERC, the organisation that runs the European cup competitions. I was there representing the RFU, with Peter Wheeler there to represent the interests of the English clubs. The first meeting I attended in 1997 was held at the East India Club in London, with Ireland's Tom Kiernan in the chair. That was a time when English clubs were debating whether or not they should be involved in the competition, which had started two years earlier without any of our clubs competing. There had been great interest in the concept of a European Cup as the rugby authorities witnessed the success of European competition in soccer. The game was still amateur when the competition was launched and the idea was that England would be represented by four teams. The RFU wanted to enter sides based on the country's four traditional regions – North, Midlands, South West and London and South East – with players drawn from leading clubs in those regions. Quite apart from anything else, it would have been a useful exercise in assessing players for international selection, as they would be seen playing outside the comfort zone of their clubs. The clubs, however, were opposed to the regional idea and wanted individual clubs, determined on merit, to take the four European places.

That caused yet another rift between club and country and, as the arguments raged, the inaugural tournament went ahead without English involvement. Both the RFU and the leading clubs soon realised that they were missing out on a competition that was to start slowly but, over the years, grow into a major competition, and common sense prevailed the following season when it was agreed that England would be represented by club sides after all. Four sides were involved – Bath, Harlequins, Leicester and Wasps – and Leicester reached the final, being beaten by Brive at Cardiff. A year on, Bath beat Brive 19–18 in an exciting final at Bordeaux in which Jon Callard, now a coach at Leeds Tykes, scored all his side's points. Unfortunately, Bath weren't able to defend their title the following season because the English clubs decided to pull out of the competition. As in the Six Nations, there was an element of distrust, with England perceived as wanting things their own way. For a start, England wanted more of their clubs involved, on the basis that there were far more top-class clubs in this country. As a result, the Shield competition was introduced to spread the net wider and ensure that all clubs playing in the English Premiership would be involved in one or other of the competitions. That got over the problem of eight English clubs being left with nothing to do on European Cup weekends but then there was further hassle because the dates weren't to everyone's liking for the following season. At the same time there were strenuous efforts by Cardiff and Swansea to join the English Premiership – a move that was firmly hit on the head by the Welsh RFU – but the English clubs withdrew from Europe and invited the two Welsh clubs to join them in a new, and unofficial, Anglo-Welsh competition. You don't have to be Einstein to work out how that went down with the rugby authorities, and by that stage I had had enough of such nonsense. I resigned as a director because I wasn't prepared to waste my time travelling to attend meetings in Dublin if no English clubs were involved.

The International Rugby Board fined England for not imposing enough sanctions on its clubs and the whole thing, like the television row, was a complete mess. Yet I could understand the desire of Cardiff and Swansea to get involved in the English league structure; if I were a businessman running a top Welsh club, I would want to play in the Premiership too. I am sure Llanelli, one of the great Welsh clubs, would also love to be involved because, historically, there have always been fixtures between the top clubs in England and Wales, and the Welsh clubs really look forward to hosting top sides from over the border. It is a tribal thing and I believe many regret not getting involved in an Anglo-Welsh league when the opportunity arose. The Celtic nations would love to get involved in the Premiership but that won't happen in the foreseeable future because it has become so very well established. That is not to say that one day we won't have a British League – an idea that was first mooted when professional rugby was in its infancy.

There is now great prestige attached to the European Cup and achieving a place in the starting line-up has become almost as big a target for clubs as winning domestic competitions.

CHAPTER TEN

A Question of Sport

If people recognise me when I am out and about, I am quite convinced that, apart from within rugby circles, they associate me more with the television quiz show *A Question of Sport* than with my spell as England captain. Without that show I wouldn't have the profile I enjoy today and would probably be little more than a statistic in the rugby record books as the captain of a Grand-Slam-winning England team. The series ensured that my face appeared regularly on the screen during a quite remarkable 13-year run as one of the team captains.

I was first invited on to the show as one of the panellists when I was England captain and I remember being very nervous about it. There was a feeling that I had 'arrived' because it was a programme that most sports people wanted to be invited on to, as it gave the opportunity to mix with some of sport's leading personalities. I was just an amateur rugby player and it gave me quite a buzz to know that I would be able to rub shoulders with professional soccer players, cricketers, boxers and athletes. The thing I was nervous about was sitting in a studio and being asked questions in front of an audience, knowing that the programme would be beamed into millions of homes. By that stage I had become accustomed to having a camera pushed in my face as I trudged off the field at the end of international matches but I wasn't accustomed to being in a studio. It was clearly going to be a very different proposition to standing in a stadium or training ground being interviewed by Nigel Starmer-Smith or Bill McLaren. I didn't want to make a complete fool of myself, and it was little consolation that, with the exception of horse racing, I had a fairly good knowledge of sport. When I played for Lancashire a group of us would spend many a coach journey pitting our wits against one another on sporting knowledge. Des Seabrook, the coach, was something of a sporting expert, and team secretary Eddie Deasey and Fran Cotton were no slouches either. Of course, my old pal Steve Smith liked to join in but he wasn't quite as knowledgeable as he thought he was!

My first appearance as a guest was in 1980, and both Hilary and I travelled to Manchester, where the show was being recorded. We joined my fellow panellists and the two captains, Emlyn Hughes and Gareth Edwards, in the hospitality suite, known as the Green Room, for a bite to eat and to get to know each other a little. They always recorded two separate shows at the one sitting, so to speak, and I was on Emlyn's team in the second show. It was quite amusing because, between shows, they used to move around the people sitting in the aisle seats so that, when the camera panned on to the audience, it would appear as though they were completely different sets of people. When I became a captain I had to remember to take two shirts or pullovers so that I could change my appearance. Eventually, demand for tickets became so great that they had to have a separate audience for each show.

I will always remember my first question on the picture board. I opted for number four, solely because that was the number I also wore on my shirt when I played rugby, and the picture that appeared was the Derby County footballer Colin Todd. It was rather an obscure shot and I managed to get it wrong, which was not an auspicious start. We did manage to win the match, however, and I recall that in the 60-second round, when you have to answer as many questions as possible in a minute, the rugby question asked which team played at St Helen's. The answer was Swansea and I had no problem getting that right because I had played there for the Barbarians.

In the end I felt I had acquitted myself quite well and was invited back the following year. The question-master was the incomparable David Coleman, and our paths crossed again shortly afterwards when I was invited to a Ford dealership in Coventry to be a guest on a quiz panel. David and Ian Robertson, who I knew quite well through rugby, ran a whole series of roadshows, and though I'm not sure if David actually had any involvement in it or not, soon afterwards I had a call from Hazel Louthwaite, the producer of *A Question of Sport*, asking if I would be interested in becoming a captain on the show.

I couldn't understand why they wanted a new captain

because I thought Emlyn and Gareth did the job so well but Hazel said they felt they needed a change of personalities. On that basis I said I would be interested but was concerned that the shows were recorded on a Sunday afternoon, which might cause difficulties for me in getting to the studio on time if England were playing in the Five Nations Championship the previous afternoon in a location like Paris or Dublin. My other concern was that, as an amateur, I wasn't allowed to receive any form of payment. The fee worked out at about £2100 for a 13-week series and, as indicated earlier, I had to arrange for the BBC to pay half to the RFU Charitable Trust and the balance to Fylde Rugby Club.

When I played in what became my final international against Scotland at Murrayfield I bumped into Gareth, who was part of the BBC commentary team with Bill McLaren. We chatted about *A Question of Sport* and I told him I was disappointed for him as I had taken over his role on the show, but he was fine and encouraged me to do it. There was no bad feeling, or anything like that, even though I am sure he was a bit fed up about losing his slot. Having agreed to take on the job I was anxious to discover who the opposing captain would be. It was Willie Carson, the jockey, and, as regular viewers of the show would testify, I knew absolutely nothing about horse-racing. Talk about the odd couple. There I was, six-feet-four inches tall and over 18 stones, and Willie was just five feet tall and barely seven stones wet through. I got on with him because I respected Willie as a sportsman and for what he had achieved, but although we would meet at the studio and have a bit of a chat I wouldn't say we were bosom pals or that he was the kind of bloke I would go off and have a drink with, unlike my two subsequent opposing captains, Emlyn Hughes and Ian Botham!

Programmes were recorded on a Sunday afternoon and there would always be a dress rehearsal in the morning, using a pub panel, one guy playing the role of Willie and another playing me. There was no audience at that stage and when the audience did take their seats a comedian called Tony Jo would take over to get them into the spirit of the occasion. Tony lives in Freckleton, which is close to where we live now and where Hilary lived before she got tangled up with me, and I got to know him well: a very funny man. Then David Coleman would come into the studio and the show would begin. I had been interviewed by him in the Grandstand studio at international games and had been greatly impressed by the guy. Quite apart from being a true professional, he had an aura about him and his knowledge of sport was second to none. Once I had finished playing and was part of the BBC team on matchdays I had the opportunity to see a master at work. His attention to detail was staggering and he would always be up to speed with what was going on in a variety of sports, even when he was busy covering a rugby international. David would be relaying soccer results to the watching public as they came in by teleprinter – very different from today's technology – and always knew the relevance of particular results. He stood for sport and professionalism. In those days, the BBC had all the real doyens of broadcasting. In golf they had Henry Longhurst and then Peter Alliss, in tennis Dan Maskell, in boxing Harry Carpenter, in rugby union Bill McLaren and in cricket people like John Arlott and Peter West. They were all professionals who really understood both the business and the sport they were commentating on. Sadly, I think the BBC has lost its way a bit in its sports coverage in that it has become too celebrity-orientated as opposed to using hard-nosed professionals. Having said that, the BBC has always been very good to me and if I have a choice of channels to watch a major sporting occasion on terrestrial television, or anything else for that matter, I will still always switch to the BBC channel.

Being so competitive, I could hardly believe it when Willie Carson won the first series. I was even more surprised when I heard that the Beeb thought Willie was better than I was at coming up with the right answers. There was one occasion when we were level in the series and they organised a decider at a hall somewhere in Cheshire. Ian Botham and Steve Davis were special guests and we could have our pick. I chose Steve, and 'Beefy' Botham ended up winning it for Willie. I think that was the occasion when one of the questions had something to do with the Queen's pigeons and Beefy quipped, 'Willie should know because he used to ride them!'

The one thing you never wanted to get wrong was the mystery guest if he came from your own particular sport, and I used regularly to quiz the rugby lads to see if any had been filmed recently by the BBC. I still failed to spot John Devereux, the former Welsh international who also played Rugby League, and England hooker Brian Moore. When he was a captain, Ian failed to pick up on Scottish rugby international John Jeffrey, even though he had had him on his panel the previous week. Willie failed to work out Lester Piggott, and Ian, a guest on that occasion, cheekily suggested that this was because he was only accustomed to seeing his back and not his face. My biggest problem was discerning the sex of the mystery guest, and Hilary would take the mickey out of me mercilessly. I confused Gillian Gilkes, the badminton player, with footballer Bryan Robson because he had permed hair at the time, and came up with Ann Hobbs the tennis player when it was, in fact, boxer Jim Watts.

Although the shows are pre-recorded and can be edited, it is still easy unwittingly to make a remark that causes offence. There was one occasion when the BBC received a lot of complaints following a totally innocent remark. Jonathan Davies, the former Welsh international fly-half, who now summarises for the BBC, was on the programme and they showed a film-clip of him dropping a high-ball. I made some remark about him not being too clever under the bomb and, because he was playing Rugby League for Warrington at the time, viewers thought I was making a comment about the dreadful IRA bombing in the town when children were killed. Nothing could have been farther from my mind; I was simply using a rugby term for what is also known as an up-and-under, when an opponent puts up a high kick in the hope that the catcher will either drop it or be put under pressure by an opponent. One upset family wrote to me personally about it. Naturally, I wrote back to offer my apologies and to explain the context in which it had been made, and thankfully everything was fine once they realised I had simply been using rugby parlance. As recompense, I invited them to the studios to watch a recording of the programme. If any of us in the studio had thought for one minute the comment could have been construed in the way that it clearly was, we would have had it edited out.

Most of the sporting personalities who came on the show were extremely nice people and it was a privilege to meet stars like Denis Law, Sir Bobby Charlton, Gary Lineker, Bryan Robson, Bernhard Langer, Nick Faldo, Frank Bruno and Steve Davies. Over the years I met people from a wide range of sports, and would do my homework by reading the sports pages of *The Daily Telegraph* from cover to cover every day. The newspaper covers just about every sport going so it is the ideal vehicle for keeping in touch with what is happening in the more fringe sports.

Very often we would arrive at the studios not knowing who the guest panellists were, but if possible I would ring the studio during the week in an effort to find out. Then I would know which sports were likely to feature more heavily than others and would do some hasty research. When Ian Botham was the rival captain we both called in assistance. Our children would sit in the front row of the audience and mouth the answers to us!

The most distinguished guest we had on the programme was Princess Anne, and everyone was on edge at the thought of being in the company of a member of the royal family in a quiz show. Cliff Morgan, who was a great chum of David

Coleman and one of the original *A Question of Sport* captains with Henry Cooper, was there that day to help entertain the royal visitor. As I said earlier, she is a super person who knows her sport, and I was also impressed by the way she turned up in the hospitality suite before the show, very much at ease with all of us. Whether or not *we* were at ease was another matter because we were very aware of trying not to say the wrong thing. I suspect one reason she felt so comfortable was that she was among sports people, everyone present respecting her for what she had achieved in the sporting arena. She was a member of Emlyn's team, and as patron of the Scottish Rugby Football Union it was perhaps fitting that she also had Scottish international John Rutherford on the same panel. I had sprint-king Linford Christie and racing-driver Nigel Mansell as my panellists, and – surprise, surprise – we got stuffed. I think the first six photographs on the picture board were of horses. I have never had any interest in horse racing whatsoever and said to the producer afterwards, 'You were determined that her team was going to win.'

As it was bit of an ordeal being a new panellist, I would always try to help them. It didn't matter if the captain came up with the wrong answers but guests could be quite self-conscious if they continually failed to get one right. Sitting in a studio with an audience and the cameras rolling can be overwhelming if you're not used to it, and the old mind can go blank at times, although David was always good at giving people time to think about their answers. Occasionally, I would give guests the answer, because it was more important that they shone than me. 'Trust me,' I would tell them, if they queried my suggestion, 'I know it's right.'

One of the more interesting characters we had on the show was snooker-player Alex Higgins. It was my very first recording as a team captain and I was petrified, wondering what he might do or say, because when he arrived he looked as though he had had a couple of good nights out. Alex was very different from the very laid-back Steve Davies, but we captains were fortunate in having David Coleman in charge. He *was* the show and, although it was one of the few programmes where the question-master was rarely on camera, he had a superb sense of timing, always ensuring that things ran smoothly. Unlike most other quiz shows, *A Question of Sport* was unscripted.

Willie and I each won a series and then he left to be replaced by Emlyn Hughes, having a second spell on the show. The only time we had met previously was when I was a guest on his team but we had some interests in common, his father having played rugby league for Barrow, and we had a lot of fun together. At the time he was playing for Wolverhampton Wanderers, having left Liverpool, but because of his family connections he knew rugby quite well and was always keen to get to internationals down in Cardiff.

After three years together we thought we were getting past our sell-by date and we clearly weren't on our own because the BBC's northern Head of Sport, Nick Hunter, called us in one day and said he would give us one more series and then that would probably be it so far as we were concerned. I loved doing the show but didn't have a problem with ending my involvement. However, we then discovered that Emlyn was leaving because he had had an offer to get involved in ITV's equivalent, a programme called *Sporting Triangles*. It wasn't the best career move Emlyn could have made, because things didn't really work out. *A Question of Sport* was a better show and has stood the test of time.

Emlyn's departure may have saved my bacon because the Beeb decided that rather than bring in two new captains they would hang on to me and bring in Ian Botham. That started a long and happy association with a fascinating guy who I had known for a number of years. I first got to know him when England won the Grand Slam in Edinburgh in 1980. Beefy had just returned from a cricketing tour and had travelled up to watch the game with his father-in-law, Gerry Waller. They were having a drink after the match and a few of us invited them into the reception. We had all had a few pints when a Scottish official went up to Ian and told him that he wasn't a guest and therefore had to leave. We told Beefy to carry on drinking with us but the official was insistent that he leave. As a form of protest we all left together and went for a drink elsewhere, unable to understand how they could have been so petty. We subsequently got into the habit of meeting up regularly at internationals, and I recall one occasion when, due to be summarising for the BBC in Paris, I flew in from Manchester while Ian arrived from Teesside. We retired straight to a bar and stayed there. We had lunch, drank some more, had dinner and drank some more, eventually collapsing into bed. The following morning I felt terrible but Ian looked even worse and we had to go in search of Terry Crystal, who was England's team doctor at the time, to get some pills to kill the headache. We retired with our tablets to a café for breakfast, during which Beefy commented, 'It's amazing but French bread tastes better in Paris than it does at home.' There were times when I really wondered about him!

Hilary and I enjoyed a great relationship with Ian, his wife Kath, and their children, and consider Ian a top bloke. I know he has his critics – who doesn't? – but I have never met anyone who has more self-confidence, a quality that has obviously served him well throughout his career. Quite apart from his great ability as a cricketer he also has a massive self-belief that he can achieve anything he wants. He proved that in 1981 when he went out to bat against the Aussies when the chips were really down and flayed them all over the park.

One year we left the children at home and the four of us – Ian, Kath, Hilary and myself – went skiing at Courcheval, and one thing I discovered there is that 'Beefy' does things in style. He made all the arrangements, and we ended up flying first class to Geneva and then the rest of the way in a private plane. It was a first time for all of us, and we spent most of it on the nursery slopes, but just a couple of days into the holiday Ian and I took to retiring to the bar for a little après ski, during which we would talk glowingly about our skiing feats, even though these probably amounted to no more than 50 metres between the pair of us!

Of my three rival captains on the show I had far more in common with Ian than with either Willie or Emlyn. Rugby and cricket are very similar games in that you spend a lot of time with team-mates who come from all walks of life, and that leads to a very particular brand of dressing-room humour. Ian and I hit it off from the first, yet we were both very competitive and wanted to win. I was delighted that he was hopeless at the cricketing questions, and loved to rub it in by coming up with the answer, but he knew his sport, was better at horse racing questions than I was, and was generally on the ball with rugby because he loves the game. I happen to think he would have made a good rugby player, probably as a flanker or in the centre, and would have done better in our game than he did at soccer, where he played for Scunthorpe United for a time.

We were so keen to win that on one occasion we both tried to cheat. We had reached the numbers game, where you pick a number between one and 12 and then try to identify the personality whose picture is on the other side of the board, when there was an unexpected fire drill, at which point we were neck-and-neck. We were all evacuated, but both of us had a quick peek at the pictures on the way out. The only problem was that the pictures had been changed when we got back into the studio!

One of the funniest interludes was when Paul Gascoigne, a guest on the show, arrived for lunch. Gazza was playing for Tottenham at the time, and his manager, Terry Venables, had warned him not to drink, but Beefy loves a challenge and finally convinced the footballer that Advocaat was non-alcoholic. He soon discovered otherwise and, for the first time, we had to rerecord something. During the numbers game he couldn't say 'Four' to save his life and, with Ian winding him up, it took about five minutes to get it right.

It was our habit to go for a meal in Manchester's Chinatown after recordings, and we had some good sessions. The only problem was that *I* had to work the following day, whereas Beefy was more a man of leisure, except, that is when he was walking the length of the country to raise money for charity. I admire him hugely for that. I walked with him once on a leg into Manchester, and that small distance left me even more impressed with his achievement.

We took *A Question of Sport* on the road to raise money for Arnold School, where my boys were studying, and staged it at Blackpool's Opera House. The guests included Wade Dooley (the alternative Blackpool Tower), former England and Lancashire cricket captain Mike Atherton and footballer Steve McMahon, who now manages Blackpool FC. On another occasion we went to Harrogate to raise money for a prep school Liam Botham attended, and I arrived late to find that we had a major problem on our hands. David Coleman had been taken ill in his dressing room and was wrapped in a blanket on the floor. I took over as question-master and did the job a couple of times until David Vine, who had done the job originally, was drafted in.

Eventually they started recording *A Question of Sport* in London, and that was more difficult for me because I was also trying to run a business. They also switched filming to a Monday evening, which made it still harder, and after 13 years

I couldn't complain when the BBC decided to ring the changes again. I had enjoyed a great time, and if I had decided to go more seriously into television I would love to have had a spell as question-master. Then again, I would never pretend that I could match the master of them all.

CHAPTER ELEVEN

The World Cup

Apart from not having won a British Lions series, my regret from a playing perspective was that I never appeared in a World Cup. During my career the highlights were to play and win something for your country and, if you were both good and lucky enough, to be selected for a British Lions tour, because that set you apart from the majority of players who attain international status. It was the ultimate, and in a sense still is when you consider that to be chosen you have to be regarded as not just the best in your own country but in the whole of Britain and Ireland.

The World Cup, however, has added a new dimension to the game and had a massive impact on the global profile of rugby union. It must be a marvellous competition to play in, although I am not too sure England would have done terribly well in the years when I was playing. Quite apart from the competition from the big-three southern hemisphere countries and the Celtic nations, it has to be remembered that, in those days, Rhodesia, as it then was, played in South Africa's Currie Cup competition, along with Namibia, and were no push-over. Japan, on their own patch, were difficult opponents and we certainly wouldn't have beaten Romania by more than 100 points as we did a couple of years ago.

I suspect that, in some ways, a World Cup in the '70s and early '80s would have been a more open competition than it is now. There would have been far more chance of a fairytale-style upset, whereas today you can't honestly see any of the smaller nations turning over one of the major contenders. In that respect, professionalism has opened a gap that the purely amateur nations will find almost impossible to bridge.

There was occasional talk about the concept of a World Cup when I was playing but one of the arguments put up against such a competition was the physical nature of the game. It was felt that it would be impossible to play back-to-back inter-national matches due to the number of bumps and bangs one tends to suffer in such games, quite apart from the fact that these drained you both physically and mentally. But rugby was a different world altogether in those days because players had jobs to go to less than 48 hours after a match and there was none of the excellent medical back-up that is available today. Even so it was still an amateur game when the first World Cup was held in New Zealand and Australia in 1987, though there is no doubt that this provided the catalyst for the sport to go professional. It was one thing to play for your country in the old Five Nations Championship and in occasional games against the southern hemisphere countries, but the potential of the World Cup to generate millions of pounds placed a very different light on the question of financial reward for the players.

The World Cup has become a very different animal from the one that sprang into life in 1987. As the game was amateur then it didn't matter all that much when the tournament took place but it matters now because of the domestic competitions, which, in a professional world, provide the bread and butter. It is a fine juggling act these days and individual nations are forced to make provision to limit disruption. The competition takes players away from their clubs for several weeks and, with a league structure in place – complete with that thorny issue of promotion and relegation – it is important to ensure that clubs providing a lot of players to an international squad aren't too disadvantaged. In England we tried scrapping relegation from the Premiership in a World Cup year, and for the 1999 event produced a different points system in an effort to produce something resembling a level playing field. Those players chosen in 2003 to represent their country in Australia weren't available until the event finished in November, which meant they effectively missed almost half the season.

Although we showed interest in the event when it was first mooted, we were pretty laid back about it in the early days, and the tournament certainly didn't generate the excitement it does today. Nor were we the ones driving it during the 1980s; it was left to the Australians and New Zealanders to do the 'big sell'. They wanted it and that's where the pressure came from. They believed themselves to be the leading sides in the world and, as much as anything else, wanted the competition to prove it. South Africa weren't involved because of the apartheid issue, but New Zealand was perceived by most as the greatest rugby nation in the world, while Australia had also suddenly come to the fore.

Rugby union was hardly a major sport in Australia, where it played second fiddle to rugby league and Australian Rules football. It still does, despite the Wallabies having won two World Cups, but the Aussies love a winner, especially someone wearing green and gold, and the game's profile has increased dramatically Down Under. The pressure for a global competition came shortly after Andrew Slack had led Australia on a Grand Slam tour of Britain and Ireland and won the Bledisloe Cup – presented by the Governor-General of New Zealand, Lord Bledisloe, in 1931 for competition between the two southern hemisphere countries. It had been abandoned because the All Blacks always won it but that has hardly been the case since its return to the rugby calendar.

The job of hosting the inaugural World Cup was split between Australia and New Zealand. Rugby union is a religion in New Zealand so interest was always going to be huge and the country was well served by stadia dedicated to the game. The situation was somewhat different in Australia; games in Sydney weren't even played in the major sporting venues. Having said that, rugby union is only really played on the east coast, with New South Wales and Queensland as the heartland of the game, and, even today, if you were to ask a man in the street about rugby he would invariably assume you were talking about the other code.

What the Aussies have achieved in winning two World Cups is quite remarkable because they have far fewer players at their disposal than we do, but the rugby union side is simply part of Australia's enduring story of sporting success. Whether it is cricket, swimming, athletics or any one of a number of other sports, you can guarantee the Australians will be up there with the best. How I envy them their training facilities. Everything is geared towards sporting excellence and they have the added benefits of a good climate and lots of space. The commitment to the cause is total and, as a nation, they spend something like £6 a head on sport. We don't even spend £1 and then we wonder why we underachieve in the sporting arena.

England head coach Clive Woodward had a spell playing first-grade rugby in Australia and would tell you what a difference a little warm sunshine makes when you have to go out training. In England our heroes go training in a pair of pumps in the pouring rain.

It took almost three years to get the inaugural World Cup off the ground and it was by invitation only. There was no qualifying competition, as there is now; the 16 countries invited to take part were Australia, New Zealand, USA, England, Japan, Canada, Wales, Ireland, Tonga, Fiji, Argentina, Italy, Romania, Scotland, France and Zimbabwe. The event was dominated by New Zealand and, considering the country's history, it was no surprise when they ended up winning. What is interesting is the fact that they haven't won it since, and have had to endure watching their old rivals and close neighbours Australia carry off the William Webb Ellis trophy on a couple of occasions.

England had the distinction of playing in the opening match of that first ever World Cup against host nation Australia in Sydney. The Aussies won 19–6 following a hotly disputed David Campese try, but England qualified for the finals after finishing second in their pool ahead of Japan and the USA. That brought them up against Wales in Brisbane and I arrived in Australia just in time for the game, having persuaded my uncle and father that I had some urgent business to attend to. I was always conscious of the time I took away from the family concern but we did have legitimate business interests in that part of the world in those days.

I had flown out with my old England team-mate Mickey Burton as part of the Gullivers Travel party, and we were no strangers to that part of the globe, having both been victims of one of the most violent Test matches I ever had the misfortune to play in. I had ended up in the dressing room needing stitches within minutes of the game starting and Mickey's game finished with an early bath, after he'd taken exception to what was being dished out to us in the name of sport. But, while I had travelled extensively as a player and understood that culture, I was a stranger to touring as a fan and found it a new experience. We flew from Heathrow, with a brief stop in India, and arrived in Sydney in the evening. Being a clean-living lad I had a bite to eat and went straight to bed. When I got up at 8 a.m. the following day I glanced into the bar to find it still packed from the previous evening. My travelling companions had not only succeeded in drinking their way to Sydney, courtesy of the airline, but had also spent the night demolishing every drink the hotel bar had on offer!

I had a ticket for the England versus Wales quarter-final and bumped into BBC producer Huw Jones at the ground in Brisbane. He said that as I was there they might as well use me so I ended up in the commentary box, trying hard not to sound too despondent as Wales deservedly beat us 16–3. Wales had been forced to bring in a young prop called David Young, who performed superbly in an area England had expected to dominate. The best-laid plans of mice and men.

When I turned up at the semi-final between France and Australia I bumped into Bill McLaren. You can guess the rest. As I was there, he said, they might as well use me so, once more, I was off to the commentary box. And what a great game of rugby it turned out to be, with France coming through to win 30–24. I don't know what it is about the French but, whenever they reach a World Cup semi-final, make sure you get a ticket because they really do turn on the style. Australia had been banking on a final against New Zealand but the French played party-poopers and Australia demonstrated how they felt about it all by losing to Wales in the play-off for third place.

The plan had been to travel to New Zealand for the final but things had got busy back in Chorley and I finished up watching the game on television before dashing off to the studios because the BBC wanted me to analyse it for the viewers. New Zealand won 29–9 but I thought the French had been rather unlucky. They were in the ascendancy up front but the All Blacks were playing in front of a passionate home crowd at Eden Park in Auckland. I suppose it was fitting though, considering the standards New Zealand had set for so many years, that they should take the prize at the first time of asking.

The World Cup wasn't quite the competition it is now, but it had been sufficiently successful for those involved to start planning the next event and it is now firmly on the calendar. The 1991 event was held in the northern hemisphere, with Twickenham as the main venue but with games also played in Scotland, Ireland, Wales and France. This was the World Cup that England should have won, because everything seemed to be in our favour, and I still find it hard to believe that we were 'conned' out of it by the Aussies.

It is necessary to set the scene. After a number of indifferent seasons Geoff Cooke had taken over as England manager following our exit from the inaugural World Cup and he laid the foundations for our successes in the future. A Cumbrian, who had settled in Yorkshire and successfully coached both the white rose county and the North, he proved a good administrator and set a target of achieving England's first Grand Slam since it had been achieved by the side I led in 1980. He brought a discipline to the squad and played to our strengths to achieve his objective. It may have taken him four years to net the elusive Grand Slam but there was hardly a better time to do so than in a year when the World Cup was being staged here.

At the time we had a big, powerful set of forwards and, with

Roger Uttley drafted in as coach, Geoff created a style of play that proved a winner, even though it was very simple. England would win the ball, it would be worked by the pack to Rob Andrew at fly-half and he would play the touchlines to put the side into a position from which it could regain possession and start the whole process again. England had a solid front row of Jeff Probyn, Brian Moore and Jason Leonard, while players of the calibre of Dean Richards, Peter Winterbottom, Mike Teague, Mickey Skinner, Gary Rees and Andy Robinson were available in the back row. Wade Dooley, had a mighty presence in the second row but, for my money, his partner Paul Ackford was the key player. Not just because of his agility at the line-out but for his ball playing skills.

The main difference between the Grand Slam sides of 1980 and 1991 was that our inherent ball skills were a lot better. In the front row we had Fran Cotton and Peter Wheeler, who were great ball-handlers and would have been outstanding as full-time professionals. All the back row trio of Roger Uttley, John Scott and Tony Neary were very strong in that department too. The exceptions were my second row partner Maurice Colclough, who wasn't quite up to the standard of the rest but a tremendous player in all other respects, and prop Phil Blakeway, who was marvellous at what he did in terms of front row craft, although we used to tell him not to touch the ball!

Had the 1991 pack had the same handling skills then it would have been outstanding. I'm not suggesting there is no place for players who aren't particularly skilled in that department. Wade Dooley was a case in point because he gave England a real physical presence. He wasn't one of the great line-out jumpers and he couldn't dummy his way downfield but opponents would think twice about trying anything on with him around, his role in the team being almost that of a minder.

England had prepared meticulously for the 1991 World Cup, and performing a Grand Slam did wonders for morale. Unfortunately, there was a danger of that dissipating when they undertook a tour to Australia and Fiji as preparation for the event. They lost the opening game against New South Wales 21–19, were beaten 20–14 by Queensland and, most worrying of all, 27–13 by Fiji B. They redeemed themselves slightly by beating the full Fiji side 28–12 but then tumbled to what, at that time, was a record 40–15 defeat by Australia. If England needed a wake-up call then that was it.

As hosts, England staged the opening game of that World Cup against the reigning holders, New Zealand at Twickenham and I had the honour of being asked to carry the English flag at the opening ceremony – not bad considering that I was still classed as a professional! There was a lot of pressure on the boys to win in order to avoid the near certainty of having to travel to Paris to play France in the quarter-finals. On the day, however, England didn't play particularly well and lost 18–12 – a result that created a doom and gloom scenario – to an All Blacks side that showed a great deal of control.

For some reason, the All Blacks seem to pose English sides more problems than the rest. There is an aura about them.

Some suggest the black playing kit makes them look much bigger than they really are; a theory reinforced by Brian Moore in his autobiography where he comments how much it helped to see them playing in the Super 12s minus their black jersey. Whatever the cause, they seemed to have a hold over us – even before the arrival on the scene of Jonah Lomu.

As expected, England beat Italy and the USA without too much difficulty and then set off for Paris, making the unusual move of leaving out Dean Richards. He had been such an immovable object in the England pack that many wondered if Geoff Cooke had lost his marbles. Geoff switched Mike Teague to number eight and brought in the abrasive Mickey Skinner at blind-side and the outcome fully justified his selection, unpopular though it had been in some quarters.

There was all the usual Gallic fervour and, not for the first time in Paris, it was no place for the faint-hearted. Nigel Heslop, the Lancashire wing, had been recalled to the side and the French players took exception to one of his early tackles on Serge Blanco, the French full-back who was bowing out after the tournament finished. We then had a demonstration of ill-discipline by the home side that helped England into a 10–6 lead by the interval, Jon Webb having kicked a couple of penalties and Rory Underwood running in a try engineered by Jerry Guscott. England were put under pressure in the second half but one massive hit by Mickey Skinner on a French forward set the tone for a side that wasn't going to take a backward step.

France did draw level but indiscipline cost them dearly, as

it did in encounters for quite a few years after that, and Webb kicked England through aided by a try from skipper Will Carling. The following day the newspapers were filled with stories claiming that French coach Daniel Dubroca had given New Zealand referee David Bishop a dose of the verbals in the corridor leading to the dressing room. I have great admiration for the way the French play their rugby, but on occasion they've let themselves down by flying off the handle or taking the law into their own hands on the field. No matter how good you are, you need to show discipline when things get a bit warm out on the park and France, under new coach Bernard Laporte, are much better in that department. Similarly, we showed great discipline when we beat Wales at Twickenham *en route* to our Grand Slam success in 1980 and Martin Johnson's side did the same when the South Africans lost their heads, along with the match, when they played England at Twickenham last year.

That victory in Paris lined up a semi-final against Scotland at Murrayfield, the Scots having won their pool and comfortably defeated Western Samoa in the quarter-finals. It was clearly going to be an interesting game because it was in Edinburgh that England had blown a glorious Grand Slam opportunity in 1990, handing that honour to the Scots. That setback was all part of a learning curve for Geoff Cooke's side and was down to a lack of discipline on our part. The media had been banging on about just how good England was and one wondered if the players had started to believe their own publicity. Everybody seemed to conveniently forget that the

Scots were on course for the Slam and also had home advantage. With respect to Will Carling I'm afraid he didn't captain the side as he should have done that afternoon and let hooker and pack leader Brian Moore take over much of the decision-making, although I don't think the old 'Pit Bull', as Brian was affectionately known, would necessarily agree with my assessment. Whoever was at fault, although we may have been the better side we didn't deserve to win, even though Jerry Guscott had set England on the right track with a typically classy try. We simply played it all wrong and ran penalties that should have been left to Simon Hodgkinson to drill over, because you take any points that are on offer in a full-blown international. Add to that the fact that New Zealand referee David Bishop didn't really referee the scrums, which worked against England, and that the Scots could not have played any better. I felt the defining moment came when Guscott almost got away again but was just halted by Scott Hastings. Had he scored then the game might have had a different outcome but, instead, we helped the Scots into the driving seat. At a scrum on half-way England tried a back row move instead of simply getting the ball back to Andrew so that he could ping the thing downfield. Someone knocked on in the move and, from the resulting scrum, Gavin Hastings kicked ahead and Tony Stanger won the race to the touchdown as the ball went over the England line.

On the day we had been outwitted by David Sole and Jim Telfer, the coach. We didn't play well, lacked leadership and, as a result, there was friction between forwards and backs that could be detected from the stands. We paid a heavy penalty, but I think Will Carling learned a valuable lesson from the experience, and he went on to lead England to three Grand Slams. He had a massive profile, one of the highest in sport at the time, yet it was a popular pastime to find fault with him – especially when he had well-publicised run-ins with the authorities. Many considered him too big for his boots and I remember one occasion when I thought my pal Fran was going to pin him against the wall during a confrontation in Cardiff. Not everyone got on with Will, that's for sure, but I never had a problem with the guy. I always found him a decent sort of bloke, and can only speak as I find. He was probably bigger than the England team at one stage and that didn't always rest comfortably with everyone at Twickenham. In any case, it's the English mentality that if someone is up there at the top then he is there to be knocked down. I don't think Aussies would see it that way and I couldn't for the life of me understand the attitude of some people on the day that Will broke my record of leading England to more victories than anyone else. They actually thought I would want to see England lose so that I could retain the record. They couldn't understand that records are only there to be broken and that I want England to win every game regardless of anything else.

The atmosphere was electric at Murrayfield for the World Cup semi-final and it proved a very tense, close contest in what was to be a low-scoring game. With the sides level at 6–6 Gavin Hastings inexplicably missed a simple penalty from almost in front of the posts; a huge psychological moment. Had the kick gone over then the pressure would really have been on England and memories would have gone flooding back to what had happened on the previous trek north of the border. In the end Rob Andrew dropped a goal and England won 9–6. I was sitting in the stand with Hilary and was given plenty of stick from the Scottish fans, but I just sat there with a quiet smile on my face.

One advantage of having a reasonably well-known face is that I had managed to 'blag' my way into the car park at Murrayfield before the game. Afterwards we were told that nobody would be allowed to leave until the Princess Royal had departed, so I just leaned against our car, and I recall thinking, as I watched all those Scots trudging out of the ground looking very downcast, that it wasn't such a bad place to be!

What brassed me off, however, was the way so many Scots used their ticket allocation for the final to attend the game decked out in Aussie colours. I found that very hard to take when we should all have been rooting for a northern hemisphere victory, and I would like to think that, had roles been reversed, I would have been shouting my head off for Scotland. There is far more nationalism around these days and I can't say that I enjoy that aspect of international rugby. Fans even boo our national anthem. I don't know just what our forebears did that was so reprehensible but everybody wants to beat us. For some teams it is a decent season if they beat England, regardless of how their other results go. I sense that the anti-English feeling is stronger in Scotland than anywhere else at present and I'm not sure that this is just because we have been successful. Everyone wanted to beat the Welsh during the '60s and '70s when *they* had the strongest side, but that is only natural. It just doesn't have to be as bitter as it has been, and I find it particularly sad because I have a great love of Scotland. Some of my best friends are Scottish, such as Andy Irvine, Jim Renwick and the late, and great, Gordon Brown. I admire their coaching set-up and have great admiration for Jim Telfer. They do remarkably well considering their resources, which are miniscule compared to those in England, and their forwards are always well organised. What they lack at present is a Renwick or an Irvine, someone among the backs with pace and vision.

The one place England can always be sure of the warmest of welcomes is Dublin. The Irish are naturally easy-going and friendly, but there is I think a special closeness going back to the days in the 1970s when both Wales and Scotland pulled out of scheduled Five Nations games there because of threats of violence to the players. England, despite threats, made the trip when they were due to play there and the team was hit by a wave of noise as they took the field at Lansdowne Road, with the standing ovation lasting five minutes. They even had to hold back the Irish team from taking the field until the noise had subsided. That was the occasion when England skipper John Pullin made his immortal statement at the post-match dinner after Ireland had won 18–9. He told his audience, 'We may not be very good but at least we turn up.' England have been well received ever since. Incidentally, Dublin is the city in which I made my international debut, and I consider it the best venue for a game away from home. There is always a hugely passionate rugby crowd who appreciate the game, and they are always too busy entertaining you to find time to rub salt in your wounds when you have lost. The Irish are generous, warm people and I can't imagine a British Lions tour without a few Irishmen on board to stop things getting too serious.

Although England had lost heavily in Australia during the build-up to the World Cup, there was a feeling that the side was on a roll and that, in front of a home crowd at Twickenham, we were capable of winning the William Webb Ellis Cup. And so we should have done. In fact we should have walked it because we had a better pack of forwards, and that's where games are won and lost if you do everything else right.

Maybe the Aussies sensed that the odds were stacking against them because the newspapers were suddenly filled with stories about how boring England were and how they couldn't play with pace and flair to save their lives. Heading the sledgers was, of course, David Campese, whose tongue was almost through his cheek, let alone in it, as he told anyone who would listen that we were no good and simply couldn't play rugby. I knew it was a wind-up and couldn't believe it when we changed our tactics on the day. It was an error that cost us the trophy.

To be fair to Geoff Cooke he had done a good job in turning England into a side capable of challenging for the game's highest honour. We had dominated the Five Nations Championship because our forwards were bigger and stronger than the opposition, and under the laws at that time it was easy to keep the ball once you had it. The usual tactic had been to win the ball, stick it up Dean Richards's shirt and drive upfield, rewinning the ball at the inevitable scrum when the move was halted. England could play the percentages because when the ball reached Rob Andrew he would kick it. It was only when there were 20 points on the board that we would start flinging the ball around.

Although I enjoy what is often called total rugby I have no criticism of the way England played. You play to your strengths and doing that had got us to a World Cup Final. Had we played in the same vein we would have won but we paid a heavy price for our ambition because running rugby was alien to that side. A 3–0 victory with the ball never going beyond Rob would have been acceptable, leaving entertainment for another day. I don't think those watching, either in the ground or in front of their television sets, would have given a stuff how we achieved it just so long as we ended up as champions.

It was a real anticlimax and the players were gutted. Brian Moore was one who knew the tactics had been wrong but many tried to defend the decision to attempt a wider game. I take the point that England had played expansive stuff in the Five Nations but, as I explained earlier, that was invariably after laying strong foundations. Nor did it take a genius to work out that the Aussie defence was up to the task and wasn't going to leave gates wide open for the English backs to run through. Defensively, they weren't quite so hot under the high-ball but that was again an underused tactic, and once the Aussies had taken a 9–0 lead – Tony Daly getting over from a line-out for Australia and Michael Lynagh kicking two goals – it was always going to be difficult hauling it back. Jon Webb kicked a penalty for England and Jon Webb dropped a goal, but not once was the Aussie defence pierced, and we ended up losing 12–6. The only time that looked likely was a controversial moment in the game, which, inevitably, involved Campese. Peter Winterbottom tried to put Rory Underwood away but Campo got between them and knocked the ball on. That gave England a penalty but some felt it should have been a penalty try. Whether it should have been isn't for me to say, but in any case we didn't deserve to win that day. Just as with the game at Murrayfield in 1990, it was another lesson that I hoped we would learn from.

The next World Cup was a momentous occasion. It was the first time that South Africa had been allowed to take part, having ridden itself of apartheid and become the Rainbow Nation after the first free elections saw Nelson Mandela installed as President. At that time there was a new spirit in the country, though today the country is unfortunately beset by problems such as high levels of unemployment and an alarmingly high crime rate. For a short period in its turbulent history, however, South Africa was a united nation and, from a rugby point of view, it gave us as a dramatic a World Cup as anyone could have wished for.

Jack Rowell had taken over as England coach and, once again, England went into the competition on the back of a Grand Slam. Two questions had to be answered: whether we had peaked too early, and whether we were capable of winning the event on foreign soil. In our favour we had a nucleus of players who had played in the previous event; the higher you go in any game, the more important experience becomes. A major problem, however, was that England very nearly ended up going without a captain, when Will Carling was sacked a few days before the squad was due to fly out from the UK. During a television documentary Carling was heard responding to a question about the possibility of the game going professional – which it did three months later – by wondering if it would still need to be run by 57 'old farts'. I was quite relieved that, at that stage, I wasn't one of them, but the media picked up on the comment and even though Will made a bit of a joke out of it the game's management went into a state of apoplexy. He was hastily summoned to a meeting and told his services as captain were no longer required – the news of his dismissal being announced on the morning of the Pilkington Cup Final featuring Bath and Wasps. The players united behind their skipper and Jack, as coach, found himself in an invidious position. He had been carefully plotting his campaign to reach the World Cup with a squad that was relaxed and very much together. Now he had to find a new captain, with no knowing what the knock-on effect of the whole sorry business might be. Within hours Rob Andrew and Dean Richards, both likely candidates for the captaincy, had let it be known to an eager media that they would refuse to take on the role not because they wouldn't feel honoured to do so but as a demonstration of their solidarity with Carling.

Being now an 'old fart' myself, I will defend the RFU position because there are a lot of guys who put a tremendous amount of unpaid effort into the game. They don't just turn up to collect their free ticket to the games and sip free gin and tonics, as some players like to believe. It is probably easier for players to accept administrators such as Fran Cotton, Jeff Probyn and I because they know we have been there as players and achieved a great deal, but they shouldn't look down on those who haven't played at the highest level, since many of those guys may have been referees or spent countless years as administrators. True, some may have only played at a fairly junior level but they probably also marked out pitches, run baths, organised club functions and sat on committees at club and county level before being elected on to the RFU. Their knowledge of the game at grassroots level is just as important to the game as a whole as the knowledge gained touring the world as an international player.

Carling was out of order in saying what he did, though I suspect he said it partly tongue in cheek; I'm glad the matter was resolved quickly anyway. At the end of the day it was a lot of fuss about very little.

Public opinion came into play in the issue, because Carling was a major sporting personality at the time, and Dennis Easby, the RFU President whose task it had been to tell Carling that he was sacked, was persuaded to meet the player and, with concessions all round, the player was eventually reinstated.

All that leads me on to a new phenomenon we have seen in rugby union in recent years: player power. There was the ridiculous situation at Cardiff a few years ago when the England players refused to talk to the BBC after they had beaten Wales. The spat was all to do with getting less money than they believed they were worth from the BBC for making themselves available for interview. The thing escalated to such a degree that on the day in question they even refused interviews to newspaper journalists. That was a pathetic and childish action on their part, because they had a responsibility to the game, to themselves and to the jersey they represented.

It was even worse when they went on strike in the build-up to an international game against Argentina, and whoever was advising them didn't do them any favours. I have seen the game from both a professional and amateur point of view and, even when I was banned, I still tried to represent the game in the best possible light. I remember having a conversation with Matt Dawson soon after the strike-threat fiasco and I told him how much I disagreed with what they had done. 'At the end of the day, Matt', I said, 'you can put 15 dustbins on the pitch, put them in a white jersey and people will turn up to watch. They don't turn up to watch you but to support England. At times when I played for England we were crap but the crowds still turned up. Although people had a difficult task just getting hold of a ticket, we always played in front of a full house. At present you are the recipient of the jersey but, ten years on someone else will be wearing it and there will still be a full house at Twickenham. I'm disappointed in the players because in my day I would have hitched a lift in order to get to London to play for England, regardless of whether or not I was getting paid. You should want to play for your country.'

I wasn't getting at Matt individually, just making a point, and I was delighted for him when he won a Grand Slam and a fiftieth cap in Dublin this year. In fact I've always respected the player because I remember how he led England on a tour to the southern hemisphere a few years ago when most of the senior players didn't travel and we suffered some heavy defeats. Matt played very well and showed a lot of character and leadership qualities. He has also played well for the Lions, but I wasn't happy when he and Austin Healey talked out of turn during the 2001 Lions tour to Australia. Matt criticised the management in a newspaper article, and in another newspaper column, Austin called one of the Australian players a plank. You have a responsibility to your team-mates and management so you don't attempt to rubbish them in public. Nor do you provide the opposition with newspaper articles they can pin up on the dressing room door to use for motivational purposes.

Anyway, to get back to the World Cup I had arranged to travel to South Africa with a group of friends from Fylde, but we were only going to be there for the semi-finals and final so we had our fingers crossed that England would reach the later stages. I watched the opening game between South Africa and Australia on television but didn't read too much into the host country's 27–18 victory, although on the day they had looked the better side and fully deserved the win. They were, after all, playing their first ever game in a World Cup, and playing on home soil, so if they weren't up for that game then they wouldn't be up for anything.

It was a great start to the competition, especially as the holders had been defeated and therefore facing a tougher route to a defence of their title. England, meanwhile, had a relatively easy group, although a somewhat physical one given that the Western Samoans invariably leave you with more than your share of bumps and bruises while the Argentinians are usually strong enough up front to give any pack a searching examination. In the event Argentina got to within six points of England's total and Italy pushed us close too, losing by a mere seven points.

There had been nothing to suggest that England could feel too confident about knocking over some of the major nations and, as I settled down to watch their quarter-final clash with Australia just hours before I was due to fly out with my buddies, I feared there was every chance that we wouldn't be watching Jack Rowell's boys in the semi-finals and that in terms of supporting England our trip would prove a waste of time. Fortunately, however, Rob Andrew ensured that it was a happy little group that flew out the following morning.

Our opening port of call was King's Park, Durban, where South Africa were due to play France in the first semi-final, and for once in my life I actually felt sorry for the French. It rained so heavily that the kick-off had to be delayed and the pitch was in such a dire state that the game should have been postponed. My abiding memory is of a whole fleet of women, armed with mops and buckets, trying to sweep water off the playing surface. On the way to the ground we had come across a guy doing a roaring trade selling umbrellas. Detecting something familiar in his accent, I asked him where he was from. It turned out that he was from Blackpool, so he must have felt quite at home in the deluge!

The game was a complete lottery but there was no doubt in my mind that the French, who had more flair, would have won on a dry day. The game's most important and prestigious competition shouldn't be decided by matches like that, and their players and supporters must have been well and truly brassed off.

With England playing New Zealand in Cape Town the following day there was no time to enjoy the delights of Durban. Instead we had to travel out to the airport and take a flight to Cape Town where, even though it was the middle of the night and freezing cold, there was still an enthusiastic band playing on the tarmac to welcome the supporters. We grabbed a few hours' sleep at our hotel outside the city and then took a minibus to the Newlands ground in good time for the match. There were thousands of English fans milling around and the atmosphere was fantastic, with the side-roads on the approach to the ground packed with little stalls selling food. That's where I bumped into Steve Smith . . . but then if there's food and drink around you will usually find my old scrum-half.

Once inside the ground I was approached by a guy who

asked if we would like to enjoy a drink in one of the hospitality suites. So off we went, and it turned out to be the hospitality box for referees. I felt a little bit like a poacher turned gamekeeper. The father of cricketer Allan Lamb was there and we had a good chat as we weighed up England's chances. We were all quite relaxed, the rest of the lads, like me, feeling that our forwards would be that much bigger and better than the New Zealand pack. As events were to reveal, it wasn't the size of their pack we should have been worried about.

That was the first time I had ever seen Jonah Lomu, and the All Blacks made such a ferocious start that the game was over after just 15 minutes. They kicked off, and Andrew Mehrtens switched the direction of the kick at the last moment such that the ball went to Lomu who simply charged through our defence as though it wasn't there. Straight from the restart the All Blacks swept back upfield and flanker Josh Kronfeld went over. England never recovered, and Lomu went on to score three more tries. He was the biggest object I had ever seen on a rugby field. From a distance you don't appreciate just how big he is; it was only when I met and chatted to him later that I realised the sheer immensity of the man. England made the mistake of hanging off him and you can't do that with a player of his size who covers the ground so quickly once he is up and running.

I believe England had been slightly complacent, imagining they could play as they had against Australia in the quarter-finals, but, of course the All Blacks are no mugs; they are steeped in the game and do their homework, probably more thoroughly than any other nation. Take away the Lomu factor and in some respects England's performance wasn't as bad as the 49–29 scoreline suggests. They were caught napping at the start, which handed the initiative to the All Blacks, and clearly not enough was known about Lomu, nor were any plans formulated to try to deal with him. Mind you, sometimes in rugby you simply know it's not going to be your day and that must have been so for England when they watched Zinzan Brooke, a forward of all people, dropping a massive goal. As it was, I thought England responded pretty well in the second half after trailing 25–3 at the interval. They ran in four tries and Dewi Morris had a good game at scrum-half.

England subsequently lost 19–9 to France in the play-off for third place and both sides looked as though they couldn't care less. Their hearts weren't in it, but they should have been thinking ahead because defeat meant that England then had the unwanted distraction of having to qualify for the 1999 event. For the major nations that can be an irritating business, the qualifying games played against sides that can't really test you and thus hardly providing meaningful preparation for the main event. But I know from my personal experience that losing in a semi-final is a bitter pill to swallow, as it is very difficult psychologically to motivate yourself for a third-place play-off.

The run-up to the final in Johannesburg was quite extraordinary. The event gripped the country such that wherever you went and whoever you talked to it was rugby, rugby, rugby. This fledgling nation was drawn together in a way it had never been before and, sadly has never been since. The atmosphere in the ground was incredibly passionate; I had never witnessed an occasion quite like it. At one stage we could see on the giant screens at Ellis Park a South African Airways jumbo jet in flight. It could have been filmed anywhere so we were all taken by surprise when the aircraft suddenly shot into view and dropped down to fly almost into the stadium. Beneath the wings someone had painted the message: 'Good Luck 'Boks'. It was a dramatic episode in a marvellous day but the moment I will never forget was the arrival in the stadium of South Africa's President, Nelson Mandela. He stepped out on to the pitch wearing a Springbok jersey bearing the number six – the number worn by skipper Francois Pienaar. To a man and woman, the crowd rose to give him a tumultuous welcome. Black, white, it didn't matter what colour you were: even the most die-hard Afrikaners applauded; a unique and highly emotional moment.

Mandela looked so happy and relaxed, and was clearly loving every minute of the occasion. I remember thinking how dignified he looked, and when I recalled everything he had been put through by the previous regime I was even more impressed by this remarkable man. Had I been locked up for all those years on Robben Island I don't think I could have been as magnanimous as he was. It was almost as though the entire nation, one that had just been reborn, was willing the Springboks to victory. Detaching myself from the emotion, however, I had to believe that the All Blacks would win. They were the better footballing side, with Andrew

Mehrtens in great form in the crucial fly-half position, and I also wondered how on earth the South Africans were going to close down Lomu, a player who had, almost single-handedly, demolished a good England side a few days earlier.

Mehrtens attempted another unorthodox kick-off in a bid to launch Lomu at the home side as in the game against England, but the ball didn't make the required ten metres, so the South Africans were awarded a scrum on half-way. There was to be no repeat of that morale-shattering semi-final and, as the drama unfolded, Ellis Park was, quite simply, an absolutely fantastic place to be. The 'Boks defended as though their lives depended upon it and even succeeded in closing down Lomu, although, in fairness, the All Blacks failed to set him up as an Exocet missile as efficiently as they had when they beat England. Every tackle on the big man was greeted with a roar of approval from the crowd and it didn't take the All Blacks long to realise they weren't just up against 15 rugby players. They were up against an entire nation.

Although New Zealand were clearly the better side on paper and should have won, there was a part of me that was almost willing South Africa to come through. I was a totally impartial observer when I arrived at the ground but it was very hard not to get caught up in the atmosphere. Despite New Zealand's perceived advantage in the build-up to the game, there was never much between the two sides when battle commenced, and the quality of both defences was such that neither was breached. The only scores were successful kicks from Mehrtens and his opposite number, Joel Stransky, and the sides were level 9–9 at the end of normal time. We were already cutting it fine to catch our flight home from the airport but I told my pals that there was no way I was leaving before the end. I had also decided that, even if it meant missing the flight, I would stay for the trophy presentation and celebrations, whichever side came out on top.

The tension was such that you could have cut it with a knife and there was near hysteria when Stransky dropped the goal that gave South Africa a 15–12 lead. All that remained was for them to survive the few remaining, agonising minutes and then, it was all over; the signal for the start of one of the biggest parties ever. Of all the World Cup Finals – and indeed all the tournaments as a whole – that was the best. It had drama, had been held in a single country for the first time and was won by a nation making its debut in the event – the host nation at that! Fortunately, the minibus driver we had booked to take us to the airport was where he had said he would be and we made it to the airport just in time for our flight home. The route to the airport was packed with people waving flags and banners, while drivers hooted their horns. It was marvellously manic and I wouldn't have missed it for the world.

That World Cup, probably more than any other, secured the ongoing success of the competition. It had had a fairly low-key start in New Zealand and Australia eight years earlier but has become the ultimate rugby event and one that all the major rugby-playing nations devote their time and energy preparing for. Yet, the 1999 World Cup, again spread over five European countries, didn't quite match the South African experience, even though it did throw up one or two memorable games and certainly didn't bear comparison to the most recent version of the event in Australia. England once again found themselves in the same pool as New Zealand, alongside Italy and Tonga. So, as in 1991, the game between England and the All Blacks was almost certainly going to have a strong bearing on pairings in the quarter-finals. Indeed, the runners-up in the pool were destined to play an extra round to qualify for the quarter-final stage whereas the pool winners would have automatic entry. England beat Italy easily and then hammered 101 points past Tonga – a scoreline matched by the All Blacks who rattled up exactly the same number of points against a hapless Italian side. Lomu again proved to be England's nemesis when we played the All Blacks. England didn't play particularly well anyway and another charge by Lomu, during which he swatted defenders nonchalantly, did the real damage.

That meant in the last 16 England had to play Fiji, a side that had pushed France all the way in the pool stages and had actually scored more points in the three games than our friends from across the Channel. In the event England won comfortably but were then due to meet South Africa at the new Stade de France stadium in Paris a few days later, the Springboks having had the advantage of a full week's rest after cruising into the quarter-finals. Had England beaten the All Blacks they would have been playing Scotland, with a much better prospect of reaching the semi-finals. England were perfectly capable of beating South Africa but were then outmanoeuvred and lost shape and direction. Nick Mallett, the Springbok coach, had done his homework and I'm told they had even planned for Jannie de Beer, who was at fly-half because of a hamstring injury to Henry Honiball, to drop goals. He did too – five of them! Time and again the Springbok pack set up the position from which de Beer, hardly one of the all-time greats, could unleash his shots, and sometimes you just sensed that everything he attempted was going to come off for him.

In the semi-finals Australia were miles better than South Africa, although the fact that there were only six points between the sides at the final whistle was an indication of Springbok resilience. They were certainly hanging in there. As I sat watching the other semi-final between New Zealand and France I was not alone in contemplating a first-ever all-Antipodean final. The All Blacks took charge, put points on the board and at half-time you wouldn't have given France a chance. In their frustration, they gave away so many penalties that, had the sin-bin been in use at that time, they would probably have been down to 12 players at one stage.

The second-half performance by France is now indelibly etched into the history of the World Cup. I don't know what was said in the dressing room at the interval, or whether the players just decided that as they weren't going to win then they might as well go out and enjoy themselves, but the result was a fabulous display of both controlled and running rugby. They ripped the All Blacks to shreds, and even I found myself on my feet applauding every try as they swept to a thoroughly deserved 43–31 victory. Abdel Benazzi had a great game at the heart of the French pack, as did flanker Olivier Magne.

By comparison, the final at the Millennium Stadium in Cardiff was something of a disappointment because Australia always had it in the bag and there was none of the drama of Ellis Park four years earlier. In truth, it was a poor game and it was obvious from the start which side was going to win. The Aussies were very professional and gave France no space in which to work their magic, so you never got the feeling that the French could pull another incredible second-half performance out of the hat. It is a pity that the game didn't match what is a truly magnificent stadium. I wasn't too impressed with the playing surface that afternoon but for watching a game it is the best rugby stadium I know.

In many ways I thought it a disjointed competition. They even had trouble pulling in the crowds in Scotland. The only real highlights were the two semi-finals, with the rest a bit of an anticlimax. Perhaps, it doesn't help to split a competition between five countries.

For me, the day of the final ended with a drinking session at the Hilton Hotel in company with the son of Prince Rainier of Monaco, together with Gordon Brown and Moss Keane, whose Irish brogue was too thick for my son Dan to decipher. We also met up there with Mark Thomas, the son of the late Clem Thomas who played for Wales and the British Lions before earning a reputation as a respected observer on the game. Mark was friendly with Prince Rainier's son, Albert, and they had planned some time earlier to meet up for the World Cup Final. After a few rounds, it was Prince Albert's turn so I suggested he got them in. At that point one of his mates said he couldn't because he didn't have any money with him, so I asked where Albert was staying. When they said he was staying at the hotel I said he didn't need money to pay for the round then because he could put it on to his room bill, which is what he did, very happily. I found him to be a very nice chap who loved and understood his sport.

This brings us to the memorable 2003 World Cup, which brought about a much-needed change in the balance of power between the two hemispheres, and I'll be saying more of that later. England had achieved their objective of completing a Grand Slam in the RBS Six Nations Championship in the build-up to the event – something they achieved prior to the 1991 and 1995 World Cups – and that provided a massive psychological boost. Had they lost then they would have been asking themselves questions about the critical pool game they faced against South Africa and I had always felt that, if they could get over that hurdle, they would reach the semi-finals by disposing of Wales, even though that hurdle proved more difficult when we arrived at it!

Watching England beat Ireland 42–6 in Dublin, when the two unbeaten sides in the Six Nations went head-to-head, will have made people sit up and take notice. There had been enormous pressure on England to win because they had lost against Scotland, Wales and Ireland in the final game in recent seasons when a Grand Slam had been at stake. They had also been kicked out of the 1999 World Cup in Paris by South African Jannie de Beer, so many have questioned England's ability to perform on the big occasion. Sides took comfort from the belief that we would choke when it really mattered. England must have been slightly worried travelling to Dublin, because Lansdowne Road is a daunting place to visit and Ireland had, on paper, been having a great season, yet when you analyse Ireland's games perhaps there was less reason for concern. In their opening match they met Scotland, who were awful. They then did well in Italy but struggled to beat France at home on a day when France also played poorly by their standards. Ireland also struggled to beat Wales in Cardiff – a side that ended up with the Wooden Spoon – so the form-book suggested an English victory.

England had played pretty well against Scotland in the penultimate game and had a lot of very seasoned and hard-nosed players in their side: people like Martin Johnson, Lawrence Dallaglio, Richard Hill and Neil Back, who had seen it all before. On the day, they gave a very professional performance. The only blip was losing the first line-out, when hooker Steve Thompson threw the ball long and Ireland grabbed possession. I always have a laugh with Clive Woodward over the fact that we always seem to lose the first line-out, and when it happened in Dublin Clive turned around in the stand and gave me a knowing look! That apart, I don't think I have ever seen England play better. Jonny Wilkinson was outstanding and Dallaglio had as good a game as I have seen him play. Johnson, as usual, was immense. I always feel comfortable when he is in the side. He put himself about, made a lot of tackles, took the ball up well and was there to win. Losing isn't in Martin's vocabulary. England had to transfer that type of clinical performance to the World Cup in Australia. I knew that if we did that then the top sides would be less confident that we could be beaten in a one-off game. Woodward had got England playing like a club side and I was relieved that the key players stayed injury free in the build-up to the tournament.

If we thought it couldn't get any better then that comprehensive victory in Dublin then we were mistaken. I suspect the rugby world wasn't ready for our fantastic results Down Under during the summer – only our second victory over the All Blacks in New Zealand and our first ever win against Australia on their home territory. Clive Woodward had been keen to test his players at the end of a long, hard season and winning back-to-back games against those two great rugby nations was a marvellous achievement.

England's defence when down to just thirteen players during the game in New Zealand was simply awesome and the side's sheer professionalism made the Aussies really sit up and take notice.

That put us in with a great chance of winning the World Cup for the first time and it was no surprise that many had us down as joint favourites with New Zealand. Interestingly, the bookies had the All Blacks down as favourites, whilst recent results had projected England to the top of the world rankings. The All Blacks were a developing side and many thought they would only get better, which sounded ominous, and the Australians were always going to be difficult in their own backyard. Just how difficult, we were about to find out.

I knew Australia had some good backs but didn't see their forwards being strong enough at that time. Nor did I think South Africa would be strong enough to beat New Zealand in the quarter-finals, which proved to be the case, and, of the major nations, that left France. They had been disappointing during the RBS Six Nations Championship but I thought that could be due to their coach, Bernard Laporte, wanting to experiment with the World Cup in mind. They had also looked out of sorts at half-back in the absence of the very influential Fabien Galthie, who had bossed the game from start to finish when France beat England in Paris the previous season. But they certainly had the potential and, having already played in two World Cup Finals, I felt they were quite capable of beating anybody on their day.

CHAPTER TWELVE

The future

Public reaction to England winning the World Cup in 2003 was incredible. The nation came to a stop as millions crowded around their television sets to watch England beat Australia in as thrilling a match as it is possible to envisage. For far too long the country had been starved of sporting success on a grand scale and the fact that it was rugby union that delivered was a reflection on the strength of the game here despite the years of political jousting by the administration, club owners and players since rugby union went professional. We had threats of breakaways by the clubs, strikes by the players, revolts among the grassroots and, at times, a lack of real leadership from Twickenham. In spite of it all we are close to having an excellent structure that should keep England competitive on the international stage for years to come and, acrimonious though it may have been at times, we will have achieved that ourselves. For better or worse the various factions wedded together to produce a national side that not only proved capable of winning major events but also captured the major, glittering prize, the William Webb Ellis Cup.

When you look at what is happening in sport generally, that is no mean achievement because we are otherwise in danger of becoming a third-rate sporting nation – ironic when you consider how we pioneered major sports and took them around the world with missionary zeal – often finding it difficult competing against countries that have far smaller populations. The difference is that many countries use sport to instil national pride, there being few better examples of that than Australia. Sadly, we have been failed by successive governments that seemed incapable of grasping the importance of sporting success, and the feel-good factor this creates, for a nation's well-being. It is almost as though our politicians have no interest in sport. If they had, they might prove better leaders. There is certainly no shortage of interest among the general public, as evidenced by the recent Commonwealth Games in Manchester; a wonderful, uplifting occasion with the public turning out in their thousands to support the event. Yet, until tabling its recent official bid, our current government has shown a reluctance to push the boat out to try to bring the Olympic Games back to London. Let's face it, if we aren't prepared to bid for the Olympics then we might just as well jack it in and become a Third World sporting nation.

We lack the facilities to encourage sporting excellence, down in part to schools selling off playing fields to raise money and in large part also to educationalists deciding that competitive sport in schools is bad for children because they can't all win and some will end up as losers. These so-called experts didn't like the idea of competition, but what is life if not competitive? It certainly is when you get out into a working environment after leaving school. Children are naturally competitive, whether it is to see who can throw a stone farthest or ride their bicycle down a hill fastest. But there has to be a discipline to winning and losing, and team sports are particularly valuable in that respect because they teach you to work with other people towards a common goal.

One of the reasons Hilary and I sent our boys to private schools, apart from the obvious academic aspects, was because we knew they would be guaranteed team sports. Games like rugby, soccer, cricket, hockey and netball help to shape you as people, and there is nothing like the changing-room culture to bring you down to earth. There's no room for prima donnas; if your mates think you are getting a little bit above yourself, they will bring you down to size fairly quickly. Being a team player can help later in life when you enter the business world because you acquire important leadership and communication skills. I'm not suggesting we should teach our children to win at all costs but it would be wrong to suggest to them that it doesn't really matter whether or not they win or lose.

I feel sorry for those youngsters who attend a school where the playing fields have been removed or where the sports teachers leave for home with everyone else at 4 p.m. We are wasting an opportunity to provide recreation for those pupils who enjoy sport and I agreed with Kate Hoey, who was an excellent Minister of Sport, when she suggested that PE teachers should start their working day at lunchtime and stay on until 7 p.m. so that sports-minded youngsters can stay on to play games or work on individual skills. That way schools can better serve the local community. Local rugby clubs could be used in the same way. We need to make better use of the facilities we possess and build new ones. It is crazy that our top young swimmers have to get up at 4 a.m. in order to train in the local baths, and, considering the lack of a major athletics stadium in this country, I can't believe that we turned over the Commonwealth Games Stadium in Manchester to a Premiership soccer club that already had a major stadium. I know that soccer is our national game but we are in danger of letting it dominate our sporting lives. The Commonwealth Games Stadium could have served the whole of the UK as a centre of athletic excellence.

It is equally frustrating that we haven't got a national stadium at present. The whole Wembley saga has been a very expensive and embarrassing shambles. We need a 100,000-seater stadium in our capital city and it is interesting that the best and biggest stadium in England at present is Twickenham. That was achieved by the game itself – there were no government handouts – and it is something of which rugby union can be very proud. We don't always get it right but the stadium is a credit to the RFU, which, as an organisation, has been making huge strides to develop the game.

Since the mid-1970s we have seen a massive increase in mini

and junior rugby at clubs throughout the country. When I was a youngster there was no such thing, and unless you went to a rugby-playing school you were unlikely to get involved in the game, but rugby union has addressed that problem. Even if the government doesn't see sport as being high on its priority list the game itself is playing a vital role in the community – anything to get kids off the streets and to stop them hanging around street corners and bus shelters because they are bored and claim they have nothing to do is worth trying. If we can get them interested in sport then we have taken a step in the right direction. Children won't develop their latent sporting talents unless they are provided with the right facilities and that includes coaches as well as playing fields and sports halls.

It is high time we stopped trailing behind the rest of the world. Tennis is a classic example. We have the biggest tournament in the world at Wimbledon but, apart from Tim Henman, we don't have anyone born-British representing us at the highest level, Greg Rusedski being Canadian. They produce good tennis players in Belgium, a much smaller country, so you have to ask what we are doing wrong or, perhaps more to the point, what we are not doing. Tim Henman was lucky because his parents were keen on the game and able to provide financial support for his coaching, so he came through, but we need to ask ourselves how many potential champions are living in our inner cities but have never been given the opportunity to hold a tennis racket, let alone own one.

So far as rugby's future is concerned we now have a major shop window in the World Cup. When England returned from Australia clutching the William Webb Ellis Cup interest in rugby union was massive and that has already been reflected in attendances at games in the Zurich Premiership and in new arrivals at the traditional mini and junior sessions at the grassroots clubs.

The impact of the World Cup has been enormous, having far-reaching implications. Major nations now gear their strategy towards peaking at the four-yearly event, and that has had an effect on one of rugby union's institutions, the British Lions. This year I took over as chairman of the Four Home Unions Committee (England, Ireland, Scotland and Wales), which is responsible for the British and Irish Lions, and I hope people still see the Lions as having an important role to play on the world stage. It is important for the players because it elevates them to a different level from playing for their country, so, despite the additional demands in the modern game, they still want to don the famous red shirt. I believe the two major brands that people want to buy, because of what they stand for historically, are the Lions and the All Blacks. To win a Test series in New Zealand is still the ultimate prize for the Lions and it has only been achieved once, in 1971. Of the 31 Tests played, the Lions have won six, two have been drawn and the All Blacks have chalked up 23 victories.

New Zealanders would be mortified if they thought Lions tours might end, so it was a very embarrassing position I found myself in when I was chairman of the England Playing Committee and the future of tours came up for debate. Several members of the committee thought the Lions were holding

England back and the recommendation was made not to support the Lions in future. Players, it was said, were returning from the tours either nursing injuries or jaded through playing non-stop rugby. The English contingent hadn't been too enamoured with the 2001 tour to Australia, which I thought had been badly run, and there was even a feeling that England could beat a Lions side made up of players from the remaining three home countries. Those who had toured South Africa under Fran Cotton's management four years earlier had a very different perspective of what Lions tours were all about and, as a former Lions captain, I fought to ensure England's future support, only to be outvoted. In retrospect, I can't defend the decision taken by the committee and, with hindsight, recognise that I should have resigned. But I was weak and carried on, even though I didn't believe in the stance being taken.

In the event, England didn't withdraw their players and I'm doubly grateful for that because I have been invited to manage the 2005 Lions tour to New Zealand, with Sir Clive Woodward heading my coaching team. It had been clear, however, that future tours would have to be organised differently because the rugby calendar is now so full that it is increasingly difficult finding a suitable window. I had come around to the idea of shorter tours of three Tests and perhaps eight to ten provincial games. In the event, we have brought that figure down to just seven provincial games, with three Tests on consecutive Saturdays at the end of the tour. With the opening game being played on 4 June and the final Test on 9 July, it will be a considerably shorter tour than those undertaken previously.

I firmly believe the future of tours by the British and Irish Lions is only going to be preserved by recognizing the demands of professional rugby at club level and we should forge a partnership where the RFU and the clubs benefit from having a player selected for a Lions tour. Shorter tours might cause a few problems for the host nations, especially New Zealand where they have a very big tradition of provincial rugby and would like to play more games against touring sides. More games also means more revenue. It would be easier in Australia because, while providing stern opposition in the Test matches, the country has a limited number of strong provincial sides so long tours only end up with the Lions playing too many easy games.

It would be a tragedy if the Lions were ever disbanded, because it is a fantastic brand. Everyone who was in Australia for the three Test matches of the last Lions tour would testify to its popularity and the coming tour to New Zealand has already created a huge level of interest both here and in the host country. It will be a massive event and a fantastic challenge for the Lions, whose only success in that country, in the history of Lions tours, was back in 1971 when Carwyn James coached them to a 2–1 win with the final Test drawn.

So far as the northern hemisphere is concerned, the Six Nations is still the competition envied by our friends on the other side of the globe but we need to address the recent problem of predictability. Sides like England and France have developed to the level where they can regularly take on New Zealand, Australia and South Africa and compete in a way the other European nations can't at present. Don't worry; I'm not suggesting a breakaway. Instead we need to work at helping the other nations to improve.

I am a passionate Englishman and I want England to win every game we play, but at present if we play Italy in particular you know there will be only one outcome. The aim has to be to improve Italian rugby, so I was delighted to see that they were the most improved side in last season's competition. New Zealander John Kirwan took over as coach and he has brought a more pragmatic approach to their game. John was a fantastic rugby player and is someone for whom I have enormous respect. Under his guidance Italy have proved quite a handful when in possession. When England played Italy they were forced to make somewhere in the region of 50 more tackles than they would normally make in an international game and, had Scotland played against Italy as poorly as they did against Ireland, the Italians would have had a second victory to their credit.

So we can expect better things from Italy in the future and that demonstrates the importance of the major countries doing everything possible to help the weaker nations to improve. It is in the interests of the global game to do that. The major weakness of rugby league is that there are only three nations strong enough to compete in a World Cup – Australia, New Zealand and Great Britain. Trying to create national sides by filling them with outsiders is a farce, and in my view that code of rugby would be far better staging a Tri-Nations competition every year and forgetting about World Cups.

Now that rugby union has gone professional it is the countries with the more sophisticated economies, the greatest number of players and the highest standard of domestic competitions that will prevail; precisely what is already happening. Even so, you will always have a period when a country suddenly produces a crop of world-class players. I feel sorry for the current Welsh side, for example, because it will always be compared with the great team of the '70s. It has to be said that if you had put JPR Williams, Barry John, Gerald Davies, Mervyn Davies and Gareth Edwards into the England side of the day then we would have ruled the roost. Largely thanks to them, the Lions won a Test series in New Zealand for the only time in 1971 and went undefeated through South Africa three years later because they had a crop of truly great players.

So, while I'm passionate about the Six Nations and accept that you will get upsets like the one England suffered in Edinburgh in 1990 and in recent seasons courtesy of Scotland, Wales and Ireland, we still need to improve the product. I don't want people not bothering to switch on their television sets at 3 p.m. on a Six Nations Saturday because they feel the result is a foregone conclusion. The wonderful thing about any sport is the nervousness you feel in the build-up to a game, and that is the same whether you are a coach, player, or supporter.

Last season, despite disappointment in some quarters

that England and France had to meet in the opening game of the tournament, the Championship still went to the wire as England and Ireland went through undefeated to set up a showdown in Dublin. That was a magnificent rugby occasion and is what makes the Six Nations such a fascinating competition. There was a vibrant atmosphere, the city's pubs were packed to overflowing as fans from both countries mingled before and after the game, and as people went through the turnstiles they were genuinely unsure of the outcome. That's what you want, a real edge.

The competition isn't just about one game. There had been great focus on the meeting between England and France, for obvious reasons, and in the clash between Wales and Ireland in Cardiff, when the outcome was vitally important to both sides, fans spent the later stages of the game on the edges of their seats as the lead changed hands in dramatic fashion.

The Six Nations underwent changes last season and not everybody likes games kicking off at odd times or on a Sunday. I hate the idea of sport on a Sunday because to me it has always been a family day. I know I wouldn't have enjoyed playing then, but thankfully it didn't happen much in my day. It seems particularly inappropriate for international matches. The whole concept of the rugby weekend was to travel on the Friday, have a good night, attend the game on Saturday afternoon, have another good night and then return home on Sunday with time to recover before work on Monday morning. You might say that I am old-fashioned wanting my rugby played at 3 p.m. on a Saturday but I do understand the commercial reasons for spreading fixtures over two days and at different times when these things are dictated by one broadcaster. Ideally, I would like to see two broadcasters involved so that any supporter can watch his or her own country in action.

There has been a lot of debate about the time of year the Six Nations games should be played. Some want the tournament to be condensed into five weeks, possibly at the end of the season while others prefer the time-honoured programme of games being played on a week on, week off, basis during the first three months of the year. Major clubs would clearly prefer not to have their players toing and froing all the time but the money generated by the games depends on Joe Public paying at the turnstile, and there are those who believe that the financial implications of forking out large sums of cash every week for five weeks might prove to be the straw that breaks the camel's back.

The problem the authorities have at present is fitting everything in because there are some excellent competitions. It was very different when I played, because club rugby was not played on a league basis and the emphasis for top players, in the North at least, was to get into their county side in order to stake an international claim. The most important games as I saw them were the five county games (seven if Lancashire made it to the final), four games in the Five Nations Championship and two games against an incoming team from the southern hemisphere – one for England and the other for either the North or North West.

In my day there was no Heineken European Cup but that is

now a well-established competition – even for English clubs, who ducked in and out like a yo-yo until the format suited them better – or until they realised what they were missing out on. It is a fantastic tournament, catering as it does for club sides in some countries and provincial teams in Ireland and Scotland. It works better in Ireland because they have an ideal set-up and their players are contracted to the Irish Rugby Union so they have more control over them in terms of how many games they play. The problem they have is finding enough meaningful games.

Initially there wasn't a television contract in place for the competition and, as a result, nobody knew when the games were taking place and the tournament wasn't given the media coverage everyone had hoped for. But there is nothing wrong with the profile today because games have become an integral part of the BBC Grandstand programme. As a consequence the European Cup has increased in popularity and the only thing that the authorities need to address – apart from the need to decide where it would fit best into the seasonal jigsaw – is the question of qualification. At present two quarter-final places are offered to the best runners-up in their pool but it is easier racking up points if your pool includes one of the Italian clubs.

There is no doubt that rugby in England has been improved by the game going professional, and this has been achieved despite the battles between the RFU, the leading clubs and those at grassroots level. I am heartily sick of all the arguments that have been raging now among these for almost a decade. Forget our external differences with our Celtic cousins over the Six Nations and Europe; we have had enough empty talk spouted over domestic issues to inflate an entire fleet of hot-air balloons. Had I not been involved in the game, but watching events from the sidelines, I would have wondered why everybody appeared to be arguing all the time. Hopefully, the different sides are slowly coming round to the idea that we can all prosper if we work together. At one stage the relationship between the RFU and the leading clubs could hardly have been any worse, but I've always been able to see both points of view and always believed it was just a question of sensible people sitting down together and sorting things out in a civilised manner. We may have some way to go but there is much more of a partnership today, however uneasy at times, between the RFU and the top clubs, and that is reflected in the performances of our national side. Success has been achieved by cooperation, the leading clubs affording England head coach Clive Woodward far more access to their players than his soccer counterpart, Sven-Goran Eriksson enjoys. Clive has taken performance and preparation to unprecedented levels but it is no good having everything in place if you have too little time to work with your raw material, the players.

It was Clive who told me once that he thought it impossible to have both the best international side and the best domestic competition. I could see where he was coming from. Soccer suffers because managers are reluctant to release their players. Without time together you can't build the club culture that Clive has achieved with England. The national side has to be the pinnacle of every sport but, sadly, I feel that Premiership soccer has become so ridiculously commercial that the national side is too often secondary to club needs. I would hate to see that situation arise in our game and feel that with goodwill on all sides we can avoid it.

The rugby Premiership is now a very good product and an excellent breeding ground for England players. Club owners are playing their part in developing our future stars and I am one of those who believes there has to be some form of ring-fencing at the top end of the game. That might not be a popular view but I want what is best for England and one way of achieving that objective is to remove the fear of relegation. I know all the arguments, both for and against, but very few clubs would be capable of realistically challenging for a Premiership place anyway because of the huge cost involved. And ring fencing would help in the development of English players. We had a classic situation last season when Rob Andrew brought in several experienced overseas players to help his Newcastle Falcons side stave off the threat of relegation. Newcastle had invested heavily in a stadium and, in fairness, Rob had also developed a lot of good young players who were all qualified to play for England. Without the threat of automatic relegation he could have saved that money and continued the process of giving youngsters a chance to test themselves in the Premiership.

Some people would say that there must be a way into the Premiership for any ambitious club. Fine. That could be achieved by an end-of-season play-off between the bottom club in the Premiership and the top team in National One.

Some might point to 2003 and argue that the fact there was automatic relegation from the Premiership kept the competition alive in the lower reaches of the division until tea-time on the final Saturday of the season, but interest would have been just as acute had the bottom side been faced with meeting the National One champions (Rotherham, in 2003), in a play-off to decide who played in the Premiership the following season. The play-off system has worked in the past and would take some of the pressure off clubs in the Premiership relegation zone whilst giving the ambitious club from National One a fighting chance of promotion.

Whilst I like the play-off idea to determine promotion and relegation, I'm not in favour of the current play-off at the top of the table to determine the champions. Under the system that operated in the 2002–3 season it was possible to finish third and still end up as champions by beating the side that finished top of the table in a championship decider at Twickenham. I understand the financial attraction of such a game but I believe that the side topping the table after meeting every other Premiership side on a home and away basis has earned the right to be declared champions.

There is already concern over the number of highly competitive games our top players have to play in and we should certainly look at either reducing the size of the Premiership or actually increasing it in size to either 14 or 16 clubs and splitting them into two conferences with meaningful play-offs at the end of the season. We also need to look at what goes on below the Premiership and I would be in favour of retaining

National One as a semi-professional league but returning the rest of the clubs to playing on a regional basis. I personally would like the game below National One to be amateur but, of course, you can't enforce that objective in what is now an open game. I would, however, want to ensure that any money those clubs received from the RFU was conditional funding. In other words it would have to be spent on developing junior rugby or to cover acceptable travelling expenses; it would not be available for the payment of players. Obviously, the game is no longer amateur, but below the top two tiers it should operate on that basis. You can't stop players being paid but if that is going to happen then the money should come out of the pocket of the local butcher or whoever, and not from the RFU. Even at the highest level the hope must be that the clubs will become self-sufficient from gate receipts and sponsorships, with less reliance on money from the centre. Lower down, in particular, it is a nonsense to think of funding inferior players. I hate the way players in the lower leagues move around like mercenaries, playing for the highest bidder. There isn't enough club loyalty these days. I spent my entire career at Fylde. The club is still a major part of my life but I wasn't happy about the money spent on trying to survive in the National leagues. I remember how they won promotion and thought they were going to receive £200,000 from the RFU, but, in the early years of professionalism, handouts from HQ didn't always reach expected levels. They went out and spent £400,000 and I can appreciate that they felt they were spending money for the right reasons, but in the end they were hundreds of thousands of pounds in debt and the only solution to the club's problem was to sell off one of their pitches for housing development. Fortunately, they were able to keep their other pitches and are now becoming a community club, which is excellent.

In France sporting facilities are provided by the municipality and a whole range of sports are played at those complexes. The facilities are available to everyone, whereas in this country it is left to individual sporting clubs to provide them, often with no local authority help whatsoever. Had Fylde not finally received planning permission for development at their ground in Lytham St Annes then the club would have been in very serious financial difficulties, and that picture is replicated at clubs up and down the country. So it is high time that we got back the old sense of community where you played for your local side throughout your career, establishing many lifelong friendships along the way. That is far better than a club financially supporting an itinerant playing membership. I don't like to harp back to the past, but when I played at Fylde, as with all top teams we would have to pay our match subscriptions to help fund such things as laundry, travel and beer for our opponents. That applied even when I was captaining England. It would be impossible now to return to those days because the best players are fully professional and we have been reaping the benefits in terms of a strong national side and a Premiership that produces games that are well worth watching. But so far as the rest of the clubs are concerned, we should be attempting to put a smile back into what is a great form of recreation.

If clubs were more intent on fun than avoiding relegation I'm sure more people would not only be attracted to the game but would stay involved in it for longer, hopefully, for life. That doesn't mean that you can't be competitive, because we should all be trying to win, but we have to remember that we are talking about sport rather than a matter of life and death. The game is serious at the highest level, as it should be with national pride at stake, but for the rest of the population it should exist as a healthy form of recreation that is open to everybody, regardless of age, sex, colour, creed or size. The beauty of rugby is that you can always find the level that suits your physique, athleticism (or lack of it) and talents. When I embarked on my playing career I had no idea what my level would be. Not for a moment, as I trotted out at full-back for Fylde's sixth team as a teenager, did I imagine I might one day have the honour of leading my country. The fact that I did should provide encouragement for youngsters from all walks of life because nothing had been preordained in my case. I was simply given the opportunity to express myself in a sporting environment and discovered a talent I had been unaware of.

Our future as a sporting nation depends on our young people being given the opportunity to participate in a whole range of sports. Speaking from personal experience, I know that involvement in sport can open up a whole new world. I had my triumphs and disappointments. I experienced a whole gamut of emotions, but, most importantly, I feel that sport helped to shape me as a human being.

CHAPTER THIRTEEN

Nothing but the best

It is always an interesting exercise to look back over your career and hypothesise over the best team you could possibly have played in, so, as a former captain of the British Lions and England, I decided to select sides choosing players who appeared in the period from my first international cap to the present day. I haven't played with or against some of the players I have selected but I have had the advantage of watching them all at close quarters.

BRITISH LIONS

15 **JPR WILLIAMS:** Without question the best full-back I have ever played with or against. In the modern game he would be an even bigger superstar than he was when he played for Wales. He had a good pair of hands, vision and

was strong and brave. The only other Lion I would look at for this position is Gavin Hastings but the talented Scot wasn't quite in the same league as the Welshman. When he emerged on to the international scene I thought Iain Balshaw had the potential to be a great full-back but, for a variety of reasons, that early promise was put on hold.

14 JASON ROBINSON: Jason is one of the few players in the world who causes the crowd to gasp in anticipation every time he gets the ball. Everyone wants to see him play, yet I don't think rugby union has seen him at his best. He was at his quickest I think when he was playing rugby league. He is a master at breaking down defences. I look back at the try he scored against France in 2002. They knew he was going to get the ball and put three men on him but he still scored under the sticks.

13 BRIAN O'DRISCOLL: The world's best centre at present. His performances for the Lions in Australia in 2001 were fantastic. Basically, he and Robinson were the back line. He has vision, pace, strength and all-round footballing ability. He will become one of the all-time greats. The other player I looked at was another Irishman, Mike Gibson, but I just felt that Brian is more explosive.

12 JEREMY GUSCOTT: The former Bath centre went on three Lions tours and was twice a factor in the Lions winning a series. He scored a crucial try under the posts to secure a series win in Australia (in 1989), and did the same in South Africa in 1997 with a drop-goal in the second test in Durban. I don't think we saw the best of him in the England team because he didn't get the service he deserved and I felt that he and his centre partner Will Carling both wanted to be the number one superstar in the team.

11 **GERALD DAVIES:** The Welshman was a great ball-player who scored some wonderful tries. He also had the ability to play in the centre and ran in four tries for the Lions against Hawkes Bay during the 1971 tour to New Zealand. I also considered Mike Slemen and John Carleton, two guys who would score for you when it came to the crunch, but Gerald gets the vote.

10 **JONNY WILKINSON:** Phil Bennett had wonderful flair but Jonny has developed incredibly in the last 18 months. Obviously, his goal-kicking and work in defence are major pluses but he is now taking on the opposition more and running different lines. Rob Andrew was a very organised fly-half but he lacked Bennett's flair. Wilkinson has it all now.

9 **GARETH EDWARDS:** There isn't really a competition for this position. Gareth has been voted the greatest rugby player ever and I'll go along with that assessment. He was strong, quick and oozing with talent. A pivotal player who

could do everything – in the modern game, he would have been absolutely fantastic.

1 **FRAN COTTON:** My great pal has to be in there somewhere and, with Graham Price also in my front row, it has to be at loose-head. Fran was one of the few props who could play with equal ability on either side of the scrum and he would be a superstar in the modern game. A good ball-handler he also had great vision, something he probably inherited from his father, who played professional rugby league.

2 **KEITH WOOD:** This was a tough one. My initial thought was to go for Peter Wheeler, who was the best hooker I played with during my career. He was probably a better technical hooker than Woody and threw the ball in better at the line-out, but Woody would give you more 'get up and go' and for that reason he has to just edge it. But it was a close call.

3 **GRAHAM PRICE:** A similar player to Fran who was also a good ball-handler as well as a great scrummager. They both went on three Lions tours and appeared in Grand Slam sides, and that experience gives them the edge over modern contenders. For speed around the park Graham probably had the edge on Fran.

4 **GORDON BROWN:** West of Scotland fans might wonder at this choice because my great friend 'Broonie' wasn't exactly the most interested guy when he played club rugby. Nor was he the biggest second row of his day but he was a big-match player. When the occasion was important enough, along with the arena, then you could guarantee that Gordon would produce the goods.

5 **MARTIN JOHNSON:** The fact that Martin became the first player to captain two British Lions tours speaks for itself. He is one tough, hard competitor and someone you would want alongside you in any pack. He is respected by team-mates and opponents alike. Fran Cotton made him captain of the 1997 Lions to South Africa because he wanted the Springboks to know they were in for a game when Martin knocked on their dressing-room door.

6 **PETER DIXON:** Peter was capped by the Lions before he played for England, which doesn't say much for national selection at that time. He covered all back row roles but I think blind-side was his best position. As a player he was ahead of his time and, if he had played in better England teams, he would have had more than one Lions tour.

7 **RICHARD HILL:** Richard is possibly the most under-rated international still playing today, but is held in the highest regard by his peers. I have picked him at open-side but he can play on either side of the scrum. It is significant

that although the Lions lost their last series in Australia, Hill was on the field for the Test they won. He keeps out players like Finlay Calder and Fergus Slattery.

8 **MERVYN DAVIES:** Merve 'The Swerve' was streets ahead of most guys who have played in this position for the Lions. His career was cut short when he suffered a brain haemorrhage and, but for that, I feel sure he would have captained the 1977 Lions. He was outstanding on the two previous tours and was a key figure in the great Welsh sides of the time. He had good hands, vision and took the ball up well.

ENGLAND

15 **JASON ROBINSON:** I hope that Iain Balshaw gets back to his best because he is talented and has real zip, which is something we are short of. If he does then he would be at full-back but, in the meantime, it has to be Jason.

14 **BEN COHEN:** You can't ignore Ben at present because he is a finisher. Big, strong and brave I think he will develop into an outstanding player. He has worked hard on his game with Northampton coach Wayne Smith. Ben isn't a natural ball-player, but through hard work he has made himself into one. He probably needs to work more on his kick-and-chase, but whereas he was once weak under the high ball he isn't any longer.

13 CLIVE WOODWARD: I haven't picked 'Woody' for any sentimental reason or the fact that he is the England head coach. He was always a bit of a maverick – someone you would want to throttle at times – but he was a match-winner. You only have to look back at his performances against Scotland in 1980 and 1981 to realise that. His ability to break down defences was outstanding.

12 JEREMY GUSCOTT: Not a difficult choice for the same reasons that he would be in my Lions team. He was a different type of player to his old partner Will Carling, who was a more direct runner whereas Guscott had the ability to win a game out of nothing.

11 MIKE SLEMEN: I would pick 'Slem' for his all-round footballing ability. He lacked a yard of pace and wasn't the best tackler but he made up for that in other ways and read the game well. That enabled him to snuff out danger and provide cover for the full-backs. Many might wonder why I didn't go for Rory Underwood but I always felt he was just a try-scorer who wouldn't have been seen much in a poor team.

10 JONNY WILKINSON: It has to be Jonny again. If you look at his record Rob Andrew would be his only major challenger, but Jonny is an all-round better player although Rob was known to make his full share of tackles, too.

9   **NIGEL MELVILLE:** I had a bit of a battle with chairman of selectors Budge Rogers to get him to pick Steve Smith ahead of Nigel in 1979 and 1980 because Nigel had come straight from school and I didn't think he was ready. But, if he hadn't been so injury prone, he would have eventually had the role for many years because he had all the skills. He was a better technician than Smithy and, while I am fond of Dewi Morris, Nigel was ahead of him. Dewi played more like a back row, and passing was never his greatest attribute. Players like Richard Hill, Matt Dawson, Kyran Bracken and Andy Gomarsall spring to mind but Melville had the edge for his overall ability. The only question mark would be over his difficulty in staying free from injury.

1   **JASON LEONARD:** Although I picked Fran Cotton at loose-head for the Lions I would move him to tight-head for England because you can't ignore Jason. He is England's most capped player and a great team man, quite apart from his ability as a scrummager.

2   **PETER WHEELER:** He was edged out of my Lions side by Keith Wood but Peter is out on his own so far as England is concerned. Brian Moore won a lot of caps but he wasn't in the same league as Peter. Like Fran, 'Wheelbrace' was a good ball-player and with Jason and Fran would have formed a formidable front row.

3 **FRAN COTTON:** No need for explanations here although some may wonder where Phil Vickery, Jeff Probyn and Phil Blakeway stand. Vickery could be a rival and has Lions tests under his belt now. Blakeway was a very strong scrummager but it is debatable whether or not he would have survived the modern game where props have to do a lot of running about and ball-handling. In normal circumstances Probyn would have been in the frame but he didn't go on any Lions tours. Fran went on three.

4 **MARTIN JOHNSON:** England have always had good second rows but Martin will take some replacing.

5 **MAURICE COLCLOUGH:** Once again, experience counts. Maurice had two British Lions tours and the only player to rival him would be Paul Ackford, who was a great ball-player and transformed the England team when he joined it. If in doubt they always threw to Paul, which took a lot of pressure off Wade Dooley, who always played better with Ackford as his second row partner. But Maurice gets the vote, although he will have a challenger soon in Ben Kay. Ben will be absolutely outstanding and has all the attributes to become the best ever.

6 **PETER DIXON:** Another of my Lions selections who was shabbily treated by a succession of England selection committees. An excellent footballer who gets my vote despite

the challenge of very good players like Roger Uttley, Lawrence Dallaglio and a host of others.

7 **RICHARD HILL:** I can't find any reason why Richard shouldn't, like Peter Dixon, figure in both back rows. No place then for either Peter Winterbottom or Tony Neary, who would certainly be his closest challengers. I played a lot of my rugby with 'Nero' but Hill was a better tackler and more versatile.

8 **DEAN RICHARDS:** From the time I first joined the England team there have been quite a few players in the number eight shirt. But my vote goes to Deano because you simply can't ignore what he has done for England. He wasn't the most mobile number eight but he read situations well, was as solid as a rock and had a good knowledge of the game that has been showing through at his club, Leicester.

CHAPTER FOURTEEN

On top of the World

Sydney is one of the finest cities in the world and it was a wonderful place to be on 22 November 2003 when England won the Rugby World Cup for the first time, in a final of high drama that brought to a close the best tournament yet and captured the imagination of a nation starved of major sporting success for far longer than befits a country that pioneered so many modern sports and introduced them to the rest of the world. For just a few short weeks, rugby union took centre stage in a country where soccer dominates the sporting scene – and will probably continue to do so – but our wonderful game had its day in the sun and succeeded in uniting the nation in a way not achieved since 1966, when England won the soccer World Cup.

To lift the William Webb Ellis Cup and return it to the land of its birth was a wonderful achievement – England not only became the first northern hemisphere side to win a

World Cup, ending the southern hemisphere's monopoly of the silverware since the first event in New Zealand in 1987, but also secured the game's top prize by beating the holders, Australia, in their own backyard. It was a magnificent achievement for head coach Clive Woodward and his back-up team, for skipper Martin Johnson and his wonderfully committed players as well as, dare I say it, for the 'blazers' in administration who backed Clive all the way and the leading club owners who made their senior players available during the years of planning.

I mean years of planning. What England achieved wasn't accomplished overnight and Clive had been building towards that November day for a long time. His planning had been meticulous and, whilst some commentators suggested that Sydney would prove too much for England's ageing pack, he knew that their experience would carry the day. There were a few scares along the way but, by the time the England team coach rolled into the Telstra Stadium for the final showdown with our hosts, I knew deep down that we were going to win. What I wasn't prepared for was the cliffhanger the game turned into and I must confess that I could hardly watch when the match went into extra time. England, in all fairness, could – and should – have had the game sewn up by half-time but that would have been a pity because it would have denied the 83,000 spectators in the stadium, and the millions watching on television, possibly the most dramatic 60 minutes of rugby ever witnessed.

I consider myself privileged to have been in Sydney for the

conclusion of a truly magnificent tournament and the Aussies are to be congratulated for their brilliant organisation, from the opening ceremony right through to a final ceremony that brought a lump to many throats – and that was before the final got under way. It was good to see the tournament staged in just one country for only the second time. New Zealand were upset at not sharing the event, as they had in the inaugural World Cup in 1987, but there were administrative issues that couldn't be solved in time and I believe we had a better tournament as a result – the Australians did a marvellous job in a land where rugby union plays second fiddle to Aussie rules and rugby league. In a global sense, this event is now the third biggest sporting tournament in the world after the soccer World Cup and the Olympics. In four years' time, although France has the stadia and infrastructure to host the entire event, for a variety of reasons some pool games will be played in Wales, Scotland and Ireland and whilst I have nothing against the Celtic nations' ability to handle events, I just think it's essential to stage future World Cups in one country if at all possible.

Australia was the ideal country in many respects because it is a nation that truly embraces sport. Aussies love all sport and they absolutely love the cut and thrust of competition. They also like having a go at us Poms and that aspect was tremendous, especially in the build-up to the final. The Pommie-bashing may have upset some people but it was largely tongue-in-cheek and there couldn't have been more generous or sporting losers after the final whistle had sounded.

Until the semi-finals I had, like most other English people, watched all the games on television and even bought an extra set to take into my office so that I wouldn't miss a thing. I had always been confident that we could win, even though we would be playing away from home, but that confidence wasn't quite so high as I watched the early games. Georgia had been a mere formality and I had always believed the big test would come when we faced South Africa in our second pool game in Perth. England ground out a victory in the end but we could have been staring defeat in the face that evening if Louis Koen had kicked his goals. The Springboks did enough during the tournament for me to believe that they could become a force again, because they have some outstanding young players like Joe Van Niekerk, Juan Smith and fly-half Derick Hougaard, who made a big impact when he took over from Koen. The young number ten also showed plenty of bottle when he got up to resume as though nothing had happened after he had been felled by a mighty tackle from Samoan centre, Brian Lima. Brian is nicknamed 'the chiropractor' and with good reason. The Samoans are some of the biggest hitters in world rugby and I suspect we will be seeing repeats of that tackle on television for years to come!

The South Africans clearly had coaching issues to sort out after the tournament, but I believe that if they keep the side together they will develop into a good team again. Yet, whilst they had looked highly competitive against England they simply didn't function against the All Blacks in the quarter-final; they looked like a group of players who didn't believe they could beat the New Zealanders. I think the same thing happened to Wales, to some extent, when they met the All Blacks in their final pool game. After an hour Wales were right in the game but I suspect they then started asking themselves if they could, realistically, win the game and probably, deep down, thought they couldn't. It reminded me of the days when I played for England in the '70s when we'd be playing against a side like Wales in their prime, take a lead and then wouldn't know how to go on and win. In those days there was also an aura about the All Blacks and to some degree the Springboks, so that you had a psychological barrier to get over anyway. The difference with the current England side is that it knows how to win games and close things down if necessary. Nowhere was that more evident than in the dying seconds of the World Cup Final.

I was confident that all would be well as I watched the Samoans give us something of a roasting. I knew we would take control eventually, but what a performance the Samoans gave, and they emerged from the tournament with a lot of credit. And nobody should have been too surprised that their direct running and powerhouse defence posed problems for England because they had done so at previous World Cups. Our boys came through because they didn't panic. There was only one game when they did show signs of panic and that was the quarter-final against Wales.

The one time my confidence failed me was at half-time in that game when I seriously believed there might be an upset. We had been outplayed and I remember walking around the garden at home, where my lads were kicking a ball around, mumbling to myself. I was due to fly to Australia the following morning and I was wondering if it would be all over for England by the time I got there. We had been playing it all wrong and making silly mistakes. At one stage Mike Tindall kicked the ball to the wing where Shane Williams, one of Wales's quick runners, found himself with just Ben Kay, a big second-row, standing between himself and the wide open spaces. The inevitable happened. They were silly mistakes, which was unusual because we have rarely seen such basic errors from England in recent times. Mike Catt came on after the interval, which was a master stroke by Woodward because Mike changed things completely and gave Jonny Wilkinson more options. At that stage we needed a little bit of magic and it came from Jason Robinson, who produced one of the best breaks of the entire tournament and ripped his way through the Welsh defence, as only he can. He could probably have dummied the last defender to score himself, but he is a great professional and wasn't prepared to take that risk when he knew Will Greenwood had come up on his outside. His off-load was selfless and all credit to Will for having got himself into the right position. But that's what Will does because he is a very good footballer with a lot of nous, something he probably learned from his father Richard, who captained England and Lancashire at a time when I was still working my way through school.

So I flew into Sydney knowing that only the semi-finals and final remained, and I had a very pleasant distraction before getting immersed in the rugby. I attended a gala dinner at which I was inducted into Sydney's Hall of Fame. It seems I was only the second Englishman to be afforded that honour, which is awarded for a contribution to world rugby during one's playing career. The only other Englishman who has been so rewarded was the late Sir Wavell Wakefield, who was a record cap holder back in the 1920s and an inspirational figure. I had never expected such an honour and I felt very humble in the company of past recipients like Colin Meads, Gerald Davies, Michael Lynargh and Gareth Edwards. Others inducted at the same time were my old Irish friend Syd Millar, former All Blacks Ian Kirkpatrick, John Kirwan and Michael Jones, former Aussie centre Tim Horan, Scotland's Gavin Hastings and Jo Maso from France. It was a fantastic evening and I invited my old friends Malcolm and Margaret Phillips to join Hilary and myself. We later teamed up with a couple of pals from back home to enjoy a few beers at a pub before things got really busy. Later in the week there was no chance of a quiet beer with anybody in a Sydney pub!

The first semi-final paired Australia with New Zealand and many people were talking about a New Zealand versus France final because they appeared to be the form teams. The Aussies had a trick up their sleeves, however, and France still hadn't been seriously tested. So far as the other home countries were concerned they had achieved their main objective, which had been to reach the quarter-finals, with anything else as a bonus. Ireland, who had been in a tough group, could have beaten Australia, so they will have been disappointed at the way they failed to reach the same level of performance against France in the quarter-finals. It was a sad way for Keith Wood to end his career. He has been a real talisman for the Irish in recent seasons and they will certainly miss his inspirational brand of leadership. I felt that Scotland were lucky to beat Fiji to reach the quarter-finals and they were generally disappointing. They needed to give their game width but failed to do so, which made them easy to defend against. They relied heavily on Chris Patterson who, along with the excellent Simon Taylor, was one of the few Scots to emerge on the credit side. It is probably right that they are to have a new broom sweeping in now in the shape of Matt Williams, who had done a good job with Leinster. Ian McGeechan moves upstairs, where his influence will still be felt, but Matt will be starting with a blank canvas and he has four years to put things right.

Wales demonstrated against the All Blacks and England that they have turned the corner. They were tremendous in the first half against England, although we were naïve and played badly. It will be great for British and European rugby to have Wales playing well again and, with a bit of luck, the Celtic League will really provide a kick start and begin to rival both the French and English domestic leagues. One reason England has had an advantage is because of the strength of the Zurich Premiership and the fact that the players are competing in a domestic league where, if you are good enough to hack it, you are good enough to enter the international arena. The Zurich Premiership is undoubtedly better than the Super 12s, which provides a sort of glorified touch rugby, in my opinion. The desire to entertain the crowds has led to some of the fundamentals of rugby being discarded and, in the Super 12s, who cares about a forward pass anyway?

So, when I settled into life in Sydney, the perception was that France and New Zealand would battle it out for the William Webb Ellis Cup whilst Australia and England would play off for third place, possibly the one game nobody ever wants to have to take part in. Sides that reach the semi-final stage are invariably those with serious ambitions of winning the title and it is interesting that, apart from Wales in 1987, the semi-finalists have always been drawn from among the big three in the southern hemisphere and France and England from north of the equator. On this occasion, however, Australia completely confounded their critics, and they had had their share, even in their own media, because they hadn't performed to the level expected of them. Yet they deservedly beat the All Blacks by playing very clever rugby, which the New Zealanders hadn't the experience to sort things out.

The All Blacks had made the mistake of giving youth its head: you don't pick a young team for a World Cup in the hope that it will be all right on the night and you don't pick a potential good team. Instead you do what Woodward did. You pick an experienced squad and if most of them retire after the final it doesn't matter so long as they have delivered the goods. Aussie coach, Eddie Jones, has had his critics but he got it right on the night and after Stirling Mortlock intercepted what could have been a try-scoring pass from New Zealand fly-half Carlos Spencer and turned it into a try at the other end, a real 14-pointer, the highly backed All Blacks didn't really have a plan B.

Stephen Larkham sensed that Spencer and centre Leon MacDonald weren't great defenders and he ran some great angles for Australia. He also always had powerful runners like Wendell Sailor and Mortlock to either side. By comparison the All Blacks didn't seem to have much of a game plan once they had fallen behind and relied too heavily on hooker Keven Mealamu taking the ball from scrum-half and fly-half and attacking down a narrow channel. Their players were also guilty of going to ground too easily, whereas on the whole better sides tend to keep the ball in hand. Games don't come much bigger than a World Cup semi-final and, on that occasion, the Aussies proved themselves far more streetwise than their old adversaries from across the Tasman Sea.

Once the dust had settled on what many deemed a major upset, attention turned to the second semi-final the following day, and I allowed myself a wry smile as I walked to the ground and watched the rain tumbling out of a leaden sky. It was a good, old-fashioned Manchester day and I don't suppose the French were overjoyed when they looked out of their windows. Not that I think the weather was a factor in their defeat. They were beaten by a better side and I don't think many in the England camp were unduly concerned when Serge Betsen scored an early try following a bad mistake at a line-out just inside England's 22. Martin Johnson's troops simply shrugged it off and settled into the task of out-scrummaging one of the most vaunted packs in the competition, cleaning out the

French at the line-out and performing such a pincer move-ment on the very influential Fabien Galthie at scrum-half that the French skipper, playing his last game for his country, was nowhere near as effective as usual. And I can't remember a game involving France where flanker Olivier Magne was quite so anonymous.

A great deal had been written about Frederic Michalak, the 21-year-old French fly-half, who had been having a marvellous tournament. With the pressure on for the first time the young-ster let it get to him and he made a string of uncharacteristic mistakes. For all the pressure on his opposite number, Jonny Wilkinson was never affected by it and that evening he silenced a few critics who thought they had detected cracks in his armour. He defended as well as ever, absorbed a few big hits in return and kicked his goals. It would have been nice to have scored a few tries, but England got the result they wanted and were very worthy victors. They absolutely battered the French and demonstrated, once again, that if you take on the French up front you are likely to beat them.

Interest in the game during the following six days was un-believable. We weren't sure how England's appearance in the final was being received back home but we had a pretty good idea that the nation was stirring and getting behind the lads. The world loves a winner and I was fairly convinced that Woodward was going to deliver. I knew we were the better side and, when I looked through their starting line-up, I couldn't think of many Australians who would have challenged for a place in the England team. Certainly none of the front five were in that category and, when the rain came down again, I was confident that we would dominate and, if necessary, grind out a victory by denying the Aussies the ball and relying on Jonny Wilkinson to kick the goals. I gave a newspaper interview in which I said that if it meant boring the Aussies and the spectators to death in order to win the World Cup then we should do just that. That didn't happen, of course, and we were treated to a game that reduced most of us to nervous wrecks. When the action moved into extra time I turned to Hilary and told her I would have to leave because I couldn't stand the tension. I didn't leave, of course, although I'm told that some spectators had to go out to escape the nerve shredding experience.

Up to half-time there had been no indication of the dramas that would unfold later. England had the majority of possession, played for field position and I wasn't unduly concerned when Larkham hoisted a pin-point kick to the corner where Lote Tuqiri out-jumped Jason Robinson to gather and plunge over for a try. The French had taken an early lead six days earlier but it hadn't done them any good and Jason repaid the debt soon afterwards following an intelligent break by Lawrence Dallaglio. Wilkinson popped up in support and his inch-perfect pass out to Robinson saw the former rugby league ace surge clear of the cover. Wilkinson was kicking his goals and England led 14–5 at the interval. The score should have been 21–5 but Ben Kay dropped a scoring pass just short of an unguarded line. That would really have put England out of sight, and it would have been a carbon-copy of the 1999

World Cup Final in Cardiff when Australia never looked like losing to France, but the game as a spectacle would have been diminished as a consequence.

One of the joys of sport is its unpredictability, and all credit to the way Australia came back in the second half. Some sides might have capitulated but the Aussies are as competitive a bunch as you are ever likely to meet on the sporting field. They had been battered for 40 minutes but kept chipping away at us and I spent rather more of the second period watching the clock on the big screen rather than the on-field action. Elton Flatley took full advantage when England conceded penalties. As many of those came from the scrummage area, I must admit to a degree of puzzlement because we had the stronger scrum and I could see no reason why we would keep infringing. But the scrum is a dark world and refereeing interpretations do vary.

When Flatley kicked the penalty that took the game into extra time I started asking what would happen if the sides remained at stalemate after ten minutes each way. I simply wasn't sure but discovered later that there would have been ten minutes of sudden-death rugby, with the first side to score taking the prize, or it would go down to drop kicks taken by five nominated players from each side. Fortunately it didn't come down to that but, when Flatley again levelled the scores with two minutes of injury time remaining, the drop kicks seemed a distinct possibility.

It was at that stage that England demonstrated their experience by not panicking. Instead, they knew exactly what they had to do in the remaining seconds of the second half of extra time and carried out the plan to perfection. Wilkinson was asked to kick long at the restart in the reasonable hope that Aussie full-back Mat Rogers would not risk trying to run the ball out of defence and would kick to touch. As it turned out Rogers obliged and England had a line-out just outside the Aussie 22. Lewis Moody, who had come on as a replacement, won the ball at the back and drove into the Aussie midfield. The ball was recycled and it was at that stage that scrum-half Matt Dawson delivered a hammer blow to his hosts by finding a gap and driving a further 20 metres into the Aussie defence. With Neil Back acting as scrum-half, Johnson had the presence of mind to drive the ball on again, knowing that Dawson needed time to get back behind his forwards in order to deliver the ball to the waiting Wilkinson. The England players knew exactly what was going to happen next, so did the Aussies, which is why flankers Phil Waugh and George Smith were straining at the leash but not daring to step offside. Indeed, everyone in the stadium knew what was going to happen next, time almost stood still and it seemed like slow motion as Dawson finally flung the ball back to Wilkinson who, on his wrong foot, sent the ball soaring between the posts. Moments later England had gathered Australia's hurried re-start and, knowing that the next time the ball went out of play the whistle would blow, Mike Catt hammered it into row Z of the stand.

The place went mad and I felt for Woodward at that moment. I felt for the players and thought about the massive responsibility they had had on their shoulders to deliver for the good of English sport. I was impressed by the way the Aussies stood to applaud both sides for a magnificent contest and they continued to demonstrate for the rest of the night just what good sports they are. They had wound us up before the game but you can never accuse them of being bad losers. They knew the better team had won and they were ready to acknowledge that fact. I went down to the dressing room and sat in a corner having a bottle of Heineken with Jason Leonard, who has been around a bit, but I knew it wasn't the place for an old has been like me to be hanging around. I settled for shaking hands and getting out because they didn't want the "blazers" around. That was their time and I left them to enjoy the moment, the culmination of months of hard work. Rugby is never going to be bigger than soccer but, on that Saturday evening in Sydney, it ruled the world.

That wasn't the end of it, of course. I don't think anyone closely connected with the game could ever have imagined that thousands of fans would descend on Heathrow Airport in the middle of the night to welcome the England players back home. People were abandoning their cars on the approach roads to the airport and it was mayhem. No wonder our boys looked bemused by it all and, if that joyous demonstration confirmed the extent to which the public had got behind them, they were left in no doubt when the victory parade was staged through the streets of London some days later.

I spent the day in a makeshift television studio hastily erected in Trafalgar Square, where the parade ended, and I couldn't believe what I was seeing. London came to a standstill with an unprecedented show of affection for a group of young men who had restored some of the pride we all feel for our country. We, perhaps, don't show that too often but then I suppose we haven't had too many opportunities to demonstrate it in recent times. Fans were climbing on to the scaffolding of our studio and seeking any vantage point. It was a welcome for heroes and one the players, and the back-up team, thoroughly deserved.

It had been a wonderful tournament and the fact that it had been won for the first time by a side from the northern hemisphere signalled a shift in the balance of power in world rugby. The important thing now is for England to build on that success but it is equally important that the other European nations learn from the English experience because you can be sure of one thing, the big three from the southern hemisphere will be hell bent on taking the trophy back across the Equator when France stages the next tournament in 2007.

So far as rugby in this country is concerned, success has provided a marvellous window of opportunity and the skill for Woodward and the game's administrators will be in building towards the next World Cup and making the game better than it is now. When Clive started building towards the 1999 World Cup the professional game had been just three years old and he was embroiled in some of the most savage infighting that has ever taken place in the sport, between the professional and amateur arms of the game. His preparations involved meaningless games against Premiership All Star sides that largely comprised players that had been press-ganged into action. One could understand their feelings. Nobody wants to be put up as cannon-fodder for an international side. Before this World Cup he took his best players Down Under to prepare by playing New Zealand and Australia. Beating the giants of southern hemisphere rugby in their own backyards gave England a psychological advantage they carried into the tournament. As a consequence, unlike their predecessors, this England side isn't scared of anybody. Home or away.

Clive has done a marvellous job of developing the players and they are a credit to him. Not just on the field either. When interviewed the players handle themselves extremely well, they are interesting to talk to and are role models not just for children but for other sportsmen. Other sports can learn massively from what Woodward has achieved and the success of the rugby union side has put pressure on our national soccer and cricket sides to succeed too. Soccer will have an early chance with the European Championships but that game will always have a problem that doesn't afflict rugby union. The truth is that soccer's truly big clubs seem bigger than the national side. The big game for many Premiership players is playing in a European Cup Final and an international against anything other than one of the major soccer nations fails to generate much interest.

Soccer could certainly learn from the loyalty factor. Clive has his own management style and built his own squad of players. To a large extent he has turned England into almost a club side and whilst he has shown loyalty to his players he expects loyalty in return. He is strong minded and, if you cross him, I suspect you will become history very quickly.

He created a good back-up team of coaches with specialists like forwards' coach Andy Robinson, defence coach Phil Larder and kicking coach Dave Aldred. He will need all those skills as he re-builds because it is unlikely that we will be seeing the likes of Martin Johnson, Neil Back, Jason Leonard, Richard Hill, Lawrence Dallaglio, Jason Robinson and Will Greenwood at the next World Cup. We will also need a new scrum-half by then and, at present, I can't see one in the offing. Our Under-21s haven't performed particularly well although we have "A" team players who can, and have, stepped in when needed. The next World Cup may be too early for us to reap the benefits from the England Academies that have been set up around the country and are invariably attached to Premiership clubs.

Somehow we have to get a conveyor belt of players coming through the clubs and academies and, whilst our recent success may boost numbers taking up the game at mini and junior level, it is our immediate needs that require attention. An encouraging sign is the way that some Premiership clubs are increasing the number of local players in their squads. My nearest club is Sale Sharks and about 60 per cent of the players are from that region. Eventually the target figure should be 80 per cent, supplemented by good overseas players who add something to the squad in terms of good practice. The "blazers" have come in for criticism over the years but we have put a lot of things into practice with a view to improving our national side and future internationals are being identified at an early age and groomed through coaching and mentoring. Our aim has to be to become the first side to actually retain the William Webb Ellis Cup.

As for future World Cups I believe we have to address the problems faced by the lesser nations and provide a level playing field. John Kirwan has done a marvellous job with Italy yet, at this most recent World Cup, the Italians were forced to play four games in 14 days whilst other sides in their pool, such as New Zealand and Wales, had bigger gaps between games and tended to play most of them at the weekend. Tonga were placed in a similar position and, like Italy, were out on their feet in the end. Italy doesn't have the resources of a country like England and probably have less than 20 players capable of playing at that level. Fortunately, the authorities are aware of the anomaly and, hopefully, that will be addressed before the next tournament.

The administration also has to look at providing greater financial help for some of the smaller nations, and particularly those from the Pacific Islands who provide so much pleasure by the way they play the game. It can't be right when players withdraw because they simply can't afford to leave their clubs to play in a World Cup and I think much of that problem would be resolved if we could move to a global season where major events, like a World Cup, could be held in June when there would be no domestic rugby in either hemisphere.

For all the difficulties, the standard is improving all the time and it is important that things move on again. Narrowing the gap between the haves and have nots of world rugby will help to achieve that but, for the moment, we should sit back and enjoy the vivid memories of an outstanding World Cup that was a credit to the people of Australia who hosted it, the players to took part in it and the spectators who packed the stadia. I feel privileged to be able to say that I was there.

CAREER RECORD

FYLDE

I made my senior debut for Fylde in 1972 against Waterloo and played around 300 games before injury forced my retirement. My final game was on January 24, 1982. It was a Lancashire Cup third round game against Merseyside Police at Sefton. We won the game 20–0.

(* denotes games as captain)

LANCASHIRE

County Championship wins with Lancashire

1977 Lancashire 17 Middlesex 6
1980 Lancashire 21 Gloucestershire 18*
1982 Lancashire 7 North Midlands 3*

NORTH

1976 North and Midlands 24 Argentina 9
1976 North West 21 Australia 16
1978 North 6 New Zealand 9*
1979 North 21 New Zealand 9*
1981 North 9 Australia 9*

ENGLAND (*denotes games as captain)

Date	Opposition	Venue	Result
18.1.75	Ireland	Dublin	Lost 12–9
24.5.75	Australia	Sydney	Lost 16–9
31.5.75	Australia	Brisbane	Lost 30–21
3.1.76	Australia	Twickenham	Won 23–6
17.1.76	Wales	Twickenham	Lost 21–9
21.2.76	Scotland	Murrayfield	Lost 22–12
6.3.76	Ireland	Twickenham	Lost 13–12
20.3.76	France	Paris	Lost 30–9
8.1.77	Scotland	Twickenham	Won 26–6
5.2.77	Ireland	Dublin	Won 4–0
19.2.77	France	Twickenham	Lost 4–3
5.3.77	Wales	Cardiff	Lost 14–9
21.1.78	France*	Paris	Lost 15–6
4.2.78	Wales*	Twickenham	Lost 9–6
4.3.78	Scotland*	Murrayfield	Won 15–0
18.3.78	Ireland*	Twickenham	Won 15–9
25.11.78	New Zealand*	Twickenham	Lost 16–6
3.2.79	Scotland	Twickenham	Draw 7–7
17.2.79	Ireland*	Dublin	Lost 12–7
3.3.79	France*	Twickenham	Won 7–6
17.3.79	Wales*	Cardiff	Lost 27–3
24.11.79	New Zealand*	Twickenham	Lost 10–9
19.1.80	Ireland*	Twickenham	Won 24–9
2.2.80	France*	Paris	Won 17–13
16.2.80	Wales*	Twickenham	Won 9–8

15.3.80	Scotland*	Murrayfield	Won 30–18
17.1.81	Wales*	Cardiff	Lost 21–19
21.2.81	Scotland*	Twickenham	Won 23–17
7.3.81	Ireland*	Dublin	Won 10–6
21.3.81	France*	Twickenham	Lost 16–12
30.5.81	Argentina*	Buenos Aires	Draw 19–19
6.6.81	Argentina*	Buenos Aires	Won 12–6
2.1.82	Australia*	Twickenham	Won 15–11
16.1.82	Scotland*	Murrayfield	Draw 9–9

BRITISH LIONS (* denotes games as captain)

NEW ZEALAND

Date	Test	Venue	Result
9.7.77	Second	Christchurch	Won 13–9
30.7.77	Third	Dunedin	Lost 19–7
13.8.77	Fourth	Auckland	Lost 10–9

SOUTH AFRICA

31.5.80	First*	Cape Town	Lost 26–22
14.6.80	Second*	Bloemfontein	Lost 26–19
28.6.80	Third*	Port Elizabeth	Lost 12–10
12.7.80	Fourth*	Pretoria	Won 17–13

INDEX